ROBERT E. LEE

THE MAN AND THE SOLDIER

CIVIL WAR BOOKS
by Philip Van Doren Stern

THE MAN WHO KILLED LINCOLN

THE DRUMS OF MORNING

AN END TO VALOR
The Last Days of the Civil War

THEY WERE THERE
The Civil War in Action as Seen by Its Combat Artists

THE CONFEDERATE NAVY
A Pictorial History

CIVIL WAR BOOKS
Edited by Philip Van Doren Stern

THE LIFE AND WRITINGS OF ABRAHAM LINCOLN

THE ASSASSINATION OF PRESIDENT LINCOLN
AND THE TRIAL OF THE CONSPIRATORS
(the original Benn Pitman report)

SECRET MISSIONS OF THE CIVIL WAR

THE SECRET SERVICE
OF THE CONFEDERATE STATES IN EUROPE
or How the Confederate Cruisers Were Equipped
By James D. Bulloch

WEARING OF THE GRAY
By John Esten Cooke

MY FATHER, GENERAL LEE
By Robert E. Lee, Jr.

PROLOGUE TO SUMTER
*The Beginnings of the Civil War from the John Brown Raid
to the Surrender of Fort Sumter*

THE CONFEDERATE RAIDER *ALABAMA*
By Admiral Raphael Semmes

ANDERSONVILLE
By John McElroy

ROBERT E. LEE

THE MAN AND THE SOLDIER

Arlington House.

A PICTORIAL BIOGRAPHY BY

Philip Van Doren Stern

Bonanza Books • New York

PICTURE CREDITS

Aerofilms Limited, Boreham-Wood, Herts., England: 13a

Andre Studio, Lexington, Va.: 25a, 141, 145, 172a, 222, 223, 224, 240a, 249a

Author's Collection: 13c, 40b, 41b, 45, 49b, 50a, 58, 59, 60b, 60c, 81, 88a, 91b, 93b, 110b, 119a, 127a, 128, 147a, 153b, 155, 157a, 163, 171b, 177a, 179a, 180, 210b, 215a, 225a, 225b, 233b, 249b

Battles and Leaders of the Civil War: 123, 131b, 134, 154b, 156a, 158, 170a, 172b, 176a, 179b, 182a, 182b, 183a

British Travel Association, New York: 11b, 12a, 13b, 14a, 14b, 15a, 21

Chicago Historical Society, Chicago, Ill.: 43 (with special permission from Mr. Charles Mason Remey), 60a, 77, 88b, 131a, 142a, 143a, 144, 188a, 228, 244a, 244b

City of Alexandria, Va.: 35a, 37

Confederate Museum, Richmond, Va.: 9, 26a, 72, 85, 129b, 135, 138a, 143c, 148, 149b, 188b, 208a, 212b, 227a, 227b, 227c, 227d, 242, 249c

Dementi Studio, Richmond, Va.: 24

Ellison, Lexington, Va.: 20, 245

Fort Hamilton Photo Laboratory, Brooklyn, N.Y.: 71a

Fort Monroe Casement Museum, Fort Monroe, Va.: 49a, 53a, 53b

Frick Art Reference Library, New York City: 17, 50b, 51c, 94

The Greenbrier, White Sulphur Springs, W. Va.: 231

Harper's *Weekly:* 114, 118, 119b, 120, 121, 122a, 126, 132a, 133, 138b, 139, 140 146a, 147b, 149a, 150, 151, 159a, 162, 165a, 181, 190, 195, 196, 197

Hartford Fire Insurance Company Group, Hartford, Conn.: 107a

Esther Holliday Green, Alexandria, Va.: 32

Henry E. Huntington Library, San Marino, Cal.: 52

Illinois State Historical Library, Springfield, Ill.: 254

The Illustrated London News: 108, 129a, 146b, 154a, 165b, 165c, 166, 168, 176b, 198, 199

W. T. Jones, Birmingham, England: 12b

R. E. Lee Memorial Foundation, Stratford, Va.: 26b, 27a, 27b, 28a, 28b, 29a, 29b, 30, 31a, 31b, 31c

Leslie's *Weekly:* 112–113, 115a, 115b, 116a, 116b, 202–203, 206

Library of Congress: 67a, 68b, 74b, 75a, 76a, 76b, 78a, 79b, 80a, 82, 83a, 84a, 84b, 87b, 132b, 137, 152a, 194, 204a, 204b, 205, 210a, 211a, 212a, 214, 218, 219, 221, 230, 232, 233a, 234, 240b, 250

Marler, Alexandria, Va.: 35b, 35c

Richard C. Marshall, Alexandria, Va.: 215b

Metropolitan Museum of Art, New York City: 75b (Gift of I. N. Phelps Stokes, Edward S. Hawes, Alice Mary Hawes, Marion Augusta Hawes, 1937)

Ed Miley, Dallas, Tex.: 252

National Archives, Washington, D.C.: 33, 36, 38b, 42b, 44, 48, 67b, 71b, 79a, 80b, 89a, 89b, 95, 106, 110a, 122b, 127b, 153a, 157b, 160, 167, 171a, 173, 175a, 175b, 177b, 183b, 184b, 185a, 189, 200, 207, 208b, 216a, 216b, 220

New York Public Library: 16, 18, 38a, 55a, 61, 68a, 70a, 86, 87a, 90, 96, 169a, 169b

Post Office Department, Washington, D.C.: 248a, 248b

Smithsonian Institution: 213a, 213b, 213c, 248c, 248d

Stone Mountain Memorial Association, Atlanta, Ga.: 253a, 253b

United States Department of the Interior, National Park Service: 15b, 46, 47, 51a, 51b, 54a, 54b, 55b, 56a, 56b, 57a, 57b, 100a, 100b, 101a, 101b, 102, 103, 104, 105, 107b, 109, 111, 143b, 174b, 174c, 184a, 185b, 209b

University of Oklahoma Press, Norman, Okla.: 97, 98

Valentine Museum, Richmond, Va.: 174a, 186a, 186b, 187, 229, 235, 236, 237, 238, 239a, 239b, 239c, 247, 251a

Virginia Historical Society, Richmond, Va.: 70b, 226, 243, 246

Virginia State Chamber of Commerce, Richmond, Va.: 25b, 130, 142b, 251b

Washington and Lee University, Lexington, Va.: 64, 65, 73

West Point Museum, West Point, N.Y.: 39, 40a, 41a, 42a, 69, 78b, 78c, 83b, 91a, 92, 93a, 217

Yale University Library, New Haven, Conn.: 74a

CONTENTS

INTRODUCTION

If Robert E. Lee's career had closed at Appomattox, he would be remembered only as a general who had fought well but had lost. Although such men are known to history, their names are nearly always obscure. Lee became truly great after the war, when he showed that a defeated soldier can, by the force of his example, teach people everywhere to surmount adversity and win respect in a new field of endeavor.

Interesting as Lee is as a soldier, he is even more fascinating as a human being. In this book, greater emphasis has been placed on him as a man than as a military figure. It is, of course, impossible to divorce the two, but more space is given here to Lee's personal life than to his exploits in the Civil War. This differs from what most other authors have done, for they usually devote most of their pages to Lee's career as a Confederate general and merely sketch in the years before and after the war. Foreign readers, encountering such books, must wonder why Americans in the North as well as in the South think so highly of a conquered general. Only someone acquainted with the facts of Lee's entire life can appreciate why he is so much more than that.

Such disproportion cannot, of course, be charged against Douglas Southall Freeman. His detailed four-volume work, which was published in 1934 under the modest title *R. E. Lee, a Biography,* covers the war years with great care but also does full justice to the other periods as well. Freeman was fortunate in being born in 1886, for that was early enough to enable him to meet many of the people who had known Lee, while it was also late enough for him to have access to most of the data made available by twentieth-century Civil War scholarship. His position as editor of a Richmond newspaper put him in touch with many of the descendants of the men he was writing about and procured for him documents and correspondence in private hands.

His monumental, thoroughly researched biography dominates the field. Anyone writing about Lee quickly realizes that Freeman has been almost everywhere before him. He can only acknowledge this and go on to examine the original sources for himself to see whether any new material is left or whether a fresh interpretation can be placed upon what his predecessor has already appraised.

The only fault reviewers found with Freeman's *Lee* was that it was biased in favor of its subject and of its author's native state. It would have been remarkable had it been otherwise, for Freeman said frankly that he had been repaid for his labors by "being privileged to live . . . for more than a decade in the company of a great gentleman." And, like Lee, he was a Virginian born and bred.

Freeman's massive work contains 2377 pages of text with 64 halftone engravings and many maps. This book attempts to do the only important thing Freeman left undone—to bring together the pictorial material which illustrates the various phases of Lee's life. The text has been written by a Northerner who has tried to present his subject as an American rather than as a Southerner and a Confederate. What Lee said and wrote after the war makes it evident that he wanted to rejoin his country.

The author feels so strongly in agreement with what Douglas Southall

Freeman had to say in the introduction to his biography of Lee that he would like to quote those words here:

I have one confession to make. For more than twenty years the study of military history has been my chief avocation. Whether the operations have been those of 1914–18, on which I happened to be a daily commentator, or those of the conflict between the states, each new inquiry has made the monstrous horror of war more unintelligible to me. It has seemed incredible that human beings, endowed with any of the powers of reason, should hypnotize themselves with doctrines of "national honor" or "sacred right" and pursue mass murder to exhaustion or to ruin. I subscribe with my whole heart to the view of General Lee that had "forbearance and wisdom been practised on both sides," the great national tragedy of 1861 might have been prevented. If . . . I have let my abhorrence of war appear . . . I trust the reader will understand that . . . [it is] only because I am not willing to have this study of a man who loved peace interpreted as glorification of war.

The author wants to thank Mrs. Casenove Lee, Washington, D.C., Mrs. George Bolling Lee, San Francisco, Cal., and Mrs. Hunter de Butts, Upperville, Va., for permission to use Lee family material; Mrs. Dorothy Mills Parker, Washington, D.C., for being kind enough to read that part of the manuscript which deals with the early history of the Lee family; Mrs. Howard Thompson, Coton Hall, Shropshire, for assistance on the English background; Mr. W. B. Hurd and Mrs. R. C. Goodale of Alexandria, Va., for making it possible to visit the places of Lee interest in that city; Mr. E. S. Mattingly, Dr. Cecil D. Eby, Jr., and Dr. Marshall Fishwick of Washington and Lee University, Lexington, Va., for information about Lee's last years; Dr. Bell I. Wiley of Emory University, Atlanta, Ga., for permitting the use of part of a speech he made on Lee; Miss India Thomas of the Confederate Museum and Mrs. Ralph Catterall of the Valentine Museum in Richmond, Dr. Chester D. Bradley of the Fort Monroe Casement Museum at Fort Monroe, Va., and Mrs. Paul M. Rhymer of the Chicago Historical Society for much help and advice.

PHILIP VAN DOREN STERN

Brooklyn, N.Y.
    April, 1963

ROBERT E. LEE

THE MAN AND THE SOLDIER

Robert E. Lee's spurs

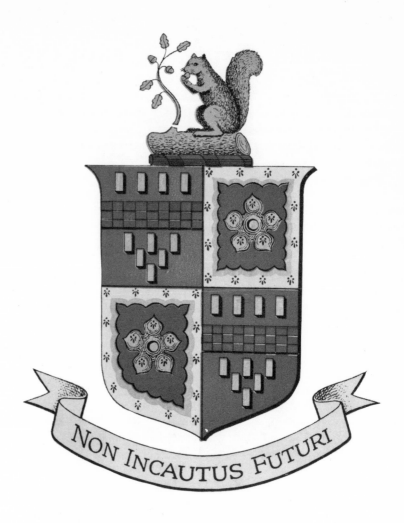

NON INCAUTUS FUTURI

THE ARMS OF THE LEE FAMILY
OF COTON HALL, SHROPSHIRE

Robert E. Lee was always interested in his family's history. In 1838, he wanted to obtain an authentic copy of the Lee coat of arms in order to have a seal cut. Writing to a cousin in Alexandria, he said: "I think [the seal] is due from a man of my large family to his posterity. . . . If, therefore, you can assist me in this laudable enterprise, I shall be much obliged. . . . I once saw . . . our family tree, and as I begin in my old age to feel a little curiosity relative to my forefathers, their origin, whereabouts, etc., any information you can give me will increase the obligation."

The man who wrote this letter had just been made a captain in the Engineers. The promotion evidently gave him reason to think about the continuity of life and the inexorable passing of time. He was then thirty-one years old.

THE LEE FAMILY IN ENGLAND

Almost without exception, the great soldiers of the world from Alexander to Napoleon had been fiercely ambitious, ruthless men. But Robert E. Lee was neither ambitious nor ruthless. The most serious charges ever made against his ability as a general were that he was too gentle, too kind, too reluctant to hurt his subordinates' feelings.

How did this modest, good-hearted man rise to fame as a military leader? What was behind the gray-and-gold uniform, the impenetrable façade of almost perfect self-control, the unrevealing eyes, the face that was never pictured with a smile—or a frown? What was Robert E. Lee really like as a soldier, as an educator, as a person?

To understand the roots of his being, one has to go far back, back for nearly seven hundred years before his birth in Virginia to the England that was just taking shape after the Norman Conquest of 1066. There in Shropshire, the county where the Lee family originated, one can trace Robert E. Lee's beginnings.

Shropshire is in the west Midlands, bordering on Wales. Its pleasant rolling hills and occasional bits of woodland are dotted with ancient structures. Watling Street, the Roman road running west to Wales, bisects the county. On it the legions marched to the Welsh border, and along it are the remains of their fortified towns. Shropshire has many quaint place names which memorialize the long continuity of human existence there. Ruyton of the Eleven Towns was once Roman Rutinium. Names like Gallowstree Elm, Halfpenny Green, and Merryhill are reminders of events that happened long ago.

About a century after the Norman Conquest, a knight named Reyner, a descendant of one of the men who had fought under William at the Battle of Hastings, built a home in a meadow near Pim Hill about five miles north of Shrewsbury, not far from the center of Shropshire. At that time the Anglo-Saxon word for a grassy clearing in the forest or an open meadow was *Leah* (also spelled *Lea, Leigh, Lay, Laye, Ley,* and *Lee* at various times and places). The knight, who was later to become the Sheriff of Shropshire, called himself Reyner de Lega (also Reyner de Lé or Lea), and it was from him that his numerous descendants—and Robert E. Lee—got their name. Reyner de Lé was the first to use the horizontal chequered bars and rectangles which still appear on the Lee arms. His dwelling was replaced in 1571 by a Tudor building, the present Lea Hall. In this fine old home, a fireplace dated 1574 has a wooden panel over it on which are carved the initials *R E L*, probably for Sir Richard Lee of Langley.

As the descendants of Reyner de Lea spread across Shropshire, they married into other leading families to form lasting alliances. In 1385, a Roger Lee married Margaret Astley of Nordley Regis. After this, the Lees quartered their arms with those of the Astleys. The shield on the Lee arms now bears the Astley cinquefoils in two of its quarters. The squirrel thoughtfully nibbling an acorn and the motto *Non Incautus Futuri* (Not Unmindful of the Future) have long indicated the family's concern for providing for the years to come and for generations yet unborn.

Locations of the Lee ancestral homes in Shropshire

Lea Hall, which stands on the site of the first Lee home in England

11

The two sons of Roger and Margaret Astley Lee were named Robert and John. Robert founded the Langley Lees, while John founded the Coton Lees. The male line of the Langley Lees ended in 1660, but the Coton Lees are still flourishing. And it was from Coton Hall that the Virginia Lees came. The country around Coton Hall is filled with associations with the Lee family which has lived in that area for nearly eight hundred years. In a church at Acton Burnell, a few miles south of Shrewsbury, is a recumbent marble effigy made about 1591 of Sir Richard Lee of the Langley Lees. Its sculptured face strongly resembles the bearded features of the leader of the Army of Northern Virginia.

St. Mary's Church in Alveley, near Coton Hall, has the fourteenth-century arms of John Lee. This church has witnessed the rites of passage of the local residents for generations. In 1349, when the Black Death struck here, two-thirds of the people died of bubonic plague. Each day's toll of corpses was interred in a common grave. But the church has also witnessed pleasanter events. Here on October 21, 1599, according to the register, Richard Lee married Elizabeth Bendy. It was their son, Colonel Richard Lee, who emigrated to Virginia and founded the Lee family in America. Near the church is the Squirrel Inn, which derives its name from the Lee coat of arms. And the boys in the Alveley School still wear a symbolic squirrel on their uniforms.

Coton Hall stands on a little hill which bears evidence of long occupation. Among the ruins there a Roman temple, a Saxon church, a Norman church, a fort, and a customs house have been identified. The manor house is far older than it looks, for the medieval structure was made into a Tudor dwelling in Elizabethan times and then was further modified about 1812 by the last of the Lees to live there. Underneath the exterior of the present mansion the stones laid by local masons hundreds of years ago still remain. Lawns and terraces cover what was once a water-filled moat dug to protect the original fortified building and its occupants.

A few yards from the manor house is a now-roofless domestic chapel which was used as a private place of worship by the Lees from 1387 to 1820—more than 400 years. Three stained-glass roundels from its ruined windows are in the church at Alveley.

Interior of the Lee Domestic Chapel at Coton Hall showing the East Window

*Two views of
Coton Hall, the ancestral
home of the Lees in Shropshire.
The present-day house is of
medieval origin, but was modified
so extensively early in the nineteenth
century that few traces of the
ancient building can be seen.*

About a mile north of Coton Hall is Kingsnordley with several ancient farmhouses. It is believed that one of these was given to Richard Lee when he married Elizabeth Bendy and that the founder of the American Lees was born here. The Lee arms, carved on an outer wall, may mark the house in which the Richard Lees lived, but there is no way of knowing.

These, then, are the historic homes and places associated with the Lee family in England. Shropshire was their home, and their careers were closely connected with the land. A. E. Housman, who was born in adjoining Worcester and who never actually lived in the Lee county, made it world famous in 1896 when *A Shropshire Lad* was first published. Contrasting its friendly rural virtues with the indifference and hostility of the city, he wrote:

*In my own shire, if I was sad,
Homely comforters I had:
The earth, because my heart was sore,
Sorrowed for the son she bore;
And standing hills, long to remain,
Shared their short-lived comrade's pain.
And bound for the same bourn as I,
On every road I wandered by,
Trod beside me, close and dear,
The beautiful and death-struck year:
Whether in the woodland brown
I heard the beechnut rustle down,
And saw the purple crocus pale
Flower about the autumn dale;
Or littering far the fields of May
Lady-smocks a-bleaching lay,
And like a skylit water stood
The bluebells in the azured wood.*

*The Lee table, designated by a will
made in 1665 to remain forever in
Coton Hall as an heirloom*

*The 500-year-old domestic chapel
on the grounds of Coton Hall.
It is now roofless and in ruins.*

Robert E. Lee knew that the Lee family in America had begun with his great-

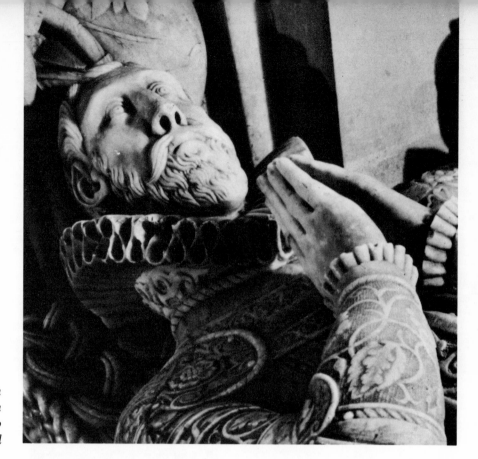

This effigy in the church at Acton Burnell of a Lee in Elizabethan times bears a close resemblance to the Confederate general

Over the fireplace at Lea Hall is this carved panel dated 1584 with the initials REL

great-great-grandfather, Richard Lee, who had settled in Virginia about 1640. The American Lees had a fairly good idea of their own history in this country and were able to trace the succeeding generations with reasonable accuracy. Oral tradition told them that Richard Lee came from Shropshire, but written records about his early life in England were scarce, and the people of R. E. Lee's generation were not able to verify their belief. It is only in very recent times that evidence has been found to settle a question which puzzled genealogists of the Lee family for so long.

Not only Robert E. Lee but even his most distinguished biographer, Douglas Southall Freeman, did not know for sure that the man who came to Virginia about 1640 was one of the Coton Hall Lees. In fact, Freeman said in his *R. E. Lee,* published in 1934, that "every effort to establish definite connection between Robert E. Lee's American ancestors and any line of English Lees has failed" (Vol. I, p. 160).

Much research and a lucky accident have proved to the satisfaction of the London College of Heralds that a connection between the English and American families does exist. The research established the *probability* that Richard, the founder of the American Lees, was the son of Richard Lee of Nordley Regis. And then the discovery of a family Bible, printed in 1765, which had been at Cobb's Hall, one of the Lee estates in Virginia, gave proof of the founder's parentage. An entry on a page in this Bible, which had been copied from a still earlier one, stated that "Colonel Richard Lee [son of Richard Lee] of Nordley Regis in Shropshire died at Dividing Creeks in the Co. of Northumberland, Va. March 1, 1664."

The entry, however, did not give a birth date, nor has this ever been determined. Since Richard Lee's parents were married in Alveley Church on October 21, 1599, it can only be said that Richard, the founder of the American Lee family, was born sometime early in the seventeenth century. The date of

14

St. Mary's Church at Alveley near Coton Hall. This ancient building contains Lee burial markers, the fourteenth-century arms of John Lee, and stained-glass roundels removed from the Coton Hall domestic chapel.

his birth has been stated conjecturally as between 1600 and 1613, with the latter more probable.

Why Richard Lee left England and came to America is not known. In fact, very little is known about his early life. As a younger son who realized that his father's estate would go to one of his elder brothers, his prospects at home were not good. He went to London to stay with an uncle or a cousin and while there acquired some knowledge of law.

Young Richard Lee is a shadowy figure; the records about him are scant, and he is as difficult to trace as a manorial ghost. But when he came to America, he soon became a very real person who left many records. An early description said that "he was a man of good Stature, comely visage, an enterprising genius, a sound head, vigorous spirit, and generous nature." What Richard Lee did after he settled in Virginia attests to the fact that he must have possessed all of these attributes, for he made a fortune there in less than twenty-five years.

Douglas Southall Freeman has pointed out that the six generations from Richard Lee to Robert E. Lee produced fifty-four male members who lived to maturity and that thirty-seven of them held public office. "These thirty-seven," he says, "included ten burgesses, ten members of the state legislature, six professional soldiers, three naval officers, six militia officers, six members of the colonial council, four members of Revolutionary conventions, three governors or acting governors, two signers of the Declaration of Independence, two diplomatists, three members of the Continental Congress, three members of the United States Congress, one member of the United States Cabinet, one secretary of the colony, one London alderman, one town mayor, one judge, five justices of the peace, two clerks and one deputy clerk of courts, and two prosecuting attorneys—a total of seventy-two offices."

The Coton Hall Bible, dated 1639

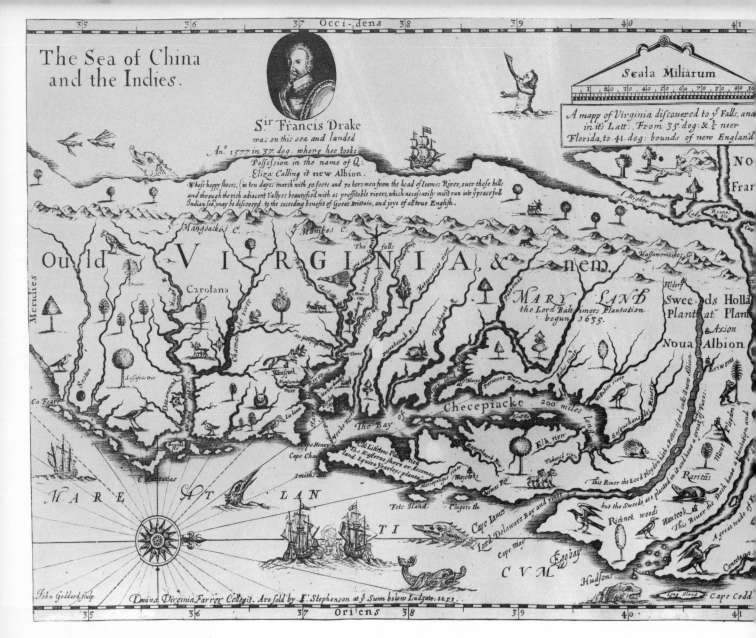

Map of Virginia
by John Goddard, 1651.
Note that north is to the right.

VIRGINIA AS IT WAS
WHEN THE FIRST LEE ARRIVED

This map of Virginia, dated 1651, shows what was then known about the country between the Atlantic Ocean and the Blue Ridge Mountains. Exploration and settlement had followed the waterways and had not gone far beyond their lower navigable stretches. The falls marked on the map at the source of the James were actually the rapids at the site of what was one day to be the city of Richmond. The unknown territory beyond the vaguely indicated mountains was thought to be a narrow strip of land bordering on the Sea of China—the Pacific Ocean. Sir Francis Drake had sailed along the coast of California and had landed near San Francisco in 1579 (not 1577, as erroneously stated below his portrait), but no one then realized that the shores he had seen were several thousand miles beyond Virginia's westernmost mountains. The bays and river systems of the Atlantic coast, however, are presented with more accuracy.

16

THE LEE FAMILY IN AMERICA

The America to which Richard Lee came was still a wild and largely unexplored land. The colony of Virginia, where the Lee family was to become so important and where Robert E. Lee was to command his armies, was then settled only along the tidewater bays and rivers. Since there were almost no roads, men and goods usually went by boat. The most desirable plantations had their own landings with natural channels leading to them that were deep enough for trading ships from England to tie up at the wharves. Land far from navigable water had little value because it was difficult to reach.

Four large rivers ran through the tidewater country: the York, the Rappahannock, the Potomac, and the James. Each was to play a major part in the migrations of the Lees and in the battles their sixth generation was to fight. The eastern theater of the great war with which Robert E. Lee's name will forever be associated was largely a struggle for possession of the capital of the North on the Potomac and the capital of the South on the James. The country in between was to be one great battlefield where the names of villages and crossroads gained dearly bought immortality.

The tidewater area is only about 160 by 120 miles in extent. But this is the heartland of Virginia, and it was here that the fate of the colony, the state, and later, the nation was to be determined. Not only the Lees, but the Washingtons, the Jeffersons, the Madisons, the Monroes, and other distinguished families had their origins here. In terms of the mother country from which the colonists came, Tidewater Virginia was about the size of Southern England without the western counties.

The seeds of the terrible internecine war of the 1860s had already been sown in this small part of the vast American continent, for here, in 1619, the captain of a Dutch trading ship had brought Negro slaves to sell them to the colonists. But here also, and in the same year, representative government in America began when the Governor and his council met in the Jamestown church with delegates from the eleven plantations.

When Richard Lee arrived in Jamestown in 1639 or 1640, more than a generation had passed since that community had been founded in 1607. During this time about 7500 white settlers and several hundred Negro slaves had populated the new colony. But in the unwanted inland areas, the Indians, who had nearly wiped out Jamestown in 1622, were still a threat. These dark and mysterious people of the forest, resentful of the encroachment of the newcomers upon the highly prized shore acres, were soon to strike again before they were driven back forever beyond the western hills.

Jamestown itself, where Richard Lee stayed when he arrived, was still a small town, although it had come a long way from the early years when its half-starved, ailing people died so fast that the only record the survivors kept was a daily list of the names of the dead.

Most of the first settlers were gone by this time. The redoubtable John Smith had died in England in 1631. Dead too, was the Indian maiden Pocahontas, who had allegedly saved his life. Legends were already gathering about the names of these pioneers. Like the people of Sir Walter Raleigh's even earlier lost colonies on the shores of North Carolina, their fate had caught the imagination of the world. John Smith and Pocahontas were to be immortalized by storytellers for centuries to come.

COLONEL RICHARD LEE

17

Jamestown Island sketched by August Kollner in 1845. The ruined tower marks the site of the church that was built in 1639–47, burned in 1676, and then rebuilt.

Since Richard Lee was required to be in Jamestown only when court was in session, he could live elsewhere. Sometime in 1640 or 1641 he married Anne Constable, who had been brought to Virginia as a member of the new Governor's household. After the wedding, the couple made their first home near the extreme southern end of the peninsula between the York and Rappahannock rivers. This was an isolated place twenty miles from Jamestown on the far side of the wide mouth of the York River. An Indian town named Capahosic Wicomico was very close to the Lee home—too close, in fact, as events of the year 1644 would prove. Pocahontas' father, Powhatan, had died in 1618 and had been succeeded by Opechancanough. The new chief was tired of seeing the white settlers devouring his people's land; toward the end of his life he tried to drive them away. On April 18, 1644, hordes of painted Indians came out of the forests to massacre the newcomers. They killed 300 of them but were repulsed in a deadly counterattack. Opechancanough was captured in 1646, brought to Jamestown and shot, but the north shore of the York River had to be abandoned during the Indian wars.

Richard Lee and his family escaped, perhaps using his trading boat to get away. In December 1644, he settled at New Poquoson on the peninsula between the York and the James, where it was safer from attack. During his residence there, he continued to acquire more land and children.

In 1649, he was appointed Secretary of State of Virginia. The same year, Charles I was beheaded and Oliver Cromwell began the series of military victories that were to keep him in power for a decade. Since the people in the distant colonies could not believe the incredible news from England, they remained loyal to the Crown and to Charles II, heir to the throne.

During this politically troubled era, Richard Lee made a voyage to Europe, was appointed to the Council, and in the winter of 1650–51 was

18

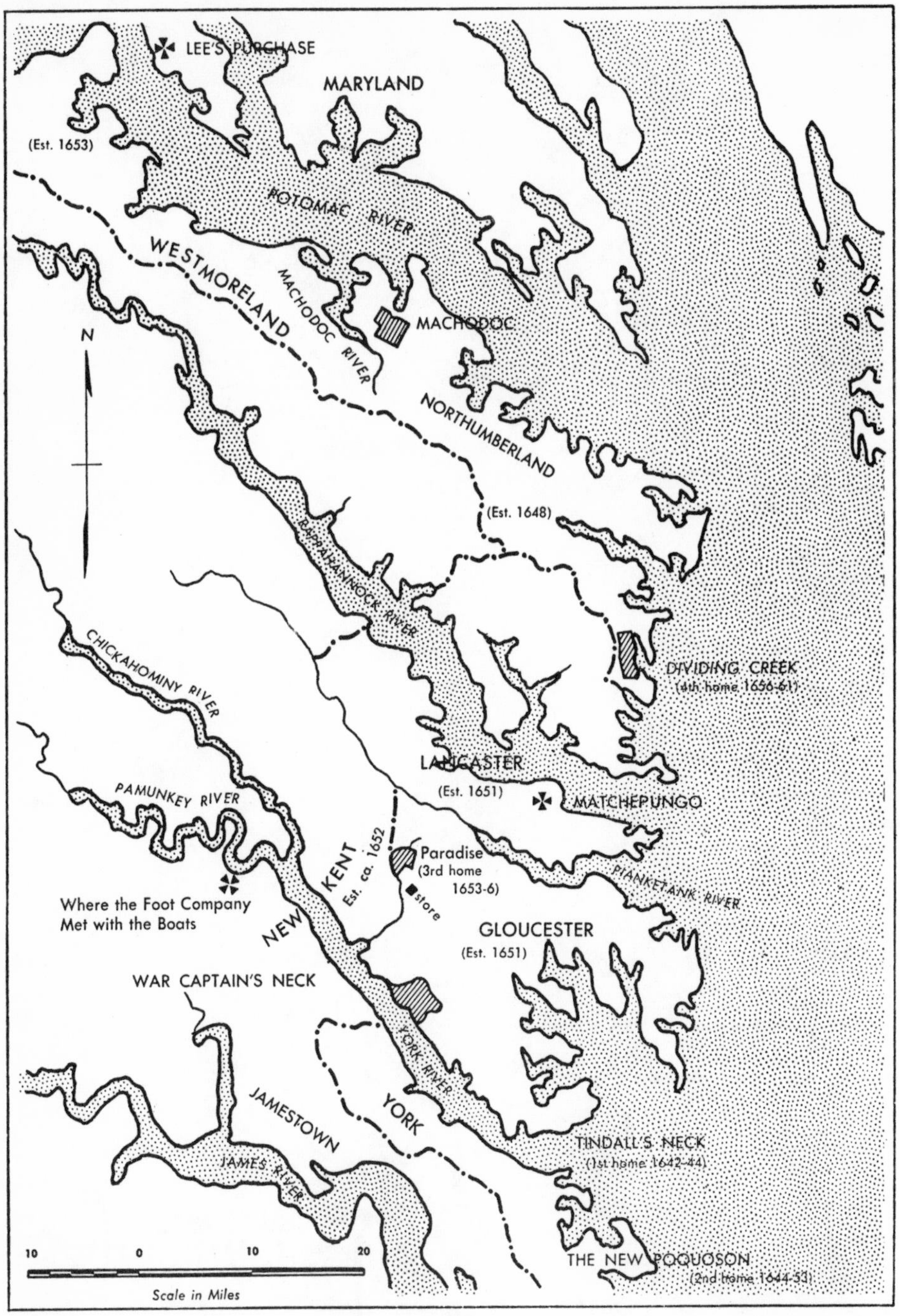

Colonel Richard Lee's landholdings from 1642 until his
death in 1664

LEE'S PURCHASE

MARYLAND

(Est. 1653)

POTOMAC RIVER

WESTMORELAND

MACHODOC RIVER

MACHODOC

N

NORTHUMBERLAND

(Est. 1648)

RAPPAHANNOCK RIVER

CHICKAHOMINY RIVER

DIVIDING CREEK
(4th home 1658-61)

LANCASTER
(Est. 1651)

MATCHEPUNGO

PAMUNKEY RIVER

PIANKETANK RIVER

Where the Foot Company
Met with the Boats

NEW KENT

Est. ca. 1652

Paradise
(3rd home
1653-6)

store

GLOUCESTER
(Est. 1651)

WAR CAPTAIN'S NECK

YORK RIVER

JAMESTOWN

YORK

TINDALL'S NECK
(1st home 1642-44)

JAMES RIVER

10   0   10   20

Scale in Miles

THE NEW POQUOSON
(2nd home 1644-53)

Reproduced from THE LEE CHRONICLE, by
CAZENOVE GARDNER LEE, JR.
Compiled and edited by
DOROTHY MILLS PARKER,
New York, 1957, by permission of
Mrs. Cazenove Lee. Map drawn by
Ludwell Lee Montague.

made a colonel, presumably because of his activity in preparing defenses
against Indian attacks. When an armed ship arrived from England to demand
that the Virginians swear allegiance to Cromwell's Commonwealth, he was
among the majority who did so early in 1652. The same year he resigned as
Secretary of State and again went abroad.

Soon after returning to Virginia, Richard moved to the northern shore
of the York River, not far from where he had first settled. Since the Indians
were no longer a menace, he was able to trade with them and expand his
landholdings rapidly. He called this third Virginia home Paradise. Despite its
pleasant name, he and his ever-growing family remained there for only three
years (1653–56), a good part of which he spent in England.

A nineteenth-century version of the genealogical tree of the Lee family in America

When he returned, he moved to his fourth and final home in Virginia, the Dividing Creek plantation at the Chesapeake Bay end of the peninsula between the Rappahannock and Potomac rivers. There his tenth and last child was born. His grandson Charles built Cobbs Hall on this land about 1720.

In 1658, Richard Lee took his eldest son John, then about sixteen years old, to England to place him in Queen's College, Oxford. The son presented to the college a silver cup which bore an engraved inscription that was to puzzle genealogists of the Lee family for centuries. The incised words stated that John was the son of Richard Lee of Morton Regis in Shropshire. But there is no place by that name in the county. Not until modern times was a reasonable explanation for the strange misspelling on the cup found. The engraver had evidently misread Nordley Regis as Morton Regis. Once this was cleared up, the presentation cup became one more link of evidence in the long chain of painstakingly sought proofs that finally established the connection between the Lees of Virginia and the Lees of Coton Hall.

While Richard Lee was in England during the winter of 1658–59, he purchased some property in Stratford Langton, which was then a verdant country place about five miles from the center of London. When he returned home, he expected to put his American landholdings in the charge of a general manager so he could move his family to his British estate, where his many children could be properly educated.

Richard Lee steadily increased his holdings. By this time he had become one of the wealthiest men in Virginia, and his acres in the rich tidewater country could be counted by the thousands. In 1660, he added 4000 more acres to his domain by claiming the headrights of eighty Negroes whom he had evidently purchased as slaves.

Richard Lee's biographer, Colonel Ludwell Lee Montague, says of him:

Richard Lee must be judged . . . in terms of his own age. There was not much difference between the transportation of an unwilling captive from Ireland and that of another from Africa, except the fact that the African could be held for life and his progeny after him. In resorting to Negro slavery Richard Lee shrewdly solved his immediate economic problem. He could not have foreseen the consequences which in 1759 caused his great-grandson, Richard Henry Lee, to make an impassioned plea to the House of Burgesses for abolition of the slave trade. He could not have foreseen the tragedy of his most famous descendant, Robert Edward Lee.

One thing is certain; Richard Lee was able to endure willingly all kinds of hardship. His many trips to England attest to that. The acute misery, discomfort, and danger of these long voyages discouraged most people from crossing the Atlantic more than once. But Richard spent a great deal of time in the small, sea-tossed sailing ships on which each successful passage was considered a happy dispensation for which the surviving passengers should give heartfelt thanks. The Lees never lacked courage. They were a venturesome family in which the willingness to take risks was handed down from generation to generation.

But Richard Lee was growing old, and with advancing age came the desire to see his family settled in comfort. When Charles II became king in 1660, Richard took his family to England a year later to live in Stratford Langton. He came back to Virginia in 1663, returned briefly to England, and made his will there in February 1664 just before sailing again to Virginia. He was evidently ill when he arrived at Dividing Creek, for he died there early in March. He was buried on the grounds of the plantation where his grave is

The silver cup which Richard Lee's eldest son, John, gave to Queens College, Oxford, in 1658

A Genealogical Chart of
The Lees of Virginia

This chart includes only the more important members of the family.

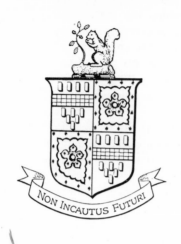

NON INCAUTUS FUTURI

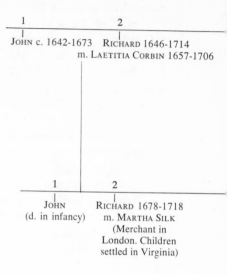

1	2
JOHN c. 1642-1673	RICHARD 1646-1714
	m. LAETITIA CORBIN 1657-1706

1	2
JOHN	RICHARD 1678-1718
(d. in infancy)	m. MARTHA SILK
	(Merchant in
	London. Children
	settled in Virginia)

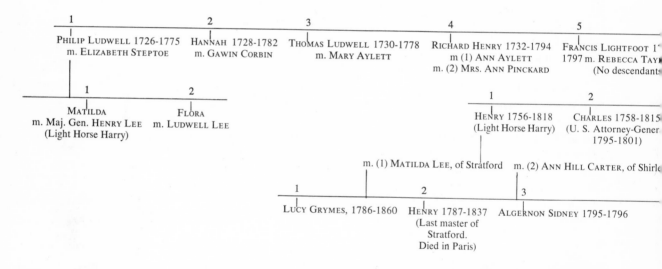

1	2	3	4	5
PHILIP LUDWELL 1726-1775	HANNAH 1728-1782	THOMAS LUDWELL 1730-1778	RICHARD HENRY 1732-1794	FRANCIS LIGHTFOOT 1
m. ELIZABETH STEPTOE	m. GAWIN CORBIN	m. MARY AYLETT	m (1) ANN AYLETT	1797 m. REBECCA TAY
			m. (2) MRS. ANN PINCKARD	(No descendants

1	2
MATILDA	FLORA
m. Maj. Gen. HENRY LEE	m. LUDWELL LEE
(Light Horse Harry)	

1	2
HENRY 1756-1818	CHARLES 1758-1815
(Light Horse Harry)	(U. S. Attorney-Gener
	1795-1801)

m. (1) MATILDA LEE, of Stratford   m. (2) ANN HILL CARTER, of Shirl

1	2	3
LUCY GRYMES, 1786-1860	HENRY 1787-1837	ALGERNON SIDNEY 1795-1796
	(Last master of	
	Stratford.	
	Died in Paris)	

1
GEORGE WASHINGTON CUS
1832-1913 (d. unmar

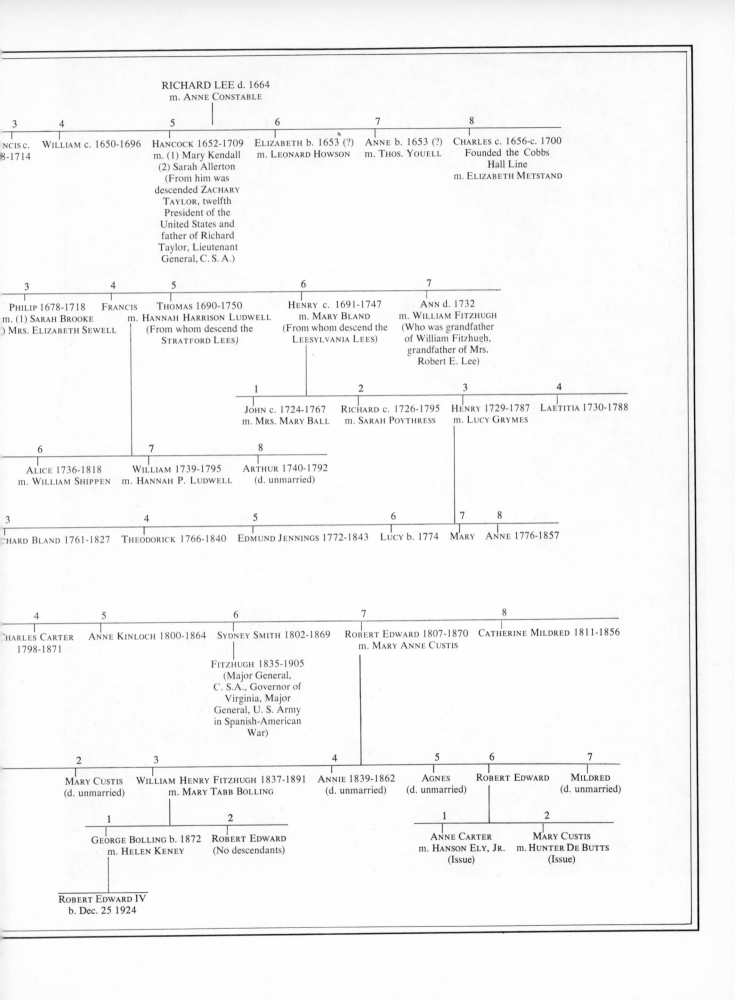

RICHARD LEE d. 1664
m. ANNE CONSTABLE

3	4	5	6	7	8
...NCIS c. ...8-1714	WILLIAM c. 1650-1696	HANCOCK 1652-1709 m. (1) Mary Kendall (2) Sarah Allerton (From him was descended ZACHARY TAYLOR, twelfth President of the United States and father of Richard Taylor, Lieutenant General, C. S. A.)	ELIZABETH b. 1653 (?) m. LEONARD HOWSON	ANNE b. 1653 (?) m. THOS. YOUELL	CHARLES c. 1656-c. 1700 Founded the Cobbs Hall Line m. ELIZABETH METSTAND

3	4	5	6	7
PHILIP 1678-1718 m. (1) SARAH BROOKE (?) MRS. ELIZABETH SEWELL	FRANCIS	THOMAS 1690-1750 m. HANNAH HARRISON LUDWELL (From whom descend the STRATFORD LEES)	HENRY c. 1691-1747 m. MARY BLAND (From whom descend the LEESYLVANIA LEES)	ANN d. 1732 m. WILLIAM FITZHUGH (Who was grandfather of William Fitzhugh, grandfather of Mrs. Robert E. Lee)

1	2	3	4
JOHN c. 1724-1767 m. MRS. MARY BALL	RICHARD c. 1726-1795 m. SARAH POYTHRESS	HENRY 1729-1787 m. LUCY GRYMES	LAETITIA 1730-1788

6	7	8
ALICE 1736-1818 m. WILLIAM SHIPPEN	WILLIAM 1739-1795 m. HANNAH P. LUDWELL	ARTHUR 1740-1792 (d. unmarried)

3	4	5	6	7	8
...CHARD BLAND 1761-1827	THEODORICK 1766-1840	EDMUND JENNINGS 1772-1843	LUCY b. 1774	MARY	ANNE 1776-1857

4	5	6	7	8
CHARLES CARTER 1798-1871	ANNE KINLOCH 1800-1864	SYDNEY SMITH 1802-1869	ROBERT EDWARD 1807-1870 m. MARY ANNE CUSTIS	CATHERINE MILDRED 1811-1856

FITZHUGH 1835-1905
(Major General,
C. S. A., Governor of
Virginia, Major
General, U. S. Army
in Spanish-American
War)

2	3	4	5	6	7
MARY CUSTIS (d. unmarried)	WILLIAM HENRY FITZHUGH 1837-1891 m. MARY TABB BOLLING	ANNIE 1839-1862 (d. unmarried)	AGNES (d. unmarried)	ROBERT EDWARD	MILDRED (d. unmarried)

1	2
GEORGE BOLLING b. 1872 m. HELEN KENEY	ROBERT EDWARD (No descendants)

1	2
ANNE CARTER m. HANSON ELY, JR. (Issue)	MARY CUSTIS m. HUNTER DE BUTTS (Issue)

ROBERT EDWARD IV
b. Dec. 25 1924

*"Light-Horse" Harry Lee, hero of the Revolution and father of Robert E. Lee.
Painted by Robert Edge Pine. Courtesy of the Pennsylvania Academy of Fine Arts.*

believed to be among others in a family cemetery under the shadow of a huge sycamore tree.

Richard Lee's extensive holdings were left to his wife and his eight surviving children. Some of them added to their original property; others moved elsewhere to improve their fortunes. But the family's chief claim to distinction is not its wealth but the fame it acquired from public service.

When Richard Lee II died in 1714, he left five children, all of whom had families. From these the Lee clan spread out rapidly. One of his sons, Thomas, had eight children. And Thomas' third son, Richard Henry Lee, was among the most distinguished men of the Revolution. He held many high offices in Virginia, was a delegate to and President of the Continental Congress, a signer of the Declaration of Independence, and the author of the Tenth Amendment to the Constitution. The fourth son, Francis Lightfoot Lee, was also a delegate to the Continental Congress and a signer of the Declaration of Independence.

Two of the younger sons, William and Arthur, were educated abroad. Arthur became a pamphleteer, the author of the *Monitor's Letters* which sharply criticized Britain's treatment of her American colonies. During the Revolutionary War, William negotiated a treaty with Holland for much-needed aid from that well-to-do country. Both brothers were active in exposing the machinations of the secret agents in Europe who were keeping the British informed about the young American republic's plans.

Thomas Lee, the father of these brilliant young men whom John Adams called "that band of brothers intrepid and unchangeable," was the builder of the great house which, more than any other, is the place around which the fortunes of this branch of the Lee family were centered for a century. This is the big brownish-red brick mansion, Stratford Hall, which has grounds bordering on the Potomac River a few miles from Wakefield, where George Washington was born in 1732.

"Light-Horse" Harry Lee, brother of Thomas, military hero of the American Revolution, and father of Robert E. Lee, was born at "Leesylvania," near Dumfries, about twenty miles south of Alexandria, Virginia. He had no claim on Stratford Hall, but when he married his cousin Matilda in 1782, he came into possession of the splendid river plantation through the alliance. During the early years of their marriage, when the young couple had plenty of money, there was much entertaining, much going and coming, much gaiety and festivity at Stratford.

At the time Harry Lee married Matilda, he seemed one of the most fortunate young men in the new American republic. He was only twenty-six years old, but he already had achieved great fame as a brilliant commander in the War of the Revolution, first in the North, where he fought at Brandywine, Germantown, Monmouth, Valley Forge, and captured Paulus Hook. Then he served with great success with General Nathanael Greene in the South. He witnessed the surrender of Cornwallis at Yorktown and from there went to the Northern Neck where he visited Stratford Hall and first met "the Divine Matilda."

Matilda bore him several children, the eldest of whom, Henry, was the heir to Stratford. "Light-Horse" Harry Lee evidently showed signs of the recklessness with money that was eventually to ruin him, for his wife made arrangements for her estate to be left in trust for the children. When she died in 1790 at the age of twenty-six, her husband was permitted to stay on in Stratford only until their son came of age. Meanwhile, he was Governor of Virginia for three terms.

Supposed portrait of Ann Carter Lee, mother of Robert E. Lee, and (below) *her home, Shirley, on the James River*

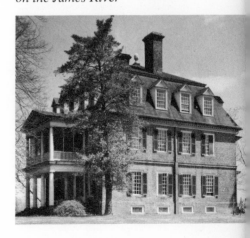

Stratford Hall. An early drawing showing the great house as it was in the days when its people traveled in coaches.

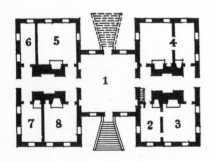

Main Floor Plan

1 Great Hall	5 Parlor
2 Nursery	6 Parlor Closet
3 Mother's Room	7 Library Closet
4 Dining Room	8 Library

STRATFORD:
THE BIRTHPLACE OF ROBERT E. LEE

Thomas Lee, grandson of Richard the Founder, had built Stratford in the 1720s. The house and its outbuildings were constructed largely of local materials. Brick was baked of clay from nearby beds; lumber was cut from the virgin forests; foundation stones were brought from Virginia quarries; and plaster and mortar were mixed by using lime made by burning Potomac oysters. Glass, hardware, and fine building stone had to be shipped in from England. Work went on for five years or more before the ambitious project was completed.

The buildings were located on a level plateau nearly a mile from the river. Then a vista was cut through the dense woods to give the main house a view of the broad Potomac and the private wharf where ships from England could unload or load their cargoes. The well-arranged group of buildings was purposely placed far from the tidal river, for its navigable waters that brought friendly ships could also bring hostile ones. A big cannon ball, fired from a British man-of-war during the Revolution and still lying on the ground near the summer kitchen, shows how wise it was to place the buildings well away from the Potomac.

The steep shores along the river were called "clifts" when Thomas Lee bought the original tract of land which he later added to until he had 4103 acres. The plantation was named Stratford, after Colonel Richard Lee's English estate at Stratford Langton.

Thomas Lee lived at Machodoc (later called Mount Pleasant) while the great house at Stratford was being built. It was a twenty-mile journey by road from one place to the other, but he must have made the trip many times in order to supervise the construction work as it proceeded. In some cases, he

STRATFORD HALL
The
Birthplace of ROBERT E. LEE
In the Northern Neck of
Virginia

·W. No 388-1

may have traveled up the Potomac by boat, since waterways were far better than Virginia roads in the 1720s.

Just before Stratford Hall was completed, Thomas Lee and his family nearly lost their lives when an incendiary fire destroyed their house at Machodoc. He had been serving as a Justice of the Peace, and some transported felons whose arrest he had ordered struck back at him by robbing his home and setting fire to it. It has been said that Stratford Hall's ready means of egress from almost every room were planned that way because of this disastrous fire, but it seems obvious that the new house was too far advanced in construction by this time to permit any major alterations.

The big, solid-looking mansion with its massive clusters of chimneys and its unusual floor plan is unique in American domestic architecture of the period. But it owes much to the Capitol at Williamsburg, to the Secretary's house there, and to the Great House at Green Spring which Governor William Berkeley had built in 1648 and in which Thomas Lee's wife, Hannah Ludwell, had grown up. Lee, who had served as a Burgess at Williamsburg, naturally knew these buildings well. He used some details from them such as the H-shaped layout of the Capitol, brickwork and roof construction from the Secretary's house, and the central hall of the Berkeley mansion in the plans for his residence. The Williamsburg prototypes and Stratford Hall itself were all derived, of course, from English manorial houses.

The great hall, 30 feet square, is literally the heart and center of Stratford; the other rooms are accessory to it. In it were held the formal receptions, the stately dances, and the family gatherings that made the big house a place to be remembered by anyone who saw it during the height of its glory. And the grounds around it, with their dependencies, stables, formal gardens, and long vista cut through the woods, all served to impress the visitor.

In addition to being a home, Stratford also had to be a fort which could be defended against a surprise attack by Indians or white outlaws. Its thick walls could withstand gunfire, and its twin groups of chimneys offered shelter to armed men who could be posted behind them. Besides being a home and a

STRATFORD HALL:
Plan of the Grounds and Buildings

1 Great House
2 Southwest Dependency—
  Thomas Lee's Office
3 Southeast Dependency—
  Kitchen
4 Northwest Dependency
5 Northeast Dependency
6 Smoke House
7 Meat House
8 Formal Garden
9 Orchard
10 Octagon House
11 Ha-Ha Wall
12 Small Stable
13 Coach House and Stable

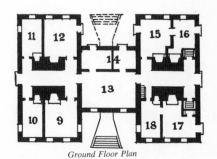

Ground Floor Plan

9 Blue Room *   14 Brick Rooms
10 Green Room *   15 White Room *
11 Red Room *   16 School Room
12 Counting House   17 Spinning Room
13 Servants' Lodging   18 Housekeeper's Room

* Bedrooms

27

Stratford Hall: Part of the Great Hall in the center of the building

The Dining Room with the portrait of Queen Caroline in the alcove

At left: the winter kitchen

Above: the private mill where flour and meal for the plantation were ground

fort, Stratford was also the center of a working plantation that was almost completely self-sustaining. It had its own mill, vegetable and herb gardens, water supply, smoke house, tobacco warehouses, cooper's shop, spinning and weaving rooms, even a school. Life was so complete on the big plantation that the Lees never had to leave it except for business trips or social visits. And they were never alone at Stratford. There was a large working population of skilled artisans, servants, and slaves, and there were guests who sometimes came to stay for a long while.

When Thomas Lee died in 1750, he left Stratford to his eldest son Philip, who occupied the house for twenty-five years. Philip in turn left it to Matilda, who married "Light-Horse" Harry Lee. Philip died in 1790.

Harry Lee was a strange and impetuous man. During the French Revolution, he wanted to volunteer his services to the men who were overthrowing the Old Regime, but his friends—George Washington among them—dissuaded him. At this time the widower was wooing twenty-year-old Ann Hill Carter of Shirley, one of the wealthiest heiresses in Virginia. Her father at first objected to the idea of his daughter marrying someone who was about to fight in what he considered a reckless cause, but when Harry Lee agreed to stay home, he gave his consent. The oddly matched couple was married on June 18, 1793.

Since Harry Lee was then the Governor of Virginia, the newlywed couple had to live in Richmond, which had been made the state capital in 1779. Ann, however, was often at her father's home, Shirley, and there her first child was born on April 2, 1795. Named Algernon Sidney Lee, the infant, like so many of his time, did not live for long. When he died at the age of sixteen months, his mother kept a lock of his blond hair as the only reminder of the baby she had borne and lost.

The Lees had moved to Stratford shortly before the death of their first child. There Ann was to bear her other children—five more—and there she was often left in isolated splendor while her husband traveled around the country on political business.

He was elected to Congress and was in Philadelphia when George Washington died in 1799. In delivering the funeral oration for Virginia's most celebrated public figure, "Light-Horse" Harry coined the undying "First in war, first in peace, and first in the hearts of his countrymen."

With the turn of the century, the fortunes of the master of Stratford Hall turned downward. Harry Lee's youth had all been glory; his declining years were to be increasingly miserable, and his wife and his children had to share his fate. He had lent Robert Morris $40,000, which he was never able to collect because Morris died. In his desperation, he turned to one mad scheme after another to regain his wealth. They all failed. Unlike his ancestors, who had built great estates in Virginia, Harry Lee seemed destined to destroy what he had. He could not touch Stratford, but he lost everything else. The once-rich tobacco lands were depleted from overplanting, and to make matters worse, a terrible drought parched the Northern Neck.

The Great House at Stratford. The birth chamber is on the main floor at the extreme right, facing south and east.

Stratford fell into disrepair; the once-big staff of servants and slaves dwindled. Ann continued to bear children, but matters became so bad at home that when she went to visit her father at Shirley in the summer of 1806, the last remaining carriage that took her there was in such poor condition that it could not be used for the return journey. And when she arrived at the big James River house, she found her beloved father dead. This was the low point in Ann Carter Lee's life. She was pregnant with her fifth child, and when she returned to Stratford in December, she had to drive through winter weather in an open vehicle her husband had somehow obtained for the trip. "Our poor old dwelling," she called the once-magnificent mansion when she wrote to a relative about Stratford.

It must have been cold there that winter, for there was not enough help to keep the vast fireplaces going. Ann had caught a severe cold in the open carriage, and she still had it when her child was born on January 19, 1807. The birth-room is a large, well-lighted chamber facing south and east. Next to it is a small room that served as a nursery. Except for the kitchen downstairs, these two rooms were probably the only warm ones in the house during that unhappy winter.

By this time Harry Lee had fathered so many children—and was so deeply immured in his own troubles—that he evidently let his wife choose a name for the infant. She called her son Robert Edward after her two brothers.

Robert Edward Lee spent the first three or four years of his life on the big plantation which had been the Lee family's pride in their prosperous days. The place evidently made a lasting impression upon him. During the war he wrote to his daughters who had just visited the old house and said: "It is endeared to me by many recollections and it has always been a great desire of my life to be able to purchase it." But it was not to be.

His memories of Stratford were not, of course, all from the years of his infancy. He visited Stratford a number of times during his boyhood. When he lived there he was too young to know anything about the disasters that were happening all around him.

On April 11, 1809, his father was arrested for debt and imprisoned in the Westmoreland County jail. He was arrested again before the year was over and sent to the Spotsylvania prison. He spent the time usefully by writing the memoirs of his experiences in the South during the Revolution. During the spring of 1809, the son he had had with Matilda came of age, so he no longer had even the right to stay at Stratford. Young Henry Lee IV had become the new master of the once-great plantation.

What Ann Carter Lee thought of all this is not known, but she seems to have been a patient and dutiful wife who was not given to complaining or to questioning her husband's decisions, although she must have wondered at times about the validity of his judgment. When they were first married and things were going well, she had no cause for uneasiness. Her youthful letters show that she was undoubtedly content with her life then.

Now things were different. She would not admit in writing that her husband was in jail; she referred to the future by saying "after his release from his present situation." But she had made up her mind that they should leave Stratford and go elsewhere—perhaps to Alexandria, where they would be close to friends and have good schools available for the children. She had to wait for Harry Lee to come home. He arrived sometime in 1810, bringing with him the manuscript of his book and boxes filled with papers. It was late in the year before he was ready to move to Alexandria. Then the one remaining wheeled vehicle in the big stable was brought out, and the four children and essential belongings were loaded into it for the long drive up the Northern Neck.

Above: the room in which Robert E. Lee was born

Below: the nursery where he spent his infancy

The fireplace in the antechamber with its guardian angels to watch over the children

An early view of Alexandria. Washington Street, looking south. The Lee home on Oronoco Street is in the left foreground.

ALEXANDRIA: THE BOYHOOD YEARS

Alexandria, then a pleasant little town of 7500 people, was older than the Federal city that was just beginning to be established on the other side of the Potomac, for it had been laid out in 1749. The surveyor who did the work was assisted by young George Washington. Washington's influence on the community eventually became so great that it touched almost every aspect of life. Christ Church, where he had worshiped, was only a few steps from the little brick house on Cameron Street which was the Lees' new home. It must have seemed small and cramped after the spaciousness of Stratford, but it was certainly easier to manage. Ann's sixth and last child, Catherine Mildred, was born there on February 27, 1811. And "Light-Horse" Harry found a publisher for his book, which was issued in Philadelphia in 1812. He was planning to write other works. All might have gone well if disaster had not followed him so doggedly.

He disapproved of the war with England that began in June 1812. His stand was unpopular in Alexandria, where many of the townspeople had suffered from British actions on the high seas. But Harry Lee was not one to be stopped by others' opinions. When the printing plant of Alexander C. Hanson's anti-war newspaper, *The Baltimore Federal Republican,* was wrecked by a hostile mob on June 22, it was moved to nearby Georgetown, so the paper could be printed there for distribution in Baltimore. Harry Lee quickly got in touch with Hanson to offer advice about protecting his office from the mob. When the paper was placed on sale in Baltimore on June 27, Harry Lee, always the defender of liberty and the freedom of the press, was there to help. A mob surrounded the house where the editor and some of his friends were staying. "Light-Horse" Harry was with Hanson when the attack began. He directed the building of barricades and took an active part in the fighting. One man in the street was wounded and another was killed by firing from the house. The militia came in time to prevent the defenders from being overwhelmed. They were locked up in a cell in the jail to prevent the mob from getting at them.

Apparently feeling that it had done its duty, the militia then disbanded and went home. The leaders of the mob regathered their followers and broke open the doors of the jail. A local butcher stood at the head of the staircase to beat each man over the head with a club as soon as he was taken out of

the cell. Then he threw the limp, unconscious forms down the stairs where the ghoulish mob was waiting. They fell upon the still-living bodies, thrust pen-knives into them, and poured hot candle grease into their eyes. One of them tried to slice off Harry Lee's nose. He bungled the job but mutilated the general's face for life. "Light-Horse" Harry Lee survived, but he would never recover from the internal wounds which the medical skill of the day could neither diagnose nor cure. Through the good offices of James Monroe, it was arranged for him to go to the warmer climate of Barbados. In the late summer of 1813, he said farewell to his wife and sailed for the British island.

Harry Lee continued to write home until the British blockade cut off all communication. He usually addressed his letters to Carter, who was nine years older than Robert. Since the father had never had a chance to become really acquainted with his youngest son, he barely mentioned him in his correspond-ence. Much of it was filled with long, ponderous passages offering good advice.

During his absence, the British fleet entered Chesapeake Bay in 1813 to burn Havre de Grace and other towns along the shore. Then, in August 1814, British ships went up the Patuxent River to put troops ashore to invade Wash-ington. They overwhelmed all opposition and marched into the city where they set fire to the new Capitol and the President's House. Smoke from the burning buildings could be seen in Alexandria six miles away.

A few days later, the much-dreaded fleet came up the Potomac to anchor off Alexandria. Militia had been organized there, but they were helpless against the greater might of the well-trained British. The mayor was forced to sur-render. The ships stayed at Alexandria for four days to load supplies taken from the well-stocked warehouses along the riverfront. When the fleet left, guns were rushed to the shores to fire a futile farewell fusillade as it sailed away.

It is not known whether Robert Edward Lee, who was seven years old at the time, witnessed any of these scenes. His mother may have kept him indoors or she may have sent him to stay with one of their many relatives in the country.

Soon afterward he went to the Carter family school at Eastern View in Fauquier County. Away from home, young Robert is said to have picked up some of the imperiousness of his cousins who were his daily companions at the school. If so, his mother evidently taught him to mend his manners when he returned.

Christ Church, Alexandria,
as it looked during the Civil War

She was having financial difficulties, for the income from her father's estate was suddenly diminished. To economize, she moved from Cameron Street to an even smaller house on Washington Street. Nevertheless, she sent her oldest son, Charles Carter, to Harvard in 1816.

In February 1818, Harry Lee wrote to tell them that he was going to try to return home. After a long wait for a ship, he embarked on one that was bound for "some Southern port . . . not yet decided." He hoped to land at Savannah and go by stage to Alexandria, but he became ill and asked to be put ashore on Cumberland Island, Georgia, which lies off the coast near the Florida border. This island was the home of General Nathanael Greene, with whom Lee had fought during the Revolution. Greene had died in 1786, but his ailing associate hoped to be welcomed by his children.

He was received cordially at Dungeness by General Greene's daughter and her husband. He seldom left the house except to walk in the garden with his host's young son. It was evident that the terribly disfigured sixty-two-year-old man, who still suffered from internal injuries, did not have long to live.

This was just before the time Spain was to cede Florida to the United States, and the combined forces of the American Army and Navy were standing by. When their commanders learned that General Lee was on the island, they called on him and sent two surgeons to attend to him. It was too late for them to be of any use. He was in great pain and sank rapidly. On March 25, 1818, he died.

He was given a full military funeral with an honor guard of Marines from the fleet and a company of infantry from the fort at Fernandina. He was buried in the Greenes' private cemetery at Dungeness. His devoted son Robert visited his grave in January 1862 while on duty on the Georgia seacoast and again in 1870, the last year of his own life. He may also have gone there as early as 1849 when he was on Cumberland Island during a tour for selecting sites for new forts.

Sometime later in 1818, Harry Lee's widow moved to a larger and more comfortable house on Oronoco Street, rented to her on favorable terms by one of the ever-protective Lee family.

In his letters, "Light-Horse" Harry had urged his sons to learn to swim, ride, shoot, box, dance, and use the sword "but [only] in self-defense." These were the accomplishments expected of a Virginia gentleman.

Dependable information about Robert E. Lee's boyhood is scarce because he was only one of thousands of Virginia youths of the same age, and there was no reason then to believe that he would ever be outstanding among them. Tradition tells us that he swam in the Potomac, went hunting and fishing, and participated in the customary outdoor sports with the other boys. It must be remembered that in those days, the organized sports which mean so much to young people now had not yet been invented. A horse, a gun, a fishing rod, and a boat were what every lad wanted then. Spectator sports, except for horse racing, were unknown. It was a do-it-yourself age when men—and boys—actually used the muscles of their arms and legs instead of sitting idly on a bench to watch paid professionals play for them.

In 1819 or 1820, Robert went to a school on Washington Street kept by a well-educated Irishman named William B. Leary. Here he learned Latin and Greek and was introduced to mathematics, a subject for which he showed great natural aptitude. His oldest brother, Charles Carter Lee, returned from Harvard to open a law office in Washington. And in 1820, Sydney Smith Lee, the second son, left home to become a midshipman in the Navy. After that, Robert was the only male in a house where his now permanently invalided mother, his older sister, Ann Kinloch Lee, who suffered from some nervous

The house on Cameron Street where the Lees first lived

Christ Church, where Washington worshiped

The Stabler-Leadbeater Apothecary shop, founded in 1792, which played a part in the lives of Washington and Lee

When young Robert E. Lee needed letters of recommendation for West Point, he got them from his cousin, W. H. Fitzhugh, from Congressman R. S. Garnett, from his half-brother, Henry Lee, from a group of members of Congress, from his former tutor, W. B. Leary, and from his older brother, Charles Carter Lee. Letters from the last two are reproduced here.

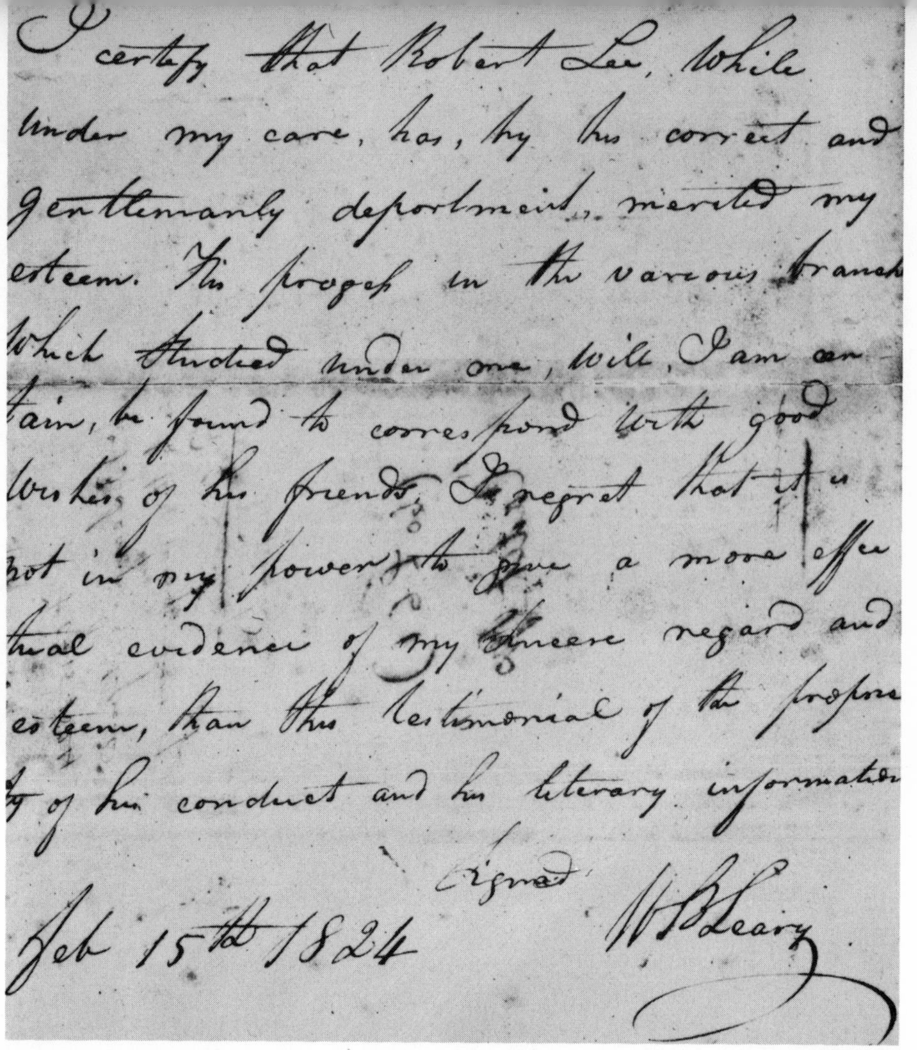

I certify that Robert Lee, while under my care, has, by his correct and gentlemanly deportment, merited my esteem. His progress in the various branches which [he] studied under me, will, I am certain, be found to correspond with good wishes of his friends. I regret that it is not in my power to give a more effectual evidence of my sincere regard and esteem, than this testimonial of the propriety of his conduct and his literary information.

Signed. W. B. Leary

Feb 15th 1824

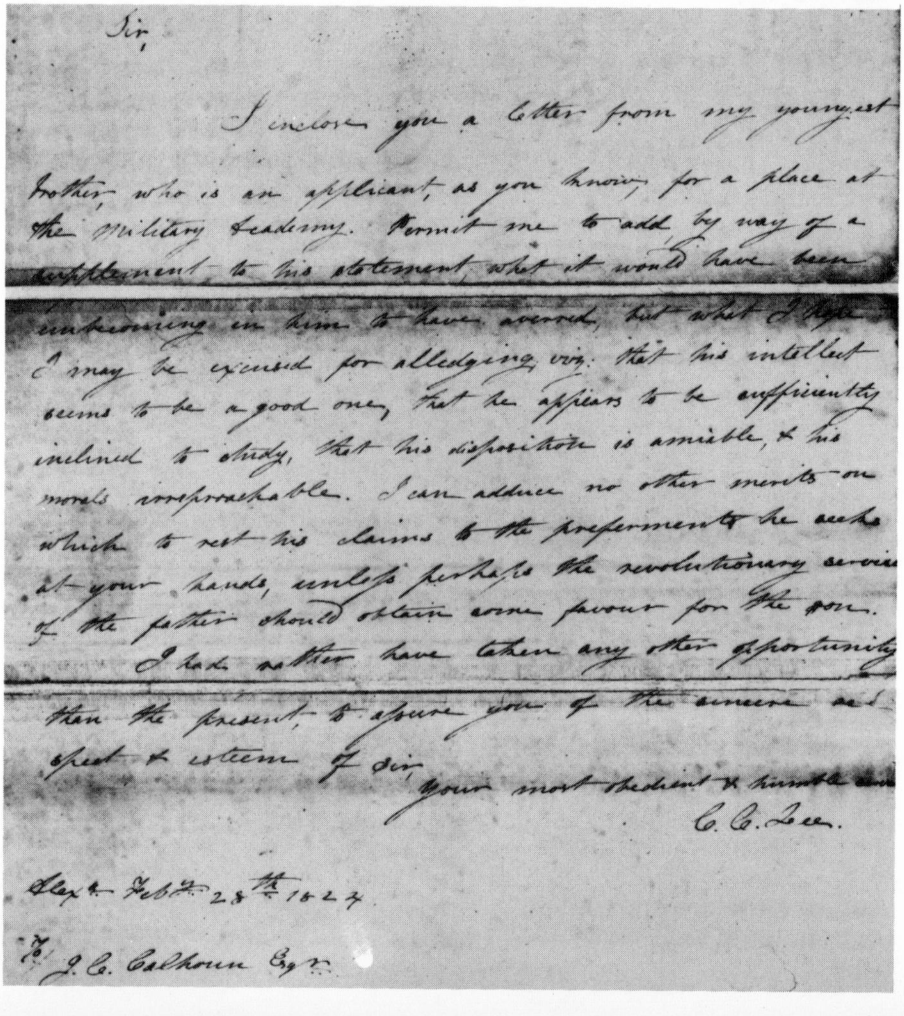

Sir,

I enclose you a letter from my youngest brother, who is an applicant, as you know, for a place at the military academy. Permit me to add by way of a supplement to his statement what it would have been unbecoming in him to have avowed, but what I hope I may be excused for alleging, viz. that his intellect seems to be a good one, that he appears to be sufficiently inclined to study, that his disposition is amiable, & his morals irreproachable. I can adduce no other merits on which to rest his claims to the preferment he seeks at your hands, unless perhaps the revolutionary services of the father should obtain some favour for the son. I had rather have taken any other opportunity than the present, to assure you of the sincere respect & esteem of sir

Your most obedient & humble servant
C. C. Lee.

Alex[andria] Feby 28th 1824.

To J. C. Calhoun Esqr.

The Oronoco Street house—Robert E. Lee's last home in Alexandria

disorder, and Catherine Mildred Lee, who was still a child, were his constant companions.

A great day came for the little family on Oronoco Street when Lafayette visited Alexandria on October 14, 1824. The celebrated French commander, who had known and admired Henry Lee during the Revolution, paid a call on his widow and doubtless conversed with her son.

Earlier this year, Robert had made up his mind that he wanted to be a soldier like his father. He could get free higher education at West Point and be trained as an army officer. He was fortunate in being so near Washington, for he could go there to see the governmental officials whose support was needed to get him the appointment. With their help, and with the fame of his father's name to aid him, there was not much doubt. On March 11, 1824, the War Department notified him that he had the much-sought-after appointment, but, because there were so many ahead of him, he could not be admitted to the Academy until July 1, 1825.

During the time he had to wait, it was decided to send the boy to a new school which a Quaker teacher, Benjamin Hallowell had opened up next door to the Lees' house. He did so well there that in later years Hallowell was able to write: "Robert E. Lee entered my school . . . in the winter of 1824–25 to study mathematics, preparatory to his going to West Point. He was a most exemplary student in every respect. He was never behind time at his studies, never failed in a single recitation, was perfectly observant of the rules and regulations of the institution; was gentlemanly, unobstrusive, and respectful in all his deportment to teachers and fellow-students. His specialty was finishing up. He imparted a neatness and finish to everything he undertook. One of the branches of mathematics he studied with me was conic sections, in which some of the diagrams were very complicated. He drew the diagrams on a slate, and although he . . . knew that the . . . drawing would have to be removed to make room for the next, he drew each one with as much accuracy and finish . . . as if it were to be engraved and printed. The same traits he exhibited at my school he carried with him to West Point."

37

West Point seen from the river

Lee accepts the appointment to the Academy

Sir

    I hereby accept the appointment to the station of a cadet in the service of the United States, with which I have been honoured by the President.

    The above is the declaration of consent which my letter of appointment ~~instructs me should accompany my acceptance.~~

        I remain with the highest respect, Sir

        your most obliged & most obedient Servant

        R. E. Lee

Alexa April 1ˢᵗ 1824

to

    The Honble J. C. Calhoun.

THE WEST POINT CADET

The United States Military Academy at West Point was unimpressive-looking when Robert E. Lee arrived there late in June 1825. Organized in 1802, the Academy had done badly for the first fifteen years of its existence. Not until Sylvanus Thayer was appointed its fourth Superintendent in 1817 did it become an efficient training school for army officers.

When Lee first saw it, the Academy consisted only of a few ugly buildings facing a desolate, windswept parade ground. There were two cheerless dormitories for the cadets, a mess hall, and a two-story structure which housed the chapel, the library, and the classrooms. A few older buildings, inherited from the time West Point was a river fort during the Revolution, completed the physical plant. The setting, however, was extraordinary, for the grounds of the Academy had a magnificent view of the Hudson River and the mountains along its shores.

Twenty-three years after its founding, West Point was still a small place, although it was large enough to supply about forty graduates each year for the officer corps of a standing army which, in 1820, had been reduced by an Act of Congress to 6000 men. Engineering was emphasized, and the Superintendent was then always appointed from that branch of the service. Other subjects were taught, but the curriculum was purposely kept narrow. The day was long, the food poor, and discipline strict with demerits and punishments dealt out swiftly for what now seem minor offenses.

Thayer had built the institution up from almost nothing, and he was generally admired for his truly notable accomplishments, but the cadets did not like him. A lifelong bachelor, the Academy was his whole existence; as a result he was not content merely to punish infractions of the rules—he sought out trouble and usually found it. Life at West Point was hard, but for a natural-born soldier like Lee, it had many rewards. Those who were not willing to work for a military education seldom lasted long. Of the 105 in the class that entered in 1825, only 46 were graduated four years later.

Among the cadets at the Academy while Lee was there were Albert Sidney Johnston, '26; Leonidas Polk, '27; Jefferson Davis, '28; Joseph E. Johnston, '29; John B. Magruder, '30; and William N. Pendleton, '30. They were all to have high places in the Confederacy; two of them were to die in the field in its defense. The West Pointers who were to be Lee's chief opponents during the Civil War were all much younger men: McClellan, '46; Burnside, '47; Hooker, '37; Meade, '35; Grant, '43; and Sheridan, '53.

With one exception, the Southerners listed above stood fairly high in their classes when they were graduated from the Academy, but none came near achieving Lee's record. He was the practically perfect cadet whose remarkable career, not only in the classroom but also on the parade ground and in training practice, is still discussed with awe at West Point. Tall, easily the handsomest man in his class and able to wear a uniform as if it had been designed for his special benefit, he attracted attention from the beginning. The first occasion on which he appeared in dress uniform was on July 1, shortly after he arrived. He then wore his new gray jacket, white trousers, and high black-plumed leather cap for a review held for Lafayette, the distinguished French visitor who had paid a social visit to the Lee home in Alexandria only a few months before. But a gulf of rank and etiquette now separated the world-famous commander and the freshman cadet.

The one future leader of the Confederacy who did not do well at West Point was the man who was to be its President. Jefferson Davis stood twenty-second in a class of thirty-three when he was graduated in 1828. And he

SYLVANUS THAYER, *the Superintendent who transformed the Academy, previously a small, ineffective training school, into an efficient, smoothly operating institution*

This picture and the one on the opposite page were painted by George Catlin about the time Lee was a cadet at West Point

THE NORTH BARRACKS (LOOKING NORTHEAST).
ERECTED IN 1817; DEMOLISHED IN 1851.

THE SOUTH BARRACKS (LOOKING SOUTHWEST).
ERECTED IN 1815; DEMOLISHED IN 1849.

THE ACADEMY (LOOKING SOUTHEAST).
ERECTED IN 1815;
DESTROYED BY FIRE FEBRUARY 19, 1838.

almost did not graduate at all, for a few weeks after Lee entered the Academy, Davis was tried by court-martial and found guilty of having gone out of bounds and—even more heinous—of having consumed "spirituous and intoxicating liquors" in Benny Havens' immortal but strictly forbidden tavern. Three cadets caught with him were dismissed, but Davis was pardoned because of his soldierly record and was allowed to remain. That did not cure him of the Benny Havens habit. On another occasion he nearly lost his life when he fell over a cliff in the darkness while attempting to get away from the prohibited premises when an instructor was reported to be on a tour of inspection. He had still more trouble over an eggnog party the next year. This led to a serious riot that caused wholesale dismissals, but Davis was lucky enough to have been confined to quarters before the more serious offenses were committed.

Thayer had so much difficulty with rowdiness that at one time he sought an interview with President John Quincy Adams to tell him that while scholastic performance at the Academy was satisfactory, he "regretted to say, the moral condition of the institution was not so favorable; that a habit of drinking had become prevalent." He also said that the ingenious cadets did their imbibing with their faces turned away from each other so they could truthfully say that they had not seen anyone drink the forbidden stuff.

But such complaints had nothing to do with the cadet from Alexandria. Perhaps because of his mother's dependence on him or because he felt that he had to uphold his father's fine military reputation, Robert E. Lee's deportment was so good that he was never given a demerit during his four years at West Point.

The page headed by Lee's name in the *Record of Delinquencies,* however, is not white and unspotted. Part of it, for November 1826 to February 1827, is covered with reports of misdoings, minor and serious. Government economy was responsible for such entries being there. Another cadet, who was dismissed in 1827, had received so many demerits that his own page was filled with them. The clerk simply put the rest on Lee's page rather than use a new sheet. The luckless cadet bore the star-studded name Pleiades Orion Lumpkin, but he was not destined to wear stars on his shoulders—or even eagles.

Lee's scholastic record was very high. Except for his first year, when he ranked third in his class, he stood second for the rest of his academic career. Ahead of him, consistently ranking first and stubbornly holding that position

40

with impregnable skill, was a young man from upstate New York who had the advantage of being nearly three years older than his rival from Virginia. One would expect that the name of this cadet would be outstanding in American military history, but it is not. The man whose chief claim to distinction is the fact that he was number one in a class at West Point in which Robert E. Lee was number two, bore a name which few people can be expected to recognize today. It was Charles Mason. After graduation he spent two years at the Academy as assistant professor of engineering; then he resigned from the Army. He read law in New York and went to Iowa, where he was appointed chief justice of the supreme court. He became a patent attorney and moved to Washington just before the Civil War. He led a long and useful life, but always as a civilian. Robert E. Lee was a patient and forebearing man. Yet, as shown below, he had good reason to dislike his invariably successful Yankee classmate.

Mason–Lee Marks at the End of Four Years

	Mason	Lee
Rank	1	2
Mathematics	300	286
Natural Philosophy	300	295
Drawing	96	97
Engineering	300	292
Chemistry & Mineralogy	100	99
Rhetoric & Moral Philosophy	200	199
French	99.5	98.5
Tactics	200	200
Artillery	100	100
Conduct	300	300
General Merit	1995.5	1966.5

A West Point cadet in the uniform of the 1820s

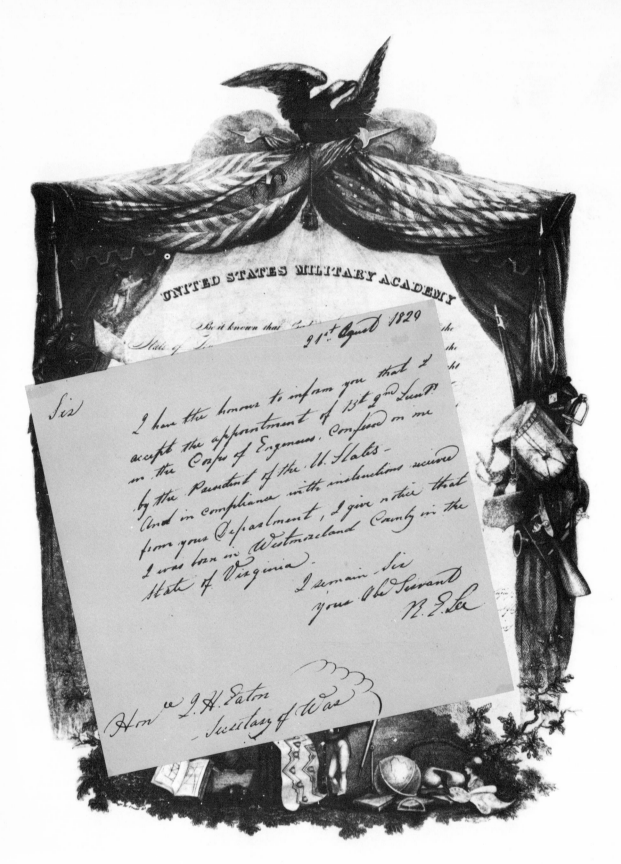

The Military Academy's diploma and Lee's letter accepting his appointment
as brevet second lieutenant in the Corps of Engineers

The rivalry between the New Yorker and the Virginian went beyond the classroom. Lee became successively Staff Sergeant, Sergeant-Major, and then Adjutant of the Corps—a very high rank indeed. But Charles Mason became Captain of the Corps. And it was he who was in command of West Point's chief public attraction—precision drilling on the parade ground. The Army lost a good officer when young Mason decided to become a lawyer.

Lee's excellent record in mathematics enabled him to become an acting assistant professor in that subject during his second year. For this he was paid $10 a month, and he was glad to have the extra income; money, as always, was scarce. His fine record also made it possible for him to return home on furlough at the end of his second year. At this time his mother was living in Georgetown, and it was evident that her always poor health was worse. A relative who saw the young West Pointer during his visit home wrote that "he was dressed in his cadet uniform . . . gray with white bullet buttons, and everyone was filled with admiration of his fine appearance and lovely manners."

Since Lee was in Georgetown in the summer of 1827, it is likely that he saw something of twenty-year-old Mary Anna Randolph Custis, the only child of George Washington Parke Custis and the heiress of the imposing house called Arlington which still stands on a ridge overlooking the the Potomac and the city of Washington. The two had known each other since they were children, when they often met at parties or during visits to country houses in the area. Mary Curtis' father did not favor the idea of his well-educated daughter marrying a penniless West Point cadet with only his army pay for her support. But the already enamored couple moved toward each other with the inevitability of gravitational attraction.

When the summer was over, Lee had to return to the unsentimental round of studies and duties at the Academy. There were to be no more furloughs, and the work became harder because science, mathematics, and technical military training were now the main subjects. The ambitious young cadet threw himself into his work and did it well, perhaps because he enjoyed what he was doing.

In June 1829, Robert Edward Lee, at the age of twenty-two, received a diploma, a two-month furlough, and $103.58 in cash. In August, orders were to come that would direct the new Brevet Second Lieutenant of the Corps of Engineers to report for duty at Cockspur Island in the Savannah River, Georgia. Meanwhile, he had two months free. He hurried south by ship and arrived in Virginia to find his mother gravely ill. She had gone to Ravensworth, the home of his cousin William Henry Fitzhugh, in Fairfax County.

Again Ann Lee's son became her nurse and watched over her day and night. But nothing could help her, and the tired, worn-out woman, old at fifty-six, died on July 26, 1829. In July 1869, when he himself had hardly more than a year to live, Lee revisited Ravensworth. When he passed the room in which she had died, he looked in and said: "Forty years-ago, I stood in this room by my mother's deathbed. It seems now but yesterday!"

He now had to settle his mother's estate. This and other business matters kept him in the Washington area until October. He doubtless visited Arlington frequently to call on Mary Custis. It is possible that the two young people may have arrived at some kind of an understanding before he left.

Then he was off; he went by ship to Savannah, taking with him an elderly slave who had served the Lee family as a coachman and house servant. It was thought that the warmer climate of Georgia might be better for the aging Negro who was slowly dying of some disease of senility that no doctor could then diagnose. But nothing could help him. The old man died and was buried somewhere along the lower reaches of the Savannah River.

CHARLES MASON, *Number One man in Lee's class at West Point*

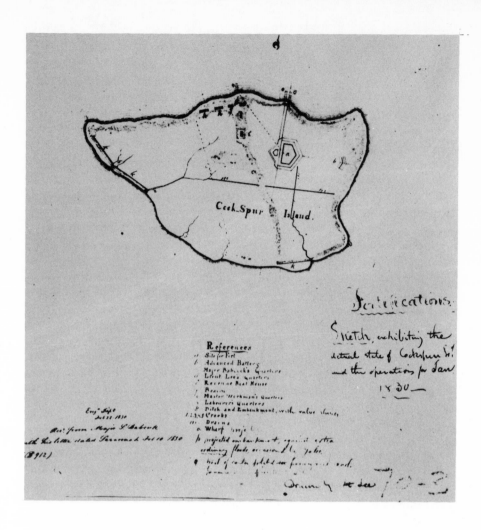

Cockspur Island and Fort Pulaski sketched by Robert E. Lee as part of his work there in 1829

FORT PULASKI AND FAMILY SCANDAL

A man's first assignment is always an important one. And when he has just come out of a school in which young people are trained to be future leaders in an elite corps, he knows that the eyes of the older men are on him and that everything he does, says, or writes will affect his career.

The fort to which Robert E. Lee was being sent in the autumn of 1824 was part of a system of defense that was being built along the Atlantic Coast. The United States had won the War of 1812, but when it was over her military men knew how weak her defenses were against the naval forces of any great European power that wanted to attack. In order to protect the entrances to key harbors and rivers, fortifications strong enough to withstand the fire of enemy ships were being constructed. This was the age of the stone fort, the presumably permanent and supposedly impregnable defensive work built of solid blocks of granite or of bricks carefully put in place by skilled masons. Such forts were expensive, but they were intended to last for centuries, so the enormous investment seemed worthwhile. By 1826, thirty-one such strongholds were ready to guard eighteen of the most vulnerable waterways leading to the interior. And by 1843, sixty-nine forts existed or were under construction at some thirty-five or forty coastal points. Army officers, especially those in the Corps of Engineers, were kept busy for many years supervising this work.

44

The fort planned for the defense of the Savannah River was located on Cockspur Island, which was so strategically located at the mouth of the river that it had already been the site of two earlier forts. It was evident that any structure intended to resist gunfire and the furious Atlantic storms that sometimes swept over the low-lying, swampy island had to be a sturdy one. General Simon Bernard, who had achieved fame as designer of fortifications for Napoleon, had been brought to the United States to help with the new defenses. His plans, however, called for so massive a fortification that its enormous weight would cause it to sink down in the Island's soft ground. Bernard's plans had to be revised, and an extensive system of wood piling and grillage was devised to support the heavy masonry that was to be placed upon it.

The fort was to be named after the Polish patriot, Count Casimir Pulaski, who had died of a wound received at the Battle of Savannah in 1779. The actual head of the project, Major Samuel Babcock, was in such poor health that he was unable to work in the field. Such efforts required a vigorous young man like Lieutenant Lee who did not mind being immersed for hours in water or mud. The assignment proved a fortunate one for the recent graduate from West Point because it gave him practical experience and compelled him to shoulder responsibilities that would ordinarily have been assumed by someone older and in a higher position of command. The fact that Lee's title was "acting assistant commissary of subsistence" did not prevent him from tackling real engineering problems.

Nevertheless, he was glad whenever a chance came to go to Savannah, where he had friends. At this time, though, the young soldier who had been born in Stratford Hall may have been reluctant to hear the name of that formerly proud place mentioned, for it had become the subject of much ugly gossip. Such talk must have been especially painful for the young lieutenant who had lost his mother only a few months before. She was closely associated with Stratford in his mind. He remembered the garden where she had planted flowers and trees, and he recalled the big sunny room which had been hers. He had been born in that room.

He knew his half-brother Henry who had taken over the estate. The talk concerned him. Relations between the children of the first and second marriage had always been friendly, so Robert had good reason to feel upset at what was happening. It came from something that had taken place some years before.

Stratford's acres were bordered on the west by a large plantation owned by Daniel McCarty. Henry had fallen in love with his neighbor's nineteen-year-old daughter, Anne Robinson McCarty, and had married her on March 29, 1817. Since her father was dead and her mother had remarried, it was only natural that she should want to bring her seventeen-year-old sister, Elizabeth, to the big house that was so near their own home.

A daughter was born to Anne in 1818. Two years later the little girl was killed by falling down the high stone steps at Stratford. This was the second Lee child to be killed by those lethal stairs; young Philip Ludwell Lee had died in the same way forty years before.

The distraught mother took to the use of morphine, which was then easily available. Her younger sister and Henry Lee, left to themselves in isolated Stratford, drifted into an affair which bore fruit in a child which is supposed to have died at birth. In those days, everyone in Tidewater Virginia knew everyone else. Scandal spread rapidly.

Henry Lee was dismissed as Elizabeth's guardian and had to pay $11,598.97, which he had been holding as part of her estate; he also had to assign about $8000 of assets to her new guardian. This was enough to put the already financially troubled Harry Lee in serious difficulty. As a result,

A diamondback terrapin sketched by Lee on Cockspur Island

A modern aerial photograph of Fort Pulaski and Cockspur Island. The building of the fort went on from 1829 to 1847. About 25 million bricks were put into the walls.

he had to sell Stratford, and on June 27, 1822, the historic old house passed forever from the possession of the Lee family. Unfortunate Elizabeth McCarty, after marrying Henry Storke in 1826, persuaded him to purchase Stratford Hall. She lived there, dressed always in black, from 1829 until her death fifty years later.

After selling his ancestral home, Henry Lee went to Fredericksburg, where he devoted himself to writing. His much-wronged wife, Anne, left him and moved to Tennessee. While she was there, she cured herself of the habit of using drugs. Some time in 1827 or 1828 she and Henry Lee were reunited.

Lee met Andrew Jackson in Tennessee and became friendly with him. When Jackson was elected President, he offered to send Lee to Algiers as United States consul. It was a minor post, but it would take him and his wife away from the unhappy scenes of their past. They sailed for that port and were in residence there when the crushing news arrived that the Senate had refused to confirm the appointment.

The same news reached Robert E. Lee in Georgia, and the public airing of the old scandal was naturally disturbing. He threw himself into the work of building Fort Pulaski, and tried to ignore the discussions and whisperings that were going on about his half-brother.

Henry and Anne never returned to America. They settled in Paris, where he wrote a number of books, among them a life of Napoleon Bonaparte. He died of influenza on January 30, 1837. His widow, desperately short of money, moved to Passy to economize. She lived there in straitened circumstances with a little dog as her only company until her death on August 27, 1840.

Construction work on Cockspur Island had to be suspended during the summer when insects and heat were a menace not only to comfort but also to health. Lee returned to Virginia, where he stayed with friends who lived

46

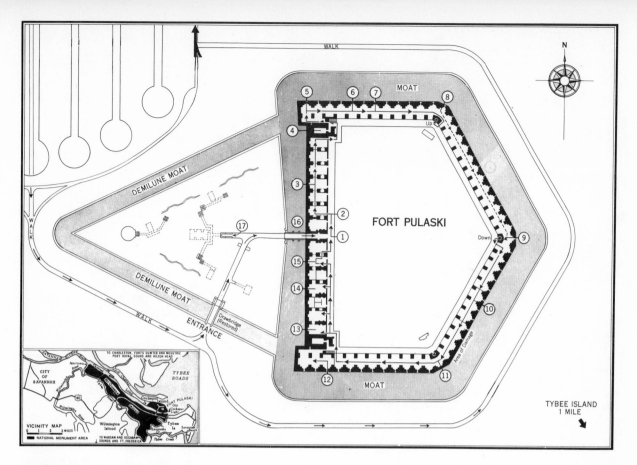

Fort Pulaski—modern map of
the fort as it is now restored

1 The Sally Port
2 The Gorge
3 Barracks Rooms
4 The North Magazine
5 The Northwest Bastion
6 The Gun Galleries
7 The Water System
8 The Terreplein
9 Terreplein, East Engle
10 The Prison
11 The Breach
12 The Southwest Bastion
13 Headquarters
14 Cistern Room
15 Bottle Room
16 The Moat
17 The Demilune

conveniently near Arlington. He was a frequent visitor there, and when Mary Custis went to spend some time at Chatham, he followed her. Nor was he unwelcome so far as she was concerned. But summer came to an end, and the young lieutenant of Engineers had to go back to Georgia.

Major Babcock was not on the island when Lee arrived on November 10. For some weeks the inexperienced lieutenant had to supervise an emergency repair job. A gale had destroyed sections of an embankment which had been built to keep the tides from flooding the area where the fort was to be placed, so he hurriedly put everyone available to work at restoring the breached wall. A drainage canal had filled up with mud, which had to be cleaned out.

Word then came that Babcock had resigned and that another man was to replace him. It was also decided that extensive changes had to be made in the plans for Pulaski. Lee had been hoping to be sent to Fort Monroe, which was nearer Arlington. He got the transfer and arrived at his new post on May 7, 1831.

His superior there was Captain Andrew Talcott of Connecticut, a capable and experienced builder of coastal forts who had also worked on the digging of the Dismal Swamp Canal from 1826 to 1828. During those two years he had been married to a young Philadelphia girl, but she had died. He was soon to marry again, this time to Harriet Randolph Hackley, a cousin of Mary Custis. Although Talcott was ten years older than Lee, the two men became close friends.

As soon as he could, Lee applied for leave to visit Arlington. According to tradition, he was reading aloud there one day from a novel by Sir Walter Scott when Mrs. Custis, thinking that he looked tired, asked her daughter to go into the dining room and get him something to eat. Lee followed the girl, and as she bent down to get a piece of fruit cake from the sideboard, he put his arm around her and asked her to marry him.

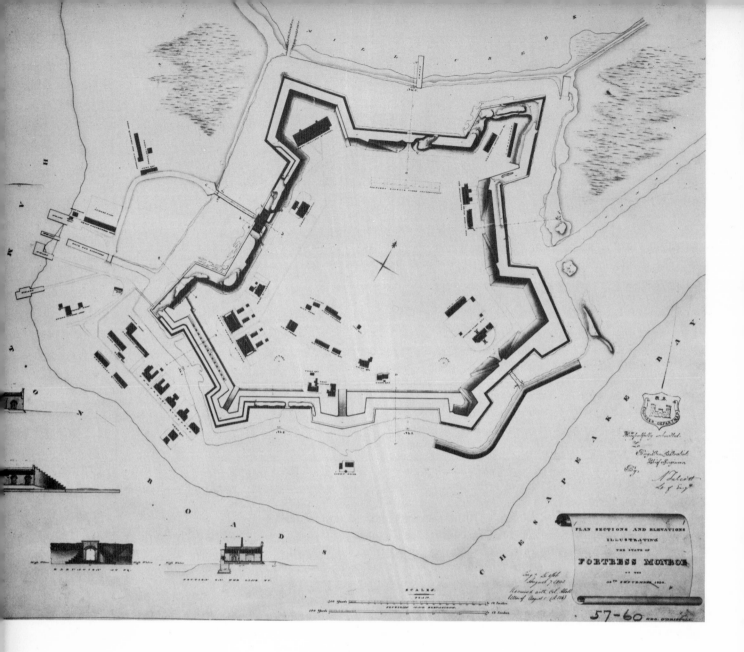

Talcott's Map of Fort Monroe

FORT MONROE AND MARRIAGE

The second lieutenant who had just volunteered to take on the responsibilities of marriage was twenty-three years old; his fiancée was not yet twenty-two. The young officer had no income except his pay, and he was in a profession where promotion was notoriously slow—especially in peacetime. But Mary Custis was the only heiress to a great estate. Her father doubtless felt that his daugher could have done much better, yet he did not oppose the marriage. Lee, of course, came from an excellent family. But so did George Washington Parke Custis. His father was Martha Washington's son by her first marriage, and when she married the first President, he had her two children placed in his care. Then he adopted Custis and his sister Eleanor and brought them up at Mount Vernon.

George Washington Parke Custis was a graduate of Princeton, a former army officer, a friend of Lafayette, and a cultured man who took such an active interest in the theater that he wrote several plays. Two of them had been produced in Philadelphia the year before his daughter's marriage. One

48

was about Pocahontas; the other introduced the first steam railroad locomotive to the American stage. Since travel by rail was then so new that most people had never seen a train, the puffing steam engine was a genuine novelty.

Custis had married Mary Lee Fitzhugh in 1804. They had four children, but after three died in infancy, they concentrated all their affection on their only daughter. Her marriage naturally meant a great deal to parents who could readily foresee how empty Arlington would be when their beloved Mary went off with her new husband.

The date June 30, 1831, was set for the wedding, and invitations were sent to relatives and friends. Meanwhile, the prospective bridegroom returned to Fort Monroe to resume work there.

Fort Monroe was called a fortress during the early years of its construction, although it did not really qualify for such a name. In his manual on military engineering published in 1836, D. H. Mahan stated that "the term fortress is applied to fortified towns alone, and the term fort to a work containing only a garrison." By this definition, Monroe was clearly a fort rather than a fortress.

It was located on the end of a long point of land that commanded the passageway leading from Chesapeake Bay to Hampton Roads. Since ships had to pass it to go up the James River to Richmond or up the Elizabeth River to Norfolk and the navy yard there, Fort Monroe was of prime importance. It dominated the wide expanse of water where the world's first battle between ironclad ships was to be fought a generation later. And inside the fort was a casemate in which the President of the Confederacy was to be imprisoned for two years after the war.

The site was of such obvious strategic value that Fort Monroe was the third defensive work to be placed there. Actual construction had started in 1819; by 1831, when Lee arrived, the fort itself was so far advanced that it housed a garrison and was being used by an artillery school to which the Army sent men from other posts for training. But the outerworks still had to be completed, and much had to be done on an offshore satellite fort that was being built on rocks sunk into deep water to serve as a foundation. There was plenty of work for the young lieutenant.

The warm June days passed rapidly, and the end of the month was soon at hand. Lee obtained leave for five or six weeks to get married and then went up the Potomac to Arlington by steamer. There many of his Army friends were gathering, and pretty Southern girls, some of them related to Mary, were staying at the house to serve as bridesmaids.

It rained on the day of the wedding. In fact it poured so hard that the clergyman who arrived on horseback was soaked to the skin. The only civilian clothes available were the host's, and they fitted badly. Fortunately, the robes of office covered them, so the minister was able to appear in proper dignity. Among those present at the ceremony was the Washingtons' Negro maid. She had been a devoted servant of the Washington family and had stood at the bedside of the first President when he died in 1799.

49

The arms
of the Custis family

The guests did not leave Arlington immediately after the wedding; in those days of difficult travel it was customary to stay on for some time. Most of them remained in the house until July 5, with much festivity going on all the time. Then the party gradually broke up.

The bridegroom paid a brief visit to the engineering office in Washington, after which he and Mary went on a honeymoon tour of relatives' houses, stopping first at Ravensworth, the home of his cousin William Henry Fitzhugh.

About a month later, the young couple arrived at Fort Monroe, where some rooms in the Talcott house had been set aside for them. The cramped apartment must have seemed confining to Mary, who had known nothing but the spacious comfort of Arlington and other big houses like it, and the wild goings-on at the Fort must have shocked her.

The enlisted men in Fort Monroe's garrison and those sent there for training in the artillery school were a rowdy lot who got drunk whenever they could and fought with each other whether drunk or sober. The three "laundresses" attached to each company often did more than merely wash clothes. Among other things, they smuggled in liquor and sold it clandestinely to the men. On at least one occasion, a trio of them were drummed out of the fort to the tune of "The Whore's March" and were forbidden to re-enter.

Young Lieutenant and Mrs. Robert E. Lee came to Fort Monroe at a time of great public disturbance. A few days after their arrival, one of the bloodiest slave insurrections ever to take place on the American mainland broke out in thinly settled Southampton County less than fifty miles from Fort Monroe. This was the famous Nat Turner revolt. Turner, a Negro preacher who had learned to read and write and who had strange visions of bloody battles between black and white spirits, organized the plot. With the help of four or five fellow slaves armed with hatchets, he slaughtered his master's family on August 22. The slaves moved rapidly, gathering recruits as they went. They slew white men, women, and children indiscriminately, and before the day was over had murdered at least fifty-five people. Then they hurried toward the Great Dismal Swamp to hide in its tangled wastes. Oddly enough, Nat Turner apparently had no special grievances and was better off than most slaves.

His actions sent a shudder of fear through the South, where every slaveholder remembered the Denmark Vesey revolt in Charleston in 1822 and recalled the tremendous outburst of violence in the French West Indies at the turn of the century when the whites had been massacred or driven from the islands.

Word of what had happened in Southampton reached Fort Monroe the next day. Local militia had already been rushed to the scene, but Regular Army troops were also to be sent there. Lee, as a staff officer engaged in construction work, was not to go. He and Mary watched anxiously at 6 A.M. on August 24 when three artillery companies and a cannon were put on board two men-of-war to be ferried across Hampton Roads to march to the scene of the revolt. A troop of cavalry was sent from Norfolk, while a company of dragoons came down from Richmond.

The isolated county bordering North Carolina was soon swarming with soldiers and militiamen. They hunted down and killed the blacks, guilty and innocent alike, so zealously that their officers had to stop them from destroying valuable slave property. About a score, including Nat Turner, were brought to trial and executed.

Lee, writing to Mrs. Custis after the troops returned to Fort Monroe, told her that there had been many instances of the slaves defending their

MRS. GEORGE WASHINGTON PARKE CUSTIS, *née Mary Lee Fitzhugh.*
Portrayed as a young girl by
Cephas Thompson

50

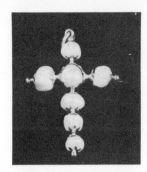

Baroque pearl cross worn by Mrs. Lee on her wedding gown

Mrs. Robert E. Lee, *née Mary Anna Custis, as a young girl, painted by Auguste Hervieu*

George Washington Parke Custis *portrayed as a young man by C. B. J. F. de St. Memin*

masters. "One poor fellow," he said, "from the inconsiderate and almost unwarrantable haste of the whites, was sadly rewarded. He . . . and two others, assisted by his master and his son, nobly defended them against twenty of the blacks; after beating them off and running in great haste after horses for them to escape on, a party of whites suddenly came up and, thinking the horses were for other purposes, shot him dead."

As a result of the uprising, more troops were soon sent to Fort Monroe to strengthen the garrison. Before long, 680 men were stationed there. This was more than 10 per cent of the entire United States Army, which had shrunk to 6055 officers and enlisted men in 1831—the lowest point it was ever to reach.

Once the Southampton scare was over, the young couple settled down to the daily routine of married life as it was lived within the stone bastions of a major coastal defense work. The new Mrs. Lee had been brought up by her mother to manage all the complexities of a great plantation. She had been taught to supervise the work of servants, minister to their needs, and take care of them in sickness and in health. But such training did not help her as a young officer's wife living in narrow quarters inside a fort. She was a loving and devoted wife, but some of her personal habits were the very opposite of her husband's. He was invariably punctual; she was nearly always late. He was fastidious in dress and appearance; she paid little attention to her clothes or hair. But he was so much in love with her that he sometimes apologized for his own striving for perfection in all things. One time, after he had evidently

51

*Some of Lieutenant Lee's first
letters to his wife*

criticized her for something, he wrote apologetically to say: "I don't know that I shall ever overcome my propensity for order and method." And there is no doubt that his love for her made him indulgent. "Do as you please, Molly, in all things," he wrote on another occasion.

He was unlikely to change Mary Custis, and he must have known it. She was a stubborn woman and a forthright one who was much more likely to speak her mind than her more tactful husband was. She had little interest in society, even though she was a good hostess. She was content to remain at home, devoting herself to reading or to sewing, for she was an expert needlewoman.

Both Mary and her husband were determined not to accept aid from her family, but when they at last had quarters assigned to them, Mrs. Custis offered to send furnishings from Arlington. Mary's husband then had to reproach her for even considering acceptance:

"I know your dear Mother will be for giving you *everything* she has; but you must recollect *one* thing, and that is that they have been accustomed to comforts all their lives, which now they could not dispense with, and that we in the commencement ought to contract our wishes to their smallest compass and enlarge them as opportunity offers."

Mary often visited her mother at Arlington, and it is because of these frequent absences from Fort Monroe that we have the letters of this period which reveal so much of the young couple's early married life. Mary spent most of the winter of 1831–32 at Arlington, but later, in 1832, when she was expecting her first child, she was at Fort Monroe. He was born there on September 16, 1832, and was named George Washington Custis after her father. In the family, the child was seldom called by any part of his long name. His mother referred to him in one letter as "Bunny" and said that "he is the most restless little creature you ever saw and very mischievous." In another letter she said: "If he wakes up in the night and cries and Robert speaks to him, he stops immediately. . . . I think he has lost much of his dove appearance and has much more of the lion about him now, though he is a very good-natured fellow." The infant she was speaking about later went to West Point and was graduated at the head of his class in 1854. Ten years after that he was a major general in the Confederate Army who fought in the bitter Appomattox campaign.

Building No. 17, Fort Monroe, where the Lees lived on the second floor of the left side of house

Among those sent to Fort Monroe after the Nat Turner revolt was Joseph E. Johnston, a Virginian who had been born two weeks after Lee and who had been in his class at West Point. Their careers were later to become closely intertwined, and the friendship that now began was to endure for the rest of their lives.

When Captain Andrew Talcott married Harriet Hackley, thereafter known as "The Beautiful Talcott," Mary gained an ally and a friend in her cousin. Life suddenly became very pleasant for the two young officers and their wives. It might have continued to be so, but the War Department artillery school was discontinued in 1834, a decision which sent Johnston into the field. During that year Talcott was removed from the construction job and Lee was ordered to work on isolated Fort Calhoun, the satellite (now called Fort Wool) being built offshore on the rip-raps. Lee felt that Talcott was badly treated, so he went to Washington to intercede for his friend. As a result, Talcott was sent to New York, while the earnest young lieutenant who had pleaded his case so well was offered a post at headquarters in Washington as assistant to the Chief of Engineers.

Fort Wool, where Lee did his final work on the defenses around Fort Monroe

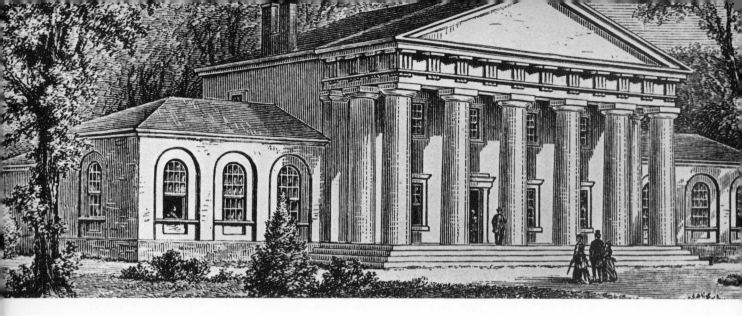

*Arlington House as it looked
when the Lees first lived there*

ARLINGTON

Mary, of course, was delighted because the transfer to Washington would bring her back to her beloved Arlington. Her husband tried to rent a house in the city, but he was unable to find one that would do, so to Arlington they went. They expected to stay only for the winter, but they were to remain for nearly four years. They arrived in November 1834, just in time for the holiday season, and the big house was made ready to receive them.

Lee had often stayed at Arlington but never for more than a few days at a time. Now it was to be his home. It was the finest he had lived in since he left Stratford when he was still a small child. Arlington's wide halls, large rooms, and extensive grounds must have reminded him of his lost home farther down the Potomac. The fact that he remembered Stratford so well and referred to it so often as a place he would like to own indicates how strong a hold it had on him. It was a link to his family's honored past, to their notable accomplishments, and to the generations before them in England where they had also been leaders. As an uprooted and landless aristocrat with only his name to mark his rank, Lee must have missed the assurance which wealth and property had given to his ancestors. He was to have a taste of luxury now, for George Washington Parke Custis lived well.

In 1802, when Custis came of age, he had begun the construction of the first sections of the house overlooking the Potomac and the nascent Federal city beyond it. Since Washington had become the capital of the United States only two years before this, Arlington was almost as old as the city itself. Washington then consisted of nothing but a few unfinished public buildings surrounded by shacks and brick kilns with unpaved streets beginning and ending in the wilderness. It grew as construction work on the house on Arlington Heights proceeded.

Washington Custis built the two separate wings of his home first, as was often the custom then. Even they, however, were not completed when he married Mary Lee Fitzhugh in 1804. The young couple had to live in three rooms temporarily partitioned off in the north wing, while they entertained guests in the south wing. Work went forward slowly—so slowly that the house, perhaps fortunately, was still unfinished when the British burned Washington in 1814. Mrs. Custis and the servants may have seen the Capitol and the President's House in flames, for Arlington provided a better view of the sad

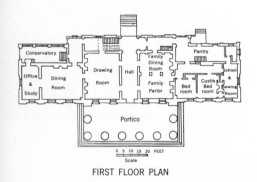

FIRST FLOOR PLAN

54

spectacle than any other place, but the master of the estate was at Bladens-
burg, fighting in the hopeless battle against the oncoming redcoats.

The central portion of Arlington, with its eight-columned portico, was
finally completed four years later. To this day, the most impressive and memorable feature of the house is that classic portico with its solid-looking Doric
columns made of brick plastered over and painted to resemble marble. The
wide porch with its superb view over the city was the family's favorite gathering place in good weather.

During the early years of the building of Arlington, Custis held annual
sheep-shearings on the grounds near the ever-dependable spring that provided
water for the lower part of the estate. On such occasions, George Washington's
big field tent was pitched on the lawn to serve as a shelter for the refreshment
table. This was only one of many Washington relics in Arlington. Custis had
inherited a number of them from his grandmother and had purchased more
when they were sold at Mount Vernon. He had made the house into a veri-
table museum of Washingtoniana, for he was very proud of his connection
with Mount Vernon and the great man who had lived there. He called his
collection the "Washington Treasury."

Since Custis enjoyed entertaining, there was an endless succession of
visitors to Arlington. Some were among the most distinguished men of the day.
Not only Lafayette but Andrew Jackson, Daniel Webster, and Sam Houston
had also been guests there. The grounds near the house were more like a
park than a working plantation. In fact, Arlington produced little profit. Its
master was interested in new agricultural ideas and had genuine concern for
preventing the already depleted soil of the South from deteriorating further,
but he was indolent by nature and preferred to talk about agricultural theories
rather than go to the trouble of putting them into practice.

Washington Custis was the soul of hospitality, though he was nearly
always short of cash. Rich in land and slaves, he seldom had much money
available because he was reluctant to dispose of any of the vast acreage he
owned at various places, and family tradition forbade selling his slaves. Besides, he felt personally responsible for the welfare of the Negroes he owned,
and he left instructions in his will that they were to be emancipated after his
death. There were 196 of them on his various estates when he died. Lack of
ready cash, however, did not prevent a wealthy plantation owner from enjoying life. When the Lees came to Arlington, the big house was at its best.
Its master was fifty-three—just old enough to be an experienced host yet not

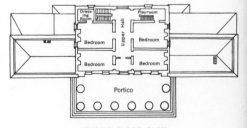

SECOND FLOOR PLAN

55

The family parlor, where the Lee wedding took place

The dining room

too old to be bored or fatigued by a role that in later years sometimes grows tiresome. Since Arlington had few field hands but many house servants, one was always standing by to anticipate every wish.

And the big, sprawling Greek Revival house, 140 feet long by 40 feet deep, was more than ample to shelter the second generation as well as the first. The exterior brick walls were covered with stucco incised with grooves to make the surface look like cut stone. The strongly made wooden framework was held together by mortises and tenons which were pinned fast with pegs.

Like most Southern houses of the same period, Arlington has a long, high-ceilinged hall running from the front entrance to the rear of the central part of the building. And another hall across the back of this section made it possible for servants and others to go from room to room without having to enter any of the main chambers. Washington Custis used this rear hall as a trophy display for his collection of deer and elk antlers. He had painted hunting scenes on the upper parts of the walls and had hung a decorative lantern from Mount Vernon from the ceiling.

The second story was given over to bedrooms although Mr. and Mrs. Custis slept on the ground floor. An office for the management of the plantation and a small conservatory for Mrs. Custis' flowers were also on this

56

The drawing room as renovated by the Lees
during their occupancy of Arlington. The painting
is a copy of the Charles Wilson Peale portrait
of Washington that used to be in the mansion.

The Lee bedroom on the second floor

Mrs. Custis' treasure chest

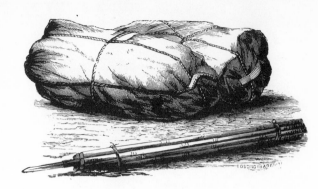

Washington's field tent

Washington's inkstand

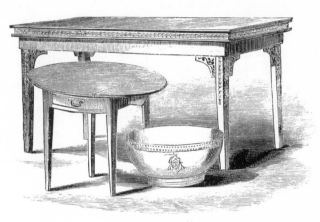

Sideboard, tea table, and punch bowl

Some of the Washington Relics at Arlington

In 1858 and 1859, Benson J. Lossing, the author of a number of popular historical works which he illustrated himself, spent some time at Mount Vernon and Arlington to sketch scenes and objects for use in his book The Home of Washington, *the first edition of which appeared in 1859.*

The Lee family was in residence when Lossing visited Arlington; they gave him every assistance. It was fortunate that he made a visual record of the Washington relics when he did, for they were widely scattered when war broke out two years later. Some were stolen, some were burned or otherwise destroyed, some simply disappeared. Those that survived the war are now in Mount Vernon, Arlington, and in public museums; others are in private hands.

Nelly Custis' harpsichord

floor. Beneath the house were the service areas—a winter kitchen, a large winecellar, and storage rooms. To keep cooking odors out of the main house and prevent the possibility of accidental fire spreading there, a summer kitchen located in the basement of a separate building behind the mansion was used during warm weather. Above it and in an adjacent building were the quarters of the house servants. In back of these were the stables and carriage houses. Flower and vegetable gardens were on either side of the mansion, and beyond them and all around, covering the slopes and the hillsides, were the great woods which have always been one of Arlington's chief glories.

Washington's silver candlestick

The house was reached by a long drive which left the river road and started up the hill at a point where the overseer's house and some of the slave houses were clustered around the famous spring. Here, too, was a dance pavilion and other buildings for the use of the public. The Georgetown and Alexandria Canal ran through the lower part of the grounds parallel with the Potomac, which it crossed on an aqueduct farther upstream.

Like Stratford, Arlington was—or at least was supposed to be—a self-sustaining plantation with its own ice house, gravel pit, smoke house, and provisions for storing food through the winter. On its grounds were cemeteries for the slaves and for the white people connected with the house. One could live, die, and be buried on the vast estate without ever having to go outside it.

But the young lieutenant had to leave the house early every weekday morning and ride to the War Department in Washington. When the weather was very bad, Lee sometimes remained in town overnight. In those early days he could be more lighthearted than his later dignified manner would lead one to believe. A slight incident tells much about his behavior then. He was about to ride back to Arlington one evening when he saw an officer he had known at West Point. He called to him and said: "Come, get up with me." His friend put his foot in the stirrup and swung up behind Lee. The two men rode gaily down Pennsylvania Avenue toward the White House. There they encountered the Secretary of the Treasury, "to whom they bowed with great dignity," as a contemporary account puts it.

Mrs. Washington's china

During most of the time that Lee was at Army Headquarters, Lewis Cass was Secretary of War and Brigadier General Charles Gratiot was in command of the Corps of Engineers. A number of organizational changes were made while they were in charge, one of which, the establishment of a Topographical Bureau in 1831, was to have a far-reaching effect upon the young lieutenant, for this branch of the service was always in need of trained men to make field surveys. When an officer became bored or unhappy with what he was doing in Washington, he could apply for such work and ordinarily stood a good chance of getting it. Sometimes, of course, orders came through that sent men to far places when they had no desire to go.

Lee's career in the War Department would have been more satisfying to him if he had not had to witness the petty bickering that constantly went on in official Washington. Personal jealousy was compounded by organizational jealousy as individuals and groups contended with one another for position and prestige. Lee was probably not sorry when he was ordered to go to the Great Lakes in the spring of 1835 to help make surveys that were needed to settle a dispute over the border between Ohio and Michigan. He spent the summer in the area, a summer that was the turning point for him between youth and middle age. When the twenty-eight-year-old lieutenant returned to Washington, he found that his wife had gone to Ravensworth, where she was seriously ill. She had given birth to their second child, a daughter named Mary Custis, and had contracted a pelvic infection which had confined her to

Washington's Cincinnati china

The War Department building where Lee worked

LEWIS CASS, *Secretary of War 1831–37*

bed for several months. She had written to her husband about it but had not told him how grave the condition was. During her long stay in bed, her hair had become so badly tangled that, with characteristic impatience, she had cut it off.

When she was able to walk again, her husband took her to the western mountains of Virginia, where the mineral springs were the chief attraction. Mary Lee recovered, but she was never to be entirely well again. And the man who had spent much of his boyhood nursing his invalid mother was now to spend the rest of his life taking care of a woman whose health became steadily worse. One of Lee's relatives who saw him returning from the springs said: "I never saw a man so changed and saddened."

Lee's character was shaped and tempered by his mother and his wife. He was fond of women and evidently preferred their company to that of men. His solicitude for them endeared him to them, and he in turn got much from them. He had grown up in a home that was without a father most of the time. Then, less than two years after his mother died, he married Mary Custis. With her, the pattern of his mother's invalidism repeated itself.

This was a time of much soul-searching for the lieutenant who was still young in years. Ordinarily outgoing, he became moody, sometimes even morose. And what was happening in the Army then was making matters worse. He became a first lieutenant on September 21, 1836, but the promotion meant little besides a small raise in pay. Actually, it brought home the fact that he had chosen a profession which was always at the whim of Congress. This was especially true of the Engineers, for the Corps' existence was largely dependent upon having plenty of construction work to do. He thought of resigning as his friend Andrew Talcott had just done, but above all he wanted to get away from Washington. Mary's health, however, made that impossible.

When they were both at Fort Monroe, he had jestingly agreed to produce a little Lee to match every little Talcott who was born, but by this time the Talcotts had five children. In May 1837, the Lees had another son, whom they named William Henry Fitzhugh after Mary's uncle. The boy was soon given a nickname, and was thereafter to be known as "Rooney" Lee.

A month before his birth, his father had received orders to proceed to St. Louis to work on the ever-changing channels of the Mississippi River. He had volunteered his services for the job in order to get away from Washington, where he was thoroughly disillusioned with official life. He purchased the instruments needed for surveying, and as soon as Mary and the child were well enough to be left in Arlington without his having to worry about them, he started west in company with Second Lieutenant Montgomery C. Meigs of Georgia, who had been graduated from West Point only the year before.

60

ST. LOUIS

The two men traveled by water most of the way, going by canal to Pittsburgh, where they took a steamer to Louisville. There they met Captain Henry Shreve, who had had a great deal of experience in clearing river channels of obstructions. He had prepared two boats for handling stone and had a steamer ready to tow them. Lee and Meigs proceeded in the riverboat which had brought them to Louisville and reached St. Louis on August 5.

Lee was now embarked on his first independent engineering job. The work he had done at Forts Pulaski and Monroe was under someone else's supervision even though he at times had had to carry on alone. But on the St. Louis assignment he had to do all the planning and make the decisions himself. Meigs had worked for a short time on the building of Fort Mifflin in the Delaware River, but that was his only experience. Shreve was a practical river man who could be depended upon for sound advice, and there were others in St. Louis who could be helpful. But the recommendations for expensive construction work had to come from Lee, who was the only one authorized to deal with the War Department.

Before undertaking any work at St. Louis, the party had to go upstream to make a survey of the rapids near the place at which the Des Moines River flows into the Mississippi. When they reached that point, Lee was only about a hundred miles from Springfield, Illinois, where a young attorney who was also to play a prominent part in the Civil War, had just been admitted to the bar. He had moved there in April from New Salem, and was sharing a friend's room because he could not afford to rent one of his own. And farther down

61

the Mississippi, just below Vicksburg, Jefferson Davis, who had been at West Point with Lee, was living in seclusion on an island plantation where his young wife had died two years before. The fourth man who was to shape the events of that future war was still a lad residing in southern Ohio with his father. He was looking forward to going to West Point. When he got there two years later, some confusion arose about his middle initial, so he allowed it to be changed on the register from Ulysses H. to Ulysses S. in order to make it agree with the way it had been entered.

The year 1837 was a bad one for the entire nation. New York banks suspended specie payments in May, and more than 600 throughout the country had to close their doors before the year was over. A long depression that paralyzed credit and froze money had begun.

The young lieutenant of Engineers, surveying the Des Moines rapids to determine where to cut a channel through them, probably heard little about these financial troubles while he was in the wilderness, but the work he was planning was to help alleviate the country's misery, for the money to be spent by the Government for river improvements would increase employment and encourage settlement in the still largely untenanted land.

The steamer carrying the surveying party ran onto the rocks in the Des Moines rapids and could not be dislodged. The men used the stranded vessel as a place to sleep and as a base of operations, leaving in small boats in the morning and returning aboard at night. After they completed their survey of the lower rapids, they went farther upstream—where they found another steamer which had been wrecked on the rocks and abandoned because its hull was stove in. The lower deck was flooded, but the cabins were above water. They moved into these and again had a ready-made base of operations. Meigs said that when the day's work was over they would "replenish the larder by fishing for blue catfish, pike, and pickerel." They must have had plenty to eat, for the virgin waters were swarming with fish.

THE BALTIMORE PORTRAITS

Lee's St. Louis assignment gave posterity two fine portraits of him and his wife. While on his way west in the spring of 1838, the Lees stopped in Baltimore to visit his sister Ann, now Mrs. William Louis Marshall. During their stay there, Lee agreed to sit for a portrait to be made by William E. West, a fifty-year-old Kentucky-born artist who had studied with Thomas Sully in Philadelphia and who had spent a number of years in Europe. While in Italy, West had painted portraits of Lord Byron and his mistress, Countess Guiccioli, and had met Shelley only a few days before he was drowned near Viareggio in 1822. West was a very uneven painter whose pictures could be excellent but were sometimes spoiled by overromanticizing. He made a bad portrait of Byron and a good one of Trelawny, the swashbuckling adventurer who was the chronicler of Shelley's death. Fortunately, the two that West did of the Lees are in his best style.

The artist was well acquainted with a glamorous and cosmopolitan world Lee had only heard about. What they discussed during the sittings was unfortunately not recorded. West left a good description of Byron, but Byron was then a world-famous figure who was to meet death at Missolonghi just two years later. The young lieutenant of Engineers, whose portrait West was painting in Baltimore, was, of course, then utterly obscure, and there was

At the end of what had doubtless been a very enjoyable summer, they returned to the lower rapids, where they found a tribe of Chippewas living in tepees while they waited for the Indian agents to distribute their annual presents. The river was rising, and Lee's party was able to refloat its steamer for the return to St. Louis.

When they arrived there, they rented space in a warehouse to prepare maps and reports. Lieutenant Lee recommended that a passageway be made through the rapids by "straightening and widening . . . the channels and by blasting and moving the rocks which obstructed navigation." This would permit steamers to run regularly into the wilderness country to bring in settlers and supplies. He also studied the local problem and drew up a report for improving the river at St. Louis.

It was at this time that Elijah P. Lovejoy, the editor of one of America's earliest antislavery newspapers, was forced to leave St. Louis. He set up a new office across the river at Alton, Illinois. One printing press after another was destroyed; when the fourth arrived by steamboat, it was placed in a shorefront warehouse which Lovejoy and some of his friends guarded. On the night of November 7, proslavery men attacked the building, killed Lovejoy, and threw his press into the river. The affair aroused a storm of controversy throughout the nation. In Boston, it brought Wendell Phillips into the ranks of the abolitionists, and in Ohio a then-unknown man named John Brown is said to have been so moved by it that he swore to devote his life to driving slavery from the land. What Lieutenant Lee thought about the killing of Lovejoy is not known. But he and Brown were to meet on the shores of another river twenty-two years later.

Since winter was now closing in and work in Missouri had to be suspended until spring, Lee and Meigs returned to Washington. When they reached Frederick, Maryland, they took one of the new Baltimore and Ohio Railroad's trains. The primitive steam locomotive had so little power that horses

continued on page 66

no reason to believe that his picture would ever be of interest to anyone except his immediate family.

Mrs. Lee wrote to her mother to tell her that she thought the portrait was "a very admirable likeness and fine painting." When West wanted to do one of her, she confided to her mother that she much preferred to be painted by Sully, but she changed her mind and allowed West to make a companion portrait.

It was fortunate that she did, for these two paintings are the only pictorial representations we have of the Lees as a married couple. The presumed portrait of Mary Custis as a young girl reproduced on page 51 has little resemblance to the thirty-year-old woman who looks gravely out of the canvas on which West recorded her features in 1838.

And the portrait of the handsome young lieutenant is, so far as is known, the first ever to be made of Robert E. Lee. At the time West was painting it, a French inventor named Louis Jacques Daguerre was vainly trying to raise money to finance a process of making pictures on a coating of silver iodide by using common salt to dissolve those parts of the camera image not affected by exposure to light. But the first practicable photographs were not to be available for another year. After 1839, Daguerreotypes spread rapidly throughout the world. They reached New York that year and immediately became popular. But it was to be some time before the lieutenant would face a camera.

MRS. ROBERT E. LEE *as painted by William E. West in 1838*

West's companion portrait of LIEUTENANT ROBERT E. LEE

had to pull the cars uphill. This was probably the first time the two young officers had ever traveled on rails. Haste along the route and this speedy new method of transportation at the end of their journey enabled them to reach Washington before Christmas.

There Lee had long discussions with his wife and her parents about the advisability of her going to St. Louis with him in the spring. It would be a difficult journey, and life in the western city would be much harder for her than at Arlington. But it was decided that she and the two boys were to go while little Mary was to remain with her grandparents. The family group started out in March, paused briefly in Baltimore for a visit to relatives, and then went to Philadelphia and Harrisburg on the new trains. There they took the canal to Pittsburgh and went by steamer to Louisville and St. Louis.

The frontier city must have seemed strange to Mary Lee, who had grown up in the comfort of long-settled Virginia. She was bothered by the mosquitoes, which she said were "as thick as a swarm of bees every evening." But, as always, she did the best she could and seldom complained.

Her husband was busy putting into effect his plans for saving the vital St. Louis waterfront which was being blocked by a huge sandbar which the industrious river was depositing on its doorstep. Most of this great mass of unwanted sand was below the city, but the bar kept extending itself toward St. Louis. Lee's scheme for getting rid of it called for building two long dikes that would deflect the fast-moving current toward the Missouri shore to wash the sand away. He had presented his report for the project to the Corps of Engineers in Washington and had obtained approval to proceed with the work, which he estimated would cost $158,000. The appropriation was slow in coming through, but the city of St. Louis put up $15,000 to get the work started. Lee threw himself into the enterprise with such vigor that he lost weight and grew lean and hard from the exercise. Although he occasionally felt dejected, he must have been elated when his captain's commission came through at the end of the summer.

Winding up the details of the season's work kept him in St. Louis so long that year that it was too late to take his family back to Arlington, so they remained in Missouri during the winter of 1838–39.

In the spring of 1839, the depression—which had not yet affected Lee—now laid its heavy hand upon what he was doing. Congress was so short of funds that it diverted money from the amount already on hand in St. Louis.

Mary was pregnant with her fourth child, which was due in June. Lee took her and the children to Arlington, where she could get better care than in the West. He then had to hurry back to St. Louis. After his arrival there, he got word that he had a second daughter, born on June 18, and named Annie Carter Lee.

He lived on board a river boat while work on the waterfront progressed. The still-unfinished dikes were beginning to send the current toward the Missouri shore to sweep the sand away. Then legal action from indignant landowners on the Illinois side of the river suddenly held up the project. Work on the Des Moines rapids was going forward, however. At the end of the season, Lee was sent on an inspection tour, after which he was allowed to return to Washington on leave. He saw his new daughter for the first time, and was able to stay at Arlington for many months because Congress could not get the funds needed to carry on the work in the West.

It was midsummer before Lee was sent back to St. Louis. By October 1840 he had finished his last work there and was on his way to Arlington, where Mary was expecting her fifth child.

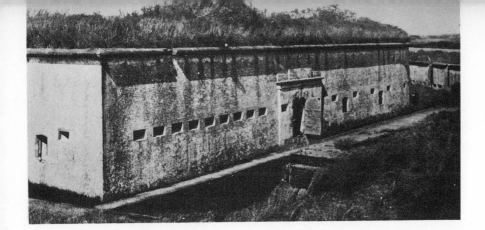

Fort Macon as it looks today

FORTS MACON AND CASWELL

Lee's work in Missouri had firmly established his reputation as a competent engineer who could be depended upon to make wise decisions and stretch the Government's limited funds as far as they would go. Since the War Department had no better assignment for him at this time, it sent him to North Carolina for the winter of 1840–41 to inspect the coastal forts in that state. His first stop was at Fort Macon near Beaufort.

The sea had flooded part of Fort Macon and damaged some of its foundations and walls. Jetties and dikes were needed to stop the invading waters. With his experience in doing such work in Missouri, Lee seemed well suited for the job. He spent some time examining the fort and made plans for repairs.

Macon, which commanded the entrance to the sound on which Beaufort was located, was to have an interesting history during the Civil War. Captured by the Confederates in April 1861, it guarded the raider *Nashville* when she arrived from England in February 1862. After the *Nashville* went to sea again by running the blockade, Macon became the object of a combined Union naval and land attack during which three batteries were built in the nearby swamps to pour in shells while a fleet ran in to bombard the fort. Macon had to be surrendered; it remained in Federal hands for the rest of the war.

There is no firm evidence to indicate that Lee ever reached Fort Caswell, although he was supposed to go there. This fort, built to defend the harbor of Smithville, North Carolina, was located in an area that was to be of prime strategic importance during the Civil War. It was built on a point of land that commanded the western entrance to the Cape Fear River and the city of Wilmington. Although not fortified in 1840, the long, low-lying spit of land along the eastern entrance to the Cape Fear River was to be the site of Fort Fisher, which became one of the strongest of all Confederate defenses. As a result of the powerful works in this area, Wilmington was able to hold out until January 1865. Into that port came hundreds of blockade-runners bringing vitally needed arms and supplies from Europe. Much of what they delivered was for the use of the Army of Northern Virginia, then under the command of Robert E. Lee.

Having finished whatever field work was necessary, Lee returned to Arlington before the end of 1840. He spent the rest of the winter preparing drawings for the repair of the forts. He was then given a chance to go to New York to supervise work on the forts defending the harbor there. Lee had visited New York briefly when he went to West Point as a very young man. Now he was to see the city as a longtime resident of the suburbs of that rapidly growing metropolis.

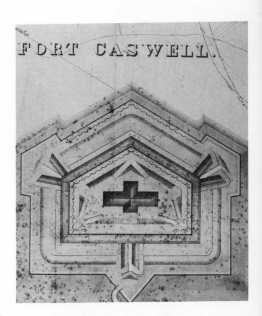

Fort Caswell, North Carolina

Brooklyn as seen from New York in 1845

*New York Harbor and the Narrows
in 1854, with Forts Hamilton and
Lafayette at the extreme right*

The period 1841 to 1846, when Lee
was at Fort Hamilton, marked the
beginning of steam for transatlantic
crossings. Steamships had made the
run as early as 1819 when the Savannah *went to Liverpool, using sails,
however, for most of the voyage. But
in April 1838, when the* Sirius *and the*
Great Western *arrived from England,*

steam had seriously started to replace
sail. Sail, however, was to have a last
glorious burst of speed and beauty
with the short-lived clipper ships in
the 1840s and 1850s. At Fort Hamilton, Lee had a front-seat view of this
race between sail and steam for mas-
tery of the high seas of the world. All
oceangoing ships passed the fort.

FORT HAMILTON

Fort Hamilton and its satellite Fort Lafayette, a few hundred feet offshore, were located on the western end of Long Island in the village of New Utrecht, about seven miles south of Brooklyn. Lee sometimes took a horse to ride along the shore road to the Brooklyn ferries in order to cross to Manhattan. Living in Brooklyn at this time was a young journalist who was to write some memorable prose and poetry about the Civil War. Since he used the Fulton Ferry almost daily, it is entirely possible that he and Robert E. Lee may, on some occasion, have crossed to Manhattan on the same boat. If they did, the tall handsome soldier, standing quietly and holding his horse as he looked out over the water where the gulls wheeled and flashed, may have been among those who made a lasting impression upon Walt Whitman, for the ever-observant poet, who was to immortalize the ferry they were riding on, said: "The hundreds and hundreds that cross . . . are more to me, and more in my meditations than you might suppose."

Manhattan was picturesque in those days. Great tides of horsedrawn traffic swept through streets where throngs of people walked or stopped to look in the shop windows or watch a sidewalk vendor sell his wares. Broadway was the main artery of traffic; it ran north, passing the lurid posters of Barnum's Museum at Ann Street to go far uptown, where crowded buildings gave way to open ground above Fiftieth Street. Whitman saw much of that lively city; Lee very little, for he was kept busy at Fort Hamilton most of the time.

His assignment was not very interesting; most of his duties were concerned with the repair, alteration, or extension of existing structures rather than the planning of new ones. The work in Missouri had been more challenging.

His first job was to recondition the rundown house that was to be his family's home. He had the forts ready for their new garrisons before the year was over, and he then had to move his wife and five children to still another house, a rented one. The Lees were to remain at Fort Hamilton for five years, but almost every winter, when cold winds made work on the fortifications impossible, they went to Arlington for a long holiday. Though they had to spend the first winter in New York's blustery climate, they were able, in 1842, to go to Virginia for Christmas.

Some diversion for Lee came during the summer of 1843 when he was called to West Point to make recommendations about new barracks that were to be built there. It was his first visit to the Academy since he had been graduated. The cadets he saw drilling on the parade ground were separated by half a generation from his. Most of them were to be majors or colonels in the great war of the 1860s, but at least two were to rise to the top. One was a boy from Ohio, Ulysses S. Grant, who was in the graduating class. He had become the best horseman in the Academy, which was noted for fine horsemanship. The other was a younger man who had entered the year before. He was a tall, shy farm boy with a strange look in his eyes. He came from the mountains of western Virginia; his name was Thomas Jonathan Jackson, although it was to change during the first big battle of the war, when he was to acquire the famous nickname by which he would continue to be known.

Lee evidently made a favorable impression that summer at West Point, for he was invited to be present at the final examinations the following June.

Uniform of an officer in the Corps of Topographical Engineers 1839–1851

At that time he spent two weeks there in close contact with members of the high command of the United States Army. They were beginning to notice him now.

On October 27, 1843, while Mary was again in Arlington, the Lees' sixth child was born. He was named after his father, and Robert E. Lee, Jr., later claimed to remember dimly—"more like dreams"—his days of infancy at Fort Hamilton.

In September 1845, Lee was made a member of a board of Army Engineers who were choosing sites for future fortifications along the coast. And in New York he had a boat assigned to him so he could go around the harbor to supervise the work. Two batteries on Staten Island were under his jurisdiction, and he had to cross the Narrows almost daily to inspect the progress of work on the other shore. On one of these short trips he rescued a dog which had probably fallen from a passing ship. Robert, Jr., wrote later: "She was a handsome thing, with cropped ears and a short tail. My father named her Dart. She was a fine ratter, and with the assistance of a Maltese cat, also a member of the family, the many rats which infested the house and stables were driven away or destroyed." Dart soon had puppies, one of which was named Spec. Robert said of the little black-and-tan terrier: "My father would not allow his tail and ears to be cropped. When he grew up, he accompanied us everywhere and was in the habit of going to church with the family."

Since the Lee children paid more attention to their dog than they did to the sermon, their father finally insisted that Spec be left at home. The next Sunday, he was confined in a room on the second story. But it was summer, and someone had left the window open. The little dog jumped out, survived the fall, and ran to overtake the family. He reached them just as they were entering the church, "much to the joy of the children." After that, he was allowed to attend the services, during which dog and children were all on their best behavior.

Lee became greatly attached to the dog. When Mary and the children were in Arlington in January 1846, he wrote: "I am very solitary and my only company is my dog and cats. But Spec has become so jealous now that he will hardly let me look at the cats. He seems to be afraid that I am going off from him and never lets me stir without him. Lies down in the office from eight to four without moving and turns himself before the fire as the side from it becomes cold. I catch him sometimes sitting up looking at me so intently that I am for a moment startled."

Some years later a Baltimore woman said: "Everybody and everything— his family, his friends, his horse, and his dog—loves Colonel Lee."

Just before Mary left for Arlington in November 1845, Rooney had what could have been a serious accident. His father wrote to Custis, then away

70

at school, a description of what had happened: "He went down to the public barn where they were putting in some hay for the horses and . . . commenced to cut some hay with the straw cutter and took off the ends of the fore and middle fingers of the left hand. The first just at the root of the nail and the second at the first joint. . . . More than an hour and a quarter elapsed before they could be dressed. All that time he sat . . . with his fingers bleeding profusely, without complaining. . . . As soon . . . as Dr. Eaton arrived . . . he sewed the ends on and bound them up. The officers who were present said they were astonished to see so young a boy behave so well, that they had seen many men under less trying circumstances behave worse. . . . We do not know yet . . . whether the ends will unite with the fingers or not. . . . He may probably lose his fingers and be maimed for life. You cannot conceive what I suffer at the thought." Fortunately, Rooney's badly hurt fingers healed without difficulty.

The house occupied by the Lees in Fort Hamilton

Lee was still at Fort Hamilton when his seventh—and last—child was born in Arlington in February 1846. She was named Mildred Childe for his youngest sister who had married and gone to Paris to live.

It was about this time that a trivial error caused Lee much annoyance. By some mistake, he had drawn his pay twice for May and June 1845. A vigilant clerk in Washington noticed the overdraft. Before preferring charges, a letter was sent to Lee asking for an explanation. His outstanding reputation for probity stood him in good stead on this unhappy occasion. Since he quickly refunded the duplicate payment, charges were not brought. When he wrote a contrite letter to the Adjutant General, he said: "I am gratified to find that you believe me incapable of intentionally committing this act; I assure you that it has caused me more mortification than any other act of my life, to find that I have been culpably negligent when the strictest accuracy is both necessary and required."

The five peaceful years in New York were now drawing to a close. Trouble was breaking out on the Mexican border, and there was much talk of war. Every Army officer in the service was wondering what his role would be if war came.

Lee writes to the Adjutant General about an error which caused him great mortification. This was on the eve of the Mexican War, when every Army officer's record was subject to even greater than usual scrutiny.

71

A photograph of Lee as Captain of Engineers, believed to have been made about the time the War with Mexico began

Although trained to be a soldier, Captain Robert E. Lee, now thirty-nine years old, had never seen the smoke of battle except as a child when the British burned Washington. The nearest he had come to war was the building of fortifications for coastal defense, while a good part of his career had been devoted to such useful peacetime pursuits as surveying state boundaries or making rivers navigable. Some of the men of his generation had fought the Indians in the Black Hawk War of 1832 and in the Second Seminole War of 1836–42, but these were minor campaigns. There had been no major American wars, no sending of troops against foreign nations during Lee's adult years. The long period of peace had reduced the Army to 826 officers and 7683 enlisted men in 1845. Congress had not only cut back again, but was also seriously debating the idea of abolishing the Military Academy at West Point. Now all this was to be changed overnight. Before 1846 ended, there would be more than 2000 officers and nearly 26,000 men in the suddenly expanded Army. There would be still more in 1847.

The United States declared war on Mexico on May 13, 1846, over issues growing out of the annexation of Texas the year before. Like the War of 1812, the war with Mexico was popular in some parts of the country, unpopular in others. Texas and states in the Mississippi Valley, which were vitally concerned, supplied 49,000 volunteers; the thirteen original states along the Atlantic Coast sent only 13,000. The war was denounced in the North as a slaveholders' plot to seize additional territory for the expansion of slavery. Young Lieutenant Ulysses S. Grant, who was with the first American troops to cross the border, felt that the Army was being "sent to provoke a fight" in a political war. He was not alone in his skepticism. "Cotton thread holds the Union together," Emerson said cynically. His neighbor in Concord, Henry David Thoreau, went to jail rather than pay a poll tax, saying that he refused to let his dollar buy "a man or a musket to shoot one with." And before the war was over, Congressman Abraham Lincoln of Illinois was to wreck his career in the House of Representatives by opposing a military expedition which his constituents favored.

But Robert E. Lee, as a professional Army officer, could only wait for Washington to make up its mind whether he was to take an active part in the war or remain at Fort Hamilton until age eventually disqualified him from service. It was three months before he got the answer. Then orders dated August 19, 1846, instructed him to come to Washington; after that he was to report to Brigadier General John E. Wool in San Antonio, Texas, for service in Mexico.

It seemed inadvisable for Mary to go back to New York while war was threatening, so she had remained at Arlington since the birth of their seventh child. Lee was with her during the few days he spent in Washington, but he had little time for anything except Army business then. He had to wind up his accounts at the War Department, and then he was off by ship to New Orleans and Texas. He made his will before he went, for he knew there was a good chance that he might not return.

He arrived in San Antonio on September 21 and reported to General Wool. The sixty-two-year-old commander, who had fought in the War of 1812, was busy assembling his troops. As an engineer, Lee was among those who had to procure tools and material for building bridges and roads. It was difficult to obtain anything in San Antonio, a town of only 2000 people, but the officers assigned to the task did the best they could. A week after Lee's arrival,

THE LAST WILL AND TESTAMENT OF ROBERT E. LEE

Dated August 31, 1846, Lee's only known will left the proceeds of his estate to his wife Mary "in full confidence that she will use it to the best advantage in the education and care of my children." After her death the estate was to be divided among the children "in such proportion to each as their situations and necessities in life may require, and as may be designated by her." He requested that his daughter Annie Carter Lee, "who from an accident . . . received in one of her eyes, may be more in want of aid than the rest, may, if necessary, be particularly provided for." (Perhaps this injury explains why no photograph of Annie has ever been found.)

Lee made his wife executrix and his eldest son, George Washington Custis Lee, executor when he came of age. Lee said that he hoped no dispute would ever arise in interpreting his intentions. He also left instructions that all his debts, "of which there are but few," were to be paid promptly.

In the schedule of property, which lists the various investments Lee had made and which shows that he estimated them to be worth $38,750, at least one venture was already of dubious value when the will was drawn up. This was one share of stock in Washington's National Theatre which he appraised at $250. Since the theater had been destroyed by fire the year before the will was made, it is not likely that this share of stock was worth much.

The schedule also lists the only slaves Lee ever owned —a Negro woman named Nancy and her children. He left instructions for them to be set free "so soon as it can be done to their advantage and that of others."

Mentioned in the schedule is Lee's "share of the claim of the property leased to the Government by my Father at Harper's Ferry." Since it was there that Lee first attracted national attention during the John Brown raid in 1859, and since many of his Civil War campaigns often involved that strategically located place, this early allusion to possible family ownership of part of it is especially interesting.

The will and the attached schedule are both in Lee's handwriting. The will was probated in the Rockbridge County Court after Lee died in 1870. At that time it was estimated that the estate did not exceed $50,000. It was probably worth far less, for many of the assets had decreased greatly in value—or had become worthless—in the financial debacle that followed the downfall of the Confederacy.

73

nearly 2000 men began to march toward the Mexican border. They reached the Rio Grande on October 8, having made good use of the roads and bridges built along the way by the Army Engineers. Pontoons carried on wagons had accompanied the troops; these were now needed to cross the Rio Grande.

By October 12, the entire column was on the other side of the river. There they got word that Monterey had surrendered to General Zachary Taylor on September 25. This was the first victory of any consequence for the United States Army since the Battle of New Orleans in 1815—more than a generation before. Wool's troops continued their march toward Monclava, sometimes having to take their supply wagons across flooded rivers by ropes or on makeshift bridges. They got there on October 29 and then had to wait for weeks because General Taylor had arranged an armistice with the Mexicans which temporarily prevented any further movement.

After the armistice expired on November 19, Wool started out again, leaving part of his army at Monclava. Lee went ahead with the engineers to prepare the road. Some time was spent at Parras on the way to Saltillo, where General W. J. Worth was waiting for them with some of Taylor's troops. They went on, traveling down a great valley with 350 wagons loaded with enough supplies for sixty days, 400,000 cartridges, and 200 rounds of artillery ammunition. They joined forces with Worth on December 21, making an army of 6000 men who were then hundreds of miles deep in enemy territory.

On Christmas Eve, Lee wrote to his two eldest sons about the animals attached to the Army: "The Mexicans raise a large quantity of ponies, donkeys, and mules. . . . These little donkeys will carry two hundred pounds on their backs, and the mules will carry three hundred on long journeys over the mountains. The ponies are used for riding and cost from ten to fifty dollars, according to their size and quality. I have three horses. Creole is my pet; she is a golden dun, active as a deer, and carries me over all the ditches and gullies that I have met with; nor has she ever yet hesitated at anything I have put her at; she is full-blooded and considered the prettiest thing in the army; though young, she has so far stood the campaign as well as any horses of the division." Captain Lee evidently missed his children: "I have frequently thought that if I had one of you on each side of me riding on ponies . . . I would be comparatively happy."

On Christmas Day there was a rumor that the Mexicans were going to attack the camp. After the excitement was over, Lee described it to his wife: "The troops stood to their arms, and I lay on the grass with my sorrel mare saddled by my side and telescope directed to the pass of the mountain through which the road approached. The Mexicans, however, did not make their appearance. Many regrets were expressed at Santa Anna's having spoiled our Christmas dinner for which ample preparation had been made. The little roasters remained tied to the tent pins wondering at their deferred fate, and the headless turkeys retained their plumage unscathed. Finding the enemy did

*The American wagon train goes
down the great valley toward Saltillo*

74

not come, preparations were again made for dinner. We have had many happy Christmases together. It is the first time we have been entirely separated at this holy time since our marriage. I hope it does not interfere with your happiness, surrounded as you are by father, mother, children, and dear friends. I therefore trust you are well and happy, and that this is the last time I shall be absent from you during my life. May God preserve and bless you till then and forever after is my constant prayer."

It was only a few days after this that Lee had one of his most interesting adventures of the war. Wool still believed that Santa Anna's forces might be near, so he called for scouts to ride out and gather information. Lee volunteered to go. He was supposed to be accompanied by a cavalry patrol, but by some mischance he did not find the horsemen. He was soon alone with a Mexican guide who was supposed to know the country. Neither Lee nor Wool trusted the young Mexican. Wool threatened to hang the boy's father if the son did not bring Lee back safely, and Lee showed the boy his pocket pistol and told him that he would shoot him if he tried to betray him.

The distrustful pair rode along in the bright moonlight until they were about five miles from the place Santa Anna's camp was supposed to be. There they saw numerous tracks made by mules and wagons. No marks of artillery could be seen, but Lee thought that a wagon party bringing up supplies and ammunition might have trampled over them. He was not satisfied, however, and insisted on following the tracks until he found the enemy's pickets. After a while he saw a number of campfires burning on a hillside. The guide showed signs of fright, for he knew that if they were captured by Santa Anna's men they would both be hanged or shot. When he refused to go any farther, Lee told him to wait and then went on alone.

He came to a slope leading down to a small stream where many white tents appeared to be gleaming on a moonlit hill beyond, and he could hear men

General Zachary Taylor watches the outcome of the battle being fought at Monterey on September 21–24, 1846. It resulted in a victory for the American troops.

GENERAL ZACHARY TAYLOR, *known as "Old Rough and Ready"*

The Island of Lobos, rendezvous of the American fleet before the attack on Vera Cruz

Landing American troops on the beach at Vera Cruz

talking on the other shore. He kept going until he reached the banks of the stream. On closer view, the scene changed from his warlike fantasy of a vast army camp to the peaceful reality of an open field where flocks of white sheep and the canvas covers of their drovers' wagons had tricked him into seeing what he expected to see.

Lee rode into the herdsmen's camp where he was informed that no Mexican troops were in the vicinity. He hurried back to headquarters to tell General Wool what he had learned. Although he had already ridden forty miles that night, he was off again after a three-hour rest, leading a troop of cavalry to try to find out where Santa Anna really was. He succeeded in locating the general area where the elusive Mexican commander was believed to be, but before a battle could be brought on, Lee was transferred to General Winfield Scott's army. A few days before he left in mid-January, a young man who had been with him at West Point came to the camp. He was Colonel Jefferson Davis, then in command of the First Mississippi Volunteers. Davis had been married to General Taylor's daughter. Her early death had brought him closer to "Old Rough and Ready," who had bought a plantation on the Mississippi River near Davis' holdings. Davis remained with Taylor and was wounded at the Battle of Buena Vista on February 22–23, when Santa Anna's troops were defeated.

When Lee reached the big encampment at the mouth of the Rio Grande, where Scott's army for the attack on Vera Cruz was being assembled, he found that it was like a reunion at West Point. Among those present were Captain Joseph E. Johnston, '29; Lieutenant George Gordon Meade, '35; Jubal Early, '37 (now major of a Virginia volunteer regiment); Lieutenant Pierre Gustave Toutant Beauregard, '38; Lieutenant D. H. Hill, '42; Lieutenant Ulysses S. Grant, '43; and Lieutenant Thomas Jonathan Jackson, who had been graduated from the Academy the year before. And waiting at Tampico to be picked up by a transport was another lieutenant who had also been in the most recent graduating class. Like Lee, he had been Number Two man. He too was to play a prominent part in the next war. His name was George Brinton McClellan.

Lee and Johnston, who were classmates and captains, managed to get a cabin together on the *Massachusetts,* which was to take them to Tampico and then to the Island of Lobos, the rendezvous for the American fleet. On the way, Lee had time to write a long letter to his sons:

We had a grand parade on General Scott's arrival [at Tampico]. The troops were all drawn up on the bank of the river and fired a salute as he passed them. He landed at the market, where lines of sentinels were placed to keep off the crowd. In front of the landing the artillery was drawn up, which received him in the center of the column and escorted him through the streets to his lodgings. They had provided a handsome gray horse, richly caparisoned, for him, but he preferred to walk with his staff around him, and a dragoon led the horse behind us. The windows along the streets we passed were crowded with people, and the boys and girls were in great glee, the Governor's Island band playing all the time. There were six thousand soldiers in Tampico. . . . We only remained there one day. I have a nice stateroom on board this ship; Joe Johnston and myself occupy it, but my poor Joe is so sick all the time I can do nothing with him. I left Jem to come on with the horses, as I was afraid they would not be properly cared for. . . . I hope they may both reach the shore again in safety, but I fear they will have a hard time. They will first have to be put aboard a steamboat and carried to the ship that lies about two miles out to sea, then hoisted in, and how we shall get them ashore again, I do not know. Probably throw them overboard, and let them swim. . . . I do not think we shall remain here more than one day longer. . . . The ship rolls so that I can scarcely write.

The fleet left Lobos on March 9, 1847. When it arrived at a beach about three miles below Vera Cruz, the work of putting men, horses, guns, and supplies ashore began. Oddly enough, the Mexicans offered no resistance. They remained inside the walls of the city or inside the even stronger Fortress of San Juan de Ulúa, which was built on a reef about half a mile from the shore. By midnight, 10,000 United States troops had been successfully landed.

General Scott had known Lee when he was working in the War Department in Washington. Now he made Lee a member of his "Little Cabinet," and a closer association between the two men began.

Batteries were built on the hills to reduce the city. Returning from one of these, Lee just missed being killed when a nervous sentry fired his pistol at him. The bullet went between the left side of Lee's chest and his arm, only a few inches from the heart.

In order to make sure that he had cannon heavy enough to breach the city's walls, Scott borrowed three 64-pounder shell guns and three long 32-pounders from the fleet. These were for a battery which Lee designed. Sailors assigned to help in the construction complained about having to work for a landlubber and protested that "they did not enlist to eat dirt." The captain of

ULYSSES S. GRANT *as a lieutenant in the Mexican War*

77

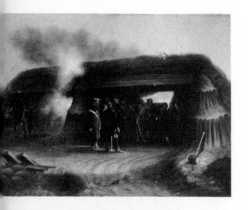

The naval battery at Vera Cruz. Sydney Smith Lee's gun is the third from the right

American siege guns at Vera Cruz, painted by the military artist James Walker

one of the ships said that it was an outrage for his men to have to dig. "They don't want any dirt to hide behind," he explained. "They'll get up on top where they can have a fair fight."

After the bombardment, during which sailors' lives were saved when enemy shells struck the protecting earthworks, the captain grudgingly admitted that the "dirt banks" had been useful. But there was no place for dirt on a ship, he said. "Besides," he added, "I don't like this land fighting anyway. *It ain't clean.*"

On the night before the bombardment, a naval officer who was to make a name for himself in the Civil War, climbed up the hill behind this battery. This was Raphael Semmes who describes the scene: "It was perfectly calm. The fleet at Sacrificios was just visible through the gloom and was sleeping quietly at its anchors without other sign of life than a solitary light burning at the gaff-end of the commodore. The castle of San Juan d'Ulloa [*sic*], magnified out of all proportion by the uncertain starlight and looking ten times more somber and defiant than ever, appeared to enjoy equal repose. Even the sea seemed to have gone to sleep after the turmoil of the recent norther, as the only sound that reached the ear from that direction was a faint, very faint, murmur, hoarse and plaintive as the lazy swell, with scarcely energy enough to break, stranded itself on the beach."

The next morning, March 24, the battery was ready to fire. Lee's brother, naval Lieutenant Sydney Smith Lee, had been assigned to one of the guns, and the two brothers fought their first action together. Lee wrote home about the warlike scene: "I stood by his gun whenever I was not wanted elsewhere. . . . I . . . am at a loss what I should have done had he been cut down before me. I thank God that he was saved. He preserved his usual cheerfulness, and I could see his white teeth through all the smoke and din of the fire. . . . The shells thrown from our battery were constant and regular discharges, so beautiful in their flight and so destructive in their fall. It was awful! My heart bled for the inhabitants. The soldiers I did not care so much for, but it was terrible to think of the women and children."

At the end of the day, gunners from the ships relieved the men in the naval battery, and firing was kept up throughout the night. It continued until March 26, when the Mexicans asked for a truce. Of the 2500 shells that had been fired, 1800 had come from the naval battery.

78

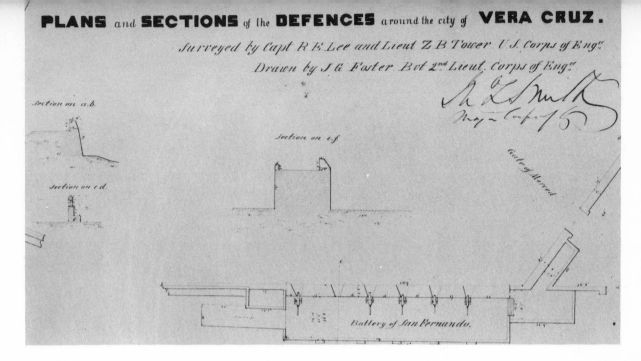

PLANS and **SECTIONS** of the **DEFENCES** around the city of **VERA CRUZ.**

Surveyed by Capt R E Lee and Lieut Z B Tower U S Corps of Engr

Drawn by J G Foster Bvt 2nd Lieut. Corps of Engr

Section on a.b.

Section on c.f

Section on c.d.

Battery of San Fernando.

Part of the survey of the defenses of Vera Cruz made by R. E. Lee after the surrender of the city

When Vera Cruz was surrendered on March 29, Scott gave the defeated army remarkably lenient terms. He set forty officers free and paroled all the prisoners. Officers were permitted to retain their side arms and horses. One person in the American army who noted Scott's generosity was young Lieutenant Grant. He had a good memory, and what he saw at Vera Cruz that day probably influenced his attitude toward the men of a conquered army when he had to set the terms for surrender at a place called Appomattox.

And the man he was to deal with at Appomattox eighteen years later also noted what Scott had done. Lee, too, was to follow the principle that a soldier should be generous—and not only to a former foe but to his own subordinates. He had good cause to remember the old general fondly, for he now got his first mention in the report of the battle which Scott sent to Washington.

C. M. Wilcox, then fresh out of West Point, but who was to be a major general in the Confederate Army, met Lee at this time. He said that the compliments the captain got were deserved, that "he was active, untiring, skillful, courageous, and of good judgment." Wilcox also said that Lee was "the handsomest man in the army."

Shortly after the surrender of Vera Cruz, Lee had an amusing experience with Scott. This took place in a Catholic church which had been damaged by the cannon fire because it was outside the walls near the American batteries. Scott wanted all the churches kept open and offered to "borrow" them and provide some of his chaplains if necessary. The idea of having a Protestant minister hold services in a Catholic church was enough to make sure that a priest was at every altar in Vera Cruz on Sunday. Henry J. Hunt, who was to fight against Lee as an artillery commander all through the Virginia campaigns, tells the story:

I found not only that the church was full, but the door was blocked by a crowd of our soldiers. . . . I finally got inside the door where I could see the altar. All present were on their knees or standing except on the left, where . . . a single bench had been . . . set against the wall. On this bench, in full uniform, epaulettes, and sword, sat General Scott and his staff, the general himself at the end nearest the altar, then his aid, Lieutenant Williams, then Captain Lee, Lieutenants Beauregard, etc. The bench seemed full, but . . . looking in that direction, I caught Captain Lee's eye. . . . He motioned me

SYDNEY SMITH LEE, *Lieutenant, U.S.N., who fought at Vera Cruz with his brother, Robert E. Lee*

toward him and made a movement indicating that there was room for me be-side him. . . . In my dilapidated old campaign dress I felt that I would be a little out of place in the brilliant party. However . . . I gradually picked my way to the bench. . . .

One of the acolytes went to the altar, lighted a large thick wax candle and brought it to General Scott. At first the general did not seem to comprehend it, but . . . he took the candle and immediately handed to Mr. Williams. The volunteers stared with open mouths. It was understood that General Scott, if succesful in his campaign, must be a Presidential candidate at the next election. Hostility to the Catholic Church was the element with the "American" [Know-Nothing] Party. The matter was getting interesting. In a moment or two the acolyte returned with another, but not so large or honorable a candle as the first. Finding the first one in the aid's hands and General Scott unprovided, he looked rather dazed, but acted promptly—blew out his light, went back to the altar, got another large one, and brought it to the general, who had to take it. I, being next to Williams, carefully looked away and saw nothing until the aco-lyte returned with the smaller candle lighted for me, which I took, and others were given to Captain Lee and the rest of the staff.

Then we were requested to rise, were wheeled "by twos" to the left, which brought General Scott in front of me and Captain Lee on my right. Soon a side door opened just in front of General Scott, and an array of priests in gorgeous vestments filed out and formed in our front. Everything was clear enough now —a Church procession in which General Scott and his staff . . . had the place of honor. I looked at Captain Lee. He had that dignified, quiet appear-ance habitual to him, and looked as if the carrying of candles in religious pro-cessions was an ordinary thing with him.

While the army got ready for the attack on Mexico City, Lee made meas-ured drawing of the fortified works around Vera Cruz. This was the first time he had had an opportunity to study defenses planned and built by foreign engineers.

General Scott was eager to press on. Hot weather would bring yellow fever to the low-lying coastal section, and his men could escape the dreaded disease only by going to the healthier mountain country as soon as possible. Wagons and other war materiel were badly needed, but Scott could not wait for them to arrive. The troops started out in the second week of April, when the weather was already unbearably hot.

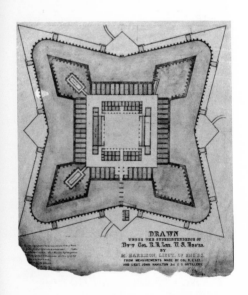

The Castle of Perote as drawn by Lee

80

Thirty miles inland, Santa Anna was waiting for them in a strongly intrenched position which blocked the road through the mountain passes near a hill named Cerro Gordo. The Mexicans were convinced that their defenses were impregnable, and the American engineers were inclined to agree with them. A direct assault was out of the question. Some way had to be found to flank Santa Anna's army of more than 12,000 men. Lee was among those who did the highly dangerous reconnaissance work needed to cut roads through the mountains. He traveled with a daredevil young scout named John Fitzwalter, whom the Mexicans called Juan Diablo. This man said that Lee at one time "was forced to take refuge beneath a fallen tree, near which was a spring to which the Mexicans frequently came for water. While he lay hidden in this perilous covert, hostile soldiers frequently passed over the tree and even sat down on it and entered into conversation, without discovering the somewhat nervous individual beneath it. He was obliged to remain there until the coming of night enabled him to retire from the dangerous locality."

Crude roads were quickly built to bring up troops and guns. To get artillery into firing position, the guns had to be drawn up a precipitous slope by hand and then let down the other side by paying out ropes. When everything was ready, Scott ordered the attack to begin on April 18. Lee described the action in a letter: "Soon after sunrise our batteries opened, and I started with a column to turn their left and to get on the Jalapa road. Notwithstanding their efforts to prevent us in this, we were perfectly successful, and the working party, following our footsteps, cut out the road for the artillery. In the meantime our storming party had reached the crest of Cerro Gordo, and, seeing their whole left turned and . . . our soldiers on the Jalapa road, they broke and fled. Those in the pass laid down their arms. . . . All their cannon, arms, ammunition, and most of their men fell into our hands. My friend Joe Johnston was wounded."

At Vera Cruz, shells from the American guns had fallen behind the walls of the city, sparing the field troops from seeing the effect they had on human beings. Cerro Gordo was Lee's first direct experience with the horrors of war. What he saw there made a lasting impression on him. In a letter to his son Custis, he described the field at Cerro Gordo. He found a Mexican drummer boy whose arm had been badly shattered. Piled on top of him was a dying Mexican soldier whose body was too heavy for a little girl from one of the villages to move. Her grief brought Lee to the scene. When he had the wounded man and boy taken to a hospital, she thanked him by saying *Mil gracias, Señor.* Lee said: "Her large black eyes were streaming with tears, her hands crossed over her breast; her hair in one long plait behind reached her waist, her shoulders and arms bare and without stockings or shoes."

Santa Anna's men, dislodged from the defenses they had thought impregnable, fled through the mountains toward Mexico City. Scott released 3000 prisoners on parole because he had no way of feeding them. Casualty figures for both Mexican and United States troops are uncertain, but Mexican losses were much greater. And about 4000 arms and 40 cannon were captured.

Again Lee was mentioned in dispatches, this time by subordinate commanders as well as by Scott himself. The general said in his report: "I am impelled to make special mention of the services of Captain R. E. Lee. . . . This officer, greatly distinguished at the siege of Vera Cruz, was again indefatigable during these operations, in reconnaissance as daring as laborious, and of the utmost in value. Nor was he less conspicuous in planting batteries and in conducting columns to their stations under the heavy fire of the enemy." In August, Lee was breveted major "for gallant and meritorious conduct at Cerro Gordo."

LT. THOMAS JONATHAN JACKSON

The next day, the victorious American army passed through Jalapa and entered the narrow Black Pass of La Hoya, where it met no resistance, and came in sight of the great brown castle of Perote, a tremendous work that could house a large garrison. But the few Mexican troops left there were almost without ammunition. When American troops occupied the place on April 22, they found fifty abandoned cannon and 500 muskets. Lee was given the task of making plans of this vast fortification. He wrote to his wife: "The castle or fort of Perote is one of the best . . . I have ever seen—very strong, with high, thick walls, bastioned fronts, and deep, wide ditch. It is defective in construction and is very spacious, covers twenty-five acres, and although there is within its walls nearly three thousand troops, it is not yet full."

Scott, who had thus far conducted a successful campaign, wanted to take Mexico City at the lowest possible cost, but the same kind of trouble that was to plague the Union at First Manassas was threatening his army. The terms of enlistment of some of his volunteers were running out, and there was no sign of replacements for them. In May he had to let a large number of them go. The rest of the army moved on to Puebla. During the long wait there, many became ill, and everyone was miserable. A few reinforcements and several hundred thousand dollars for the payroll came from Vera Cruz in July, but it was August before enough fresh troops and supplies arrived to make Scott feel sure enough to order an advance.

More than 10,000 men started out on August 7 to march toward Mexico City. It was a route no one was likely to forget, for it led through the high mountains. Finally the troops came to a place where they could 'see the great Valley of Mexico stretched out below them. It was a spectacular sight. In front of a backdrop of volcanoes, a number of lakes, fields, canals, roads, houses, and churches formed a vast green and silver carpet in the center of which shone the fabulous city that Cortez and his men had conquered more than three centuries before. And Cortez, too, had landed at the same place they had and had marched from the coast through the mountains to come upon just such a view of this splendid prize, once the Venice of the Aztecs, now the Venice of the mountains, the capital of Mexico.

Ahead, the main road led directly to the city. But this was the most difficult of all routes, for the way was blocked by the strongly fortified hill of Peñon. Lee was among those who were sent to examine it. There was no doubt of El Peñon's might. Santa Anna and all his men were waiting there.

Scott decided to go the long way around, which meant slogging through the marshes south of the two big lakes, Chalco and Xochimilco. When he got beyond the lakes and came to the road running from Acapulco to Mexico City, he found that it was fortified at a town named San Antonio. To the west lay a wide expanse of broken lava called *pedregal*. There was no chance of getting artillery across such a rough surface. There was supposed to be another road farther west that roughly paralleled the Acapulco road, but no one knew whether there was any way of getting through—or around—the *pedregal* to reach it. Heading an exploratory party was the daring soldier Phil Kearney, who was to die early in the Civil War when he rode unknowingly into the Confederate lines at Chantilly. Lee went with him into the lava field. They found that a poor road went part of the way through the southern part of the *pedregal* to a hill named Zacatepec; after that the engineers would have to make a new surfaced passage for artillery and wagons. From the top of Zacatepec they could see that the Mexicans were fortifying their position across the road running north to Mexico City.

The next day, August 19, Lee and about 500 men accompanied by two light batteries marched to Zacatepec to build the road. And on that day, ac-

GENERAL WINFIELD SCOTT, *portrayed at the time of the War with Mexico*

The Battle of Churubusco—the capture of the bridgehead

cording to Douglas Southall Freeman, Lee met, "perhaps for the first time," Thomas Jonathan Jackson.

Construction work proceeded rapidly, but it soon became evident that the Mexicans would have to be driven back before the road could be completed. Artillery went into action, and a steady stream of reinforcements sent up by Scott pressed forward until the road leading to Mexico City was under their control. Rain came that night, making the desolate *pedregal* even more forbidding than usual. Someone had to cross it on foot to tell General Scott about the plans for the next day. Lee, always the good soldier, promptly volunteered to go. It was a nightmare journey through a land where every rock was armed with sharp cutting edges and lightning was the only source of illumination. When he finally arrived at headquarters, Scott was so much impressed by his daring that he said that it was "the greatest feat of physical and mental courage performed by any individual, in my knowledge, pending the campaign."

Lee spent the rest of the night guiding troops back over the route he had just taken. At dawn the American troops went into action. It took them just seventeen minutes to capture the earthworks built across the road. Then they pressed on to the river and village of Churubusco, where the Mexicans were holding a strongly fortified bridgehead with a wide water-filled ditch in front of it.

The fields around the river were high with corn, which made it difficult for the attackers to see what they were doing. But they went on, breaking and reforming several times until two brigades, which had been sent across the river to fall upon the Mexican position from the rear, finally cracked the solid defenses. Then the troops in front of the bridgehead half-waded and half-swam across the watery ditch to take the stubbornly held fortification by desperate hand-to-hand combat.

During the pursuit of the fleeing defenders, Phil Kearney was badly wounded. Riding one of the dapple-gray horses he had bought for his squadron, he was struck by a grape-shot that shattered his left arm. Grant, too, had been in the thick of the fighting instead of staying with the quartermaster

Picking up the wounded. Detail from a painting by James Walker.

83

Chapultepec

Mexico City

Chapultepec and Mexico City

Chapultepec was said to be the key of Mexico City, and such it proved to be. The steep hill was crowned by a stone fort and buildings of the national military academy. Cadets from this took part in the battle. American troops are shown before scaling ladders were brought up to enable them to storm the walls.

The lower picture shows General Scott and his staff entering the city on the morning of September 14. The capture of the capital of Mexico was the final act of the war. The Treaty of Guadalupe Hidalgo, signed February 2, 1848, ceded California and New Mexico to the United States for payment of $15,000,000.

wagons where he belonged. Lee came out of the battle with honors and later got the brevet of a lieutenant colonel.

An armistice with the Mexicans was signed on August 24. During it, the American army remained within sight of the city it had come to conquer. The armistice accomplished nothing. When it expired on September 7, Scott quickly made plans for attack.

The city, which stood in the bed of what had once been a lake, was surrounded by broad stretches of marshy lands across which a number of causeways ran. It was a major problem to decide which of these to use as an approach, for they all ended in strongly fortified gates where they entered the city. To the southwest was Chapultepec, a large fortified hill commanding the Tacubaya causeway which terminated at the Belen Gate. West of it was El Molino del Rey, where there was said to be a cannon foundry. Scott got word that church bells had been sent there to be melted down to provide more artillery for the defense of the city.

On September 8, American troops attacked El Molino and captured it. The rumor about the cannon foundry proved false, although a few molds for casting guns were found. The hard-won position was soon abandoned because it did not seem worth holding. This futile action cost the American army nearly eight hundred killed or wounded—losses it could not afford to sustain so far from the coast.

A meeting of generals and engineers was held on the eleventh. Scott obviously favored taking Chapultepec and using it as a base to attack the city. Lee spoke out against him, favoring the causeways leading up from the south. But the general overruled him, and preparations began for the assault on the 200-foot hill which had been Montezuma's summer palace. About 7200 men were available for the attack.

On September 12, American and Mexican guns barked at each other for hours. But cannon fire was not enough. The next day, troops with scaling ladders had to make a direct assault on the stone fort's outerworks. The men reached the walls before the ladders did, and there was a dreadful wait under fire until the ladders arrived. Then the men scrambled up the walls and dashed into the fort. There was no stopping them until the entire hill was in their possession.

Lee had gone for two nights without sleep. When Scott sent him to the San Cosme Gate, he was wounded slightly on the way. Then, when he got back, fatigue, excitement, and perhaps loss of blood caused him to faint. This was the only time he was ever even a minor battle casualty.

During the evening, American troops fought their way to the gates of the city. At 4 A.M. on September 14, a flag of truce was displayed. At sunrise, the victorious army marched into the city, and before the morning was over, the Marines who had accompanied the troops were guarding the Halls of the Montezumas which they were to immortalize in song.

Santa Anna had released the convicts from the jails. The suddenly freed prisoners rioted in the streets just as convicts from the Richmond penitentiary were to do eighteen years later when the Confederate capital was evacuated. It was now the American Army's job to recapture them. Since the prisoners had obtained guns which they fired irresponsibly from rooftops, they had to be hunted down one by one. After that, peace settled on the capital of Mexico. American troops, however, had to remain in occupation for many months.

Lee got the brevet of a colonel for his work in the campaign. He settled down for the winter to make maps for the War Department's records. It was June before he could sail from Vera Cruz to New Orleans. He arrived home on June 29, after having been away for nearly two years.

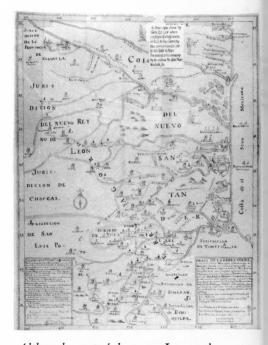

Although most of the maps Lee made in Mexico were for current military use, he copied this one from a work printed in Spanish in 1746. It bears his signature in the lower left-hand corner.

Baltimore as it looked when the Lees were there from 1849 to 1852. Behind the tall Washington Monument, Charles Street runs down to the river.

BALTIMORE AND FORT CARROLL

When Lee arrived at Arlington, his youngest son, Robert E. Lee, Jr., who was to be his father's chronicler, was old enough to remember the event, perhaps because he was personally involved in it. He wrote: "I had a frock or blouse of some light wash material. . . . Of this I was very proud and wanted to wear it on this important occasion. . . . Clothed in this, my very best, and with my hair freshly curled in long golden ringlets, I went down into the large hall where the whole household was assembled, eagerly greeting my father, who had just arrived on horseback from Washington. . . . There was visiting us at this time . . . a friend of my mother's, with her little boy, Armistead, about my age and size, also with long curls. Whether he wore as handsome a suit as mine I cannot remember, but he and I were left together in the background, feeling rather frightened and awed. After a moment's greeting to those surrounding him, my father pushed through the crowd, exclaiming: 'Where is my little boy?' He then took up in his arms and kissed—not me, his own child in his best frock with clean face and well-arranged curls—but my little playmate, Armistead! I remember nothing more of any circumstances connected with that time, save that I was shocked and humiliated. I have no doubt that he was at once informed of his mistake and made ample amends to me."

When Lee unpacked his luggage, he took out a bottle of fine old whiskey which a lady had given him before he left. He returned it to her unopened with a note thanking her and hoping that she might be convinced that he could get on without liquor.

He spent the summer at Arlington, where he finished his Mexican maps. He was assigned to office work in Washington, reappointed to the Board of Engineers in charge of coast defenses, and then in the autumn ordered to go to Baltimore to begin construction work on a new fort on Sollers' Flats. It was later to be named Fort Carroll for the last surviving signer of the Declaration of Independence. He went there for two weeks in November and then advised that work on the project be put off until spring.

In January 1849, he was sent to Florida and Alabama to recommend sites for future fortifications. Since his journey took him to Cumberland Island, he may have visited his father's grave at Dungeness. While he was away his name appeared as one of the managers of the ball which was to celebrate President Zachary Taylor's inauguration in March. Many distinguished men were serving as managers for this. Among them was a still-unknown attorney from Illinois,

Abraham Lincoln, then finishing his single term in the House of Representatives.

After Lee's return from Florida in April, he rented a small brick house in Baltimore for his family. By this time Baltimore, the small town where "Light-Horse" Harry had received the wounds which brought on his death, had become an important city. With a population of nearly 200,000, it had large industrial interests, active markets for flour and tobacco, and extensive docks for transatlantic and coastal shipping. And it was also a railroad junction for lines coming from all parts of the country. Baltimore was proud of its many monuments, its numerous churches, and its active cultural life. It had a seamier side, however, and was famous for its "plug-uglies." Its politics were crooked; so were its elections. In the autumn of the year the Lees took up residence there, a fellow Virginian (who had been at West Point in 1830–31 for a short time) was found unconscious from drink or drugs on election day. When he was taken to the hospital to die, it was discovered that he was the well-known writer, Edgar Allan Poe. He was exactly two years younger than Lee.

When Lee began his work, he found that the site chosen for the new fort was so soft that piles would have to be driven into it to support the weight of the masonry walls. He drew up plans for a steam pile driver and other construction machinery. During the summer he came down with a fever that may have been malaria—his first recorded illness.

At this time there was much talk about purchasing Cuba from Spain, or, if that failed, seizing it by force with the help of exiled revolutionists then in the United States. Jefferson Davis' second wife, Varina, says that her husband refused $200,000 to direct such a scheme. When asked to recommend someone, he said: "The only man I could indicate to you just now is one in whom I have implicit confidence: Robert E. Lee." The Cubans went to Baltimore to ask Lee to join them. A few days later, Mrs. Davis wrote, an Army officer came to their house in Washington. She thought he was "the handsomest person I had ever seen." He introduced himself and then went in to discuss the Cuban offer with Davis. Lee soon came to the conclusion that it would not be consistent with his duty to the United States Government to accept the offer. Less than two months later the Cubans who had proposed it were captured and garroted. Several Americans who had joined them were also executed.

There has been much speculation about what might have happened if Lee had accepted the offer to lead an expedition to Cuba. But such speculation is futile. There are no ifs in history, and Lee's whole background and training

*The golden epaulets
of Robert E. Lee*

made it inevitable that he would refuse to serve a foreign cause for money but volunteer his services freely to his native state when Virginia seceded from the Union in 1861.

Work on the fort proceeded, and since Lee was able to be home every night he spent a great deal of time with his family in their home on Madison Street. Robert, Jr., tells how he sometimes accompanied his father to work: "We went to the wharf in a bus, and there we were met by a boat with two oarsmen, who rowed us down to Sollers' Point, where I was generally left under the care of the people who lived there, while my father went over to the Fort, a short distance out in the river. These days were very happy ones for me. The wharves, the shipping, the river, the boat and oarsmen, and the country dinner we had at the house at Sollers' Point, all made a strong impression on me; but above all I remember my father, his gentle, loving care of me, his bright talk, his stories, his maxims and teachings. I was very proud of him and of the evident respect for and trust in him every one showed. . . . He was a great favorite in Baltimore, as he was everywhere, especially with ladies and little children. When he and my mother went out in the evening to some entertainment, we were often allowed to sit up and see them off; my father, as I remember, always in full uniform, always ready and waiting for my mother, who was generally late. He would chide her gently, in a playful way and with a bright smile. He would then bid us good-bye, and I would go to sleep with this beautiful picture in my mind, the golden epaulets and all—chiefly the epaulets."

The admiring young boy also tells one of the tenderest and most intimate stories we have about his father's relationship to his children: "Our greatest treat was to get into his bed in the morning and lie close to him, listening while he talked to us in his bright, entertaining way. This custom we kept up until I was ten years old and over. Although he was so joyous and familiar with us, he was very firm on all proper occasions, never indulged us in anything that was not good for us, and exacted the most implicit obedience. I always knew that it was impossible to disobey my father. I felt it in me, I never thought why, but was perfectly sure when he gave an order that it had to be obeyed. My mother I could sometimes circumvent . . . but exact obedience to every mandate of my father was a part of my life and being at that time. He was very fond of having his hands tickled, and, what was still more curious, it pleased and delighted him to take off his slippers and place his feet in our laps in order to have them tickled. Often . . . the enforced sitting would be too much for us, and our drowsiness would soon show itself in continued nods. Then, to arouse us, he had a way of stirring us up with his foot—laughing heartily at and with us. He would often tell us the most delightful stories, and then there was no nodding. Sometimes, however, our interest in his wonderful tales became so engrossing that we would forget to do our duty—when he would declare, 'No tickling, no story!' "

Custis, the eldest son, was appointed to the Military Academy in 1850. His career at West Point was to be far more checkered than his father's, but he was luckier, for there was no Charles Mason there to plague him by remaining unshakably at the head of his class. As a result, Custis was Number One man in 1854. During his first two years at the Academy, the young cadet received many letters of advice from his father, who naturally wanted him to do well. These letters which Lee often sent to his children served later as the model for a famous forgery, first published during the Civil War in the New York *Sun* on November 26, 1864. It was dated April 5, 1852, and was supposedly written from Arlington to Custis at West Point. Known as the "Duty" letter, because the words "Duty is the sublimest word in our language" occur

Colonel R. E. Lee, *photographed
by Mathew Brady sometime
in 1850 or 1851*

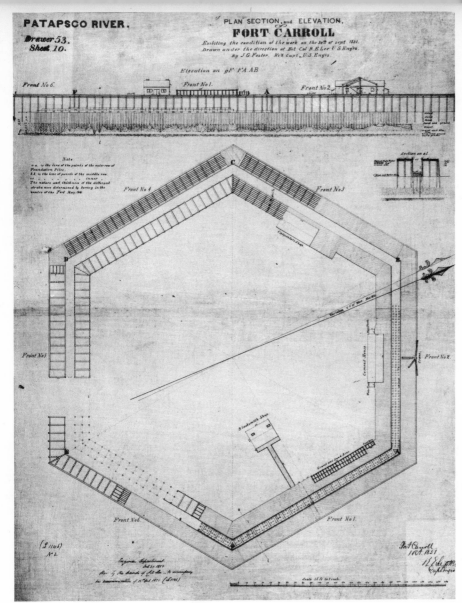

*Plan of Fort Carroll, Maryland,
showing state of construction on
September 30, 1851. Drawn under
Lee's direction and signed by
him in the lower right-hand corner.*

in it, the forgery was exposed by Lee himself when it was reprinted in Richmond soon after it appeared in New York.

Lee did not have to communicate with Custis by letter for very long. On May 28, 1852, he received orders to proceed to West Point to take command of the post on September 1 as Superintendent. More than once in his life, Lee, when offered a promotion or a new and tempting position of some kind, was to be seized with doubt about his ability to do what was expected of him. This was not false modesty, nor was it pretended reluctance in order to make his services seem more desirable. Lee was incapable of such dealing. When he wrote his reply, he meant it when he said: "I learn with much regret the determination of the Secretary of War to assign me to that duty, and I fear I cannot realize his expectations in the management of an Institution requiring more skill and experience than I can command." Then he asked that someone else be appointed.

Lee, of course, may have been even more than usually hesitant to accept the post because his son was at the Academy, and he would not want anyone to feel that he might be in a position to favor one cadet more than another. Fortunately, the War Department had no reservations about Lee's ability to administer the affairs of the Academy impartially. It denied his request.

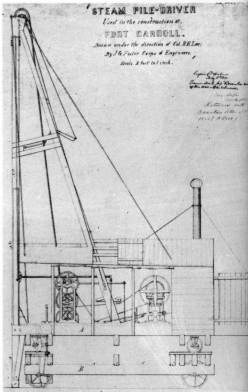

*Plans for a steam pile driver used
in the construction of Fort Carroll.
Drawn under Lee's direction.*

West Point in the mid-1850s

SUPERINTENDENT OF WEST POINT

And so to West Point the Colonel went. Once there, he did such a good job that he is remembered to this day as one of the best men who ever headed the Academy. The position had certain advantages, not the least of which was the privilege of occupying the Superintendent's house. This gave Lee and his family a chance to have a home of their own, something they had not had since they left Fort Hamilton in 1846. And the new post brought Lee to public and Congressional notice.

By an unfortunate coincidence, however, he got off to a bad start. The Secretary of War was then a peppery Southerner named C. M. Conrad. On September 13, 1852, a day less than two weeks after Lee had taken office, the Academic Board sent a letter to Conrad protesting his peremptory reinstatement of two cadets who had failed in their examinations. The War Department returned the letter to the Acadamy for Lee's signature as the new president of the Board. He, of course, had no knowledge of the controversy, but he signed the letter as a matter of official duty. Two weeks later he received a snarling reply from Conrad, who said: "As the letter was not addressed to you . . . I am at a loss to understand how 'justice' to yourself requires you to answer it. As you have thought proper to do so, however, and to unite with the other members of the Board in vindicating their course, it may be well, in order to prevent a repetition of the mistake, that I should say to you what I have . . .

said to them; that I shall receive with pleasure, and shall treat with respect, any suggestions or advice from the Board touching the management of the Academy. But when they undertake to criticise or censure an order given to them by the Head of this Department . . . I cannot but consider it as officious, not to say disrespectful. . . . I hope I shall not again be called upon to notice a similar departure from official propriety."

Lee was not used to such treatment. But he swallowed his pride and merely said: "I affixed my signature in conjunction with the Secretary to authenticate the paper adopted by the Board, presenting the result of proceedings commenced prior to my becoming a member, and in which I considered I was not individually concerned. It was not for the purpose of doing myself 'justice' or offering 'my views,' and entirely opposed to being officious or disrespectful."

Fortunately for Lee, Conrad's term of office expired on March 4, 1853, when he was replaced by Jefferson Davis, a graduate of West Point and a friend of its new Superintendent. Annoying criticism ceased, and Lee was allowed to run the Academy without tight supervision.

Shortly after the change in the administration at Washington took place, Mrs. Custis became seriously ill. She died before her daughter could reach Arlington. Her death was grieved by the entire family, and Lee was among those who missed her most. Washington Custis was now seventy-two years old and was alone in the big house. Mary Lee stayed with him until her husband could join her early in July after graduation ceremonies at the Academy.

Mrs. Custis' death evidently made a deep impression on Lee. Although a religious man, he had never joined the church. When two of his daughters were confirmed at Christ Church in Alexandria on July 17, he asked to be confirmed with them. The place where he knelt at the chancel is now marked by a silver plaque.

During Lee's two years and seven months of office at the Military Academy he came in contact with some of the men who were to play major roles in the war that was now less than a decade away. Outstanding among them were two cadets who were destined to be cavalry commanders. One was a Virginian named James Ewell Brown (J.E.B.) Stuart, '54; the other was Philip Henry Sheridan, '53, who had been appointed from Ohio. Cavalrymen were noted for their short tempers. Both these future leaders of horse soldiers got into trouble at the Academy.

Stuart, although devoutly religious, was always ready to fight. When a cadet in his company once made a remark he thought insulting, Orderly Sergeant Stuart pitched into him. Three others happily joined the fight; all five were arrested. When Lee decided the case, he said of Stuart: "Courtesy, as well as duty, forbade recourse to the method pursued, and such a resort is entirely at variance with the regulations of the Academy." But the Superintendent found extenuating circumstances; he returned the erring cadets to duty.

A month later Stuart was brought up again, this time for speaking disrespectfully to one of the Academy's instructors. Lee then said: "It is as difficult to understand how one of Cadet Stuart's intelligence should have failed to see the impropriety of his course as it is to believe that he intentionally committed a fault so utterly at variance with his generally correct deportment. . . . The . . . acknowledgment of error on the part of Cadet Stuart has satisfied his instructor that he did not intentionally commit the offense with which he is charged. But the Superintendent cannot consider even such an·avowal a sufficient excuse for his act. The freedom from intentional error is a poor plea for the commission of positive wrong. He is, however, convinced that Cadet Stuart now sees his fault, and trusts that its further prosecu-

The Superintendent's house, photographed in 1870

The Superintendent's house as it looks today

The modern cadet full-dress hat (1952)

tion is not necessary. . . . Cadet Stuart is released from arrest and returned to duty."

Sheridan was still at the Academy when Lee was there, but the offense which had caused him to be suspended for a year had taken place before the new Superintendent arrived. The touchy little fighter described the incident in his *Memoirs*: "Cadet William R. Terrill . . . was a Cadet Sergeant, and, while my company was forming for parade, having given me an order in what I considered an improper tone, to 'dress' in a certain direction when I believed I was accurately dressed, I fancied I had a grievance and made toward him with a lowered bayonet, but my better judgment recalled me before actual contact could take place. Of course Terrill reported me for this, and my ire was so inflamed by his action that when we next met I attacked him . . . in front of barracks."

Sheridan later regretted what he had done, admitted that he deserved even greater punishment, and sought out Terrill in 1862 to renew acquaintanceship with him. He apologized just in time, for Terrill was killed a few days later at the battle of Perryville.

Other future Civil War generals who were cadets at West Point during Lee's superintendency were Lee's nephew, Fitzhugh Lee, John B. Hood, John Pegram, William D. Pender, O. O. Howard, James B. McPherson, and John M. Schofield. Fitz John Porter was Lee's adjutant at the Academy.

Undoubtedy, the most embarrassing discipline case which Lee had to handle as Superintendent was one concerning his brother's son. Young Fitzhugh Lee was a high-spirited lad, destined to make a fine soldier, but he was restless under discipline. When he was twice brought up for being absent at night without leave, his uncle recommended court-martial, and Fitz Lee escaped dismissal only because his classmates pledged themselves not to commit the same offense for a year. Final decision was left to Washington, but the high command there approved.

Lee regretfully had to dismiss one cadet who was to achieve fame in a field far removed from military affairs. This was James McNeill Whistler. He led his class in drawing but when asked to define silicon in a chemistry examination, he called it a gas. Many years later he said: "Had silicon been a gas I would have been a major general."

Whistler protested his dismissal on the grounds that his marks were better than those of two cadets who had been allowed to remain at the Academy. After reviewing his case sympathetically, the Superintendent said: "I can only regret that one so capable of doing well should have so neglected himself and must now suffer the penalty. The application of Cadet Whistler is herewith returned."

Whistler was not the only cadet Lee dismissed from the Academy. He often advised the parents of a failing student to allow the boy to resign in order "to save him and his friends this disappointment and mortification." Many other young men benefited from Lee's understanding attitude toward those who got in trouble because of West Point's stiff rules of conduct. Some of the things then forbidden may seem laughable today, but it must be remembered that the general rules of deportment were much stricter then than they are now. Lee was kind and reasonable, but the record shows that there was no relaxation of discipline during his administration. Only one cadet finished a complete year without receiving a single demerit while he was Superintendent.

Robert E. Lee, Jr., who was going to a day school at West Point, had a sympathetic helper in his father. He remembered that he would often "come into the room where I studied at night, and sitting down by me, would show me how to overcome a hard sentence in my Latin reader or a difficult sum in arithmetic, not by giving me the translation of the troublesome sentence or the answer to the sum, but by showing me, step by step, the way to the right solutions. . . . When I was able to bring home a good report from my teacher, he was greatly pleased . . . but he always insisted that I should get the 'maximum,' that he would never be perfectly satisfied with less."

The elder Lee was very much aware of the fact that the eyes of everyone at the Academy were on him and his family. He once wrote, in a letter to his daughter Annie, "I do not know what the Cadets will say if the Superintendent's children do not practice what he demands of them. They will naturally say he had better attend to his own before he corrects other people's children."

That so upright and august a father should have even one failing was a matter of rather shocked surprise to his youngest son, especially since it had to do with behavior in church. Writing of West Point, Robert, Jr., said: "My father was the most punctual man I ever knew. He was always ready for family prayers, for meals, and met every engagement, social or business, at the moment. He expected all of us to be the same and taught us the use and necessity of forming such habits. . . . I never knew him late for Sunday service at the Post Chapel. He used to appear some minutes before the rest of us, in uniform, jokingly rallying my mother for being late and for forgetting something at the last moment. When he could wait no longer for her, he . . . would march along to church. . . . There he sat very straight—well up the middle aisle—and, as I remember, always became very sleepy and sometimes even took a little nap during the sermon. At that time, this drowsiness of my father's was something awful to me, inexplicable. I know it was very hard for me to keep awake, and frequently I did not; but why he, who to my mind could do everything that was right without any effort, should sometimes be overcome, I could not understand."

The Superintendent may have drowsed occasionally while seated in a pew but there was no doubt of his splendid horsemanship when in the saddle. He taught young Robert to ride the family pony. And he insisted that the boy use the dragoon seat which did not permit posting. One day while they were out riding, they saw three cadets far beyond the Academy's limits. They jumped over a wall and ran into the woods to escape notice. Lee had not recognized them. "Did you know those young men?" he asked his son. Then he checked himself hastily and said: "But no, if you did, don't say so."

Other horsemen dressed in the uniform of the United States Army who were patrolling the Far West at this time were meeting trouble. The discovery of gold in California had brought a horde of miners and settlers into country which the Indians had always considered their own. There were twenty-two Indian wars during the 1850s, and more men were needed in the Army to cope with the resentful tribes. This decade of internal growth, territorial expansion, and sudden rise in immigration called for a larger armed force to police the new West, and officers were needed to take command of regiments that were being formed. Among those detailed to active duty in the field was the Superintendent of the United States Military Academy at West Point.

On March 3, 1855, appointments were made for the new Second Cavalry; Albert Sidney Johnston was to be its colonel and Robert E. Lee its lieutenant colonel. This meant parting with the Corps of Engineers to which Lee had been so long attached, but it also meant service in the field where promotion was more likely now that the Army was coming to life again. On March 15, Lee took the oath of allegiance required by law. At the end of the month he turned over command of West Point to his successor and went to Washington to settle his affairs there.

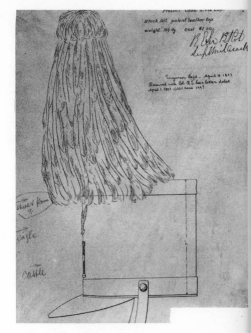

Lee's original sketch for the cadet full-dress hat (1853)

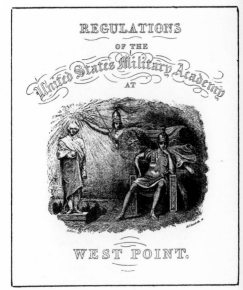

Frontispiece to the 1853 edition of the Regulations

R. E. LEE *as Superintendent of the Military Academy at West Point. Painted from life by Robert W. Weir.*

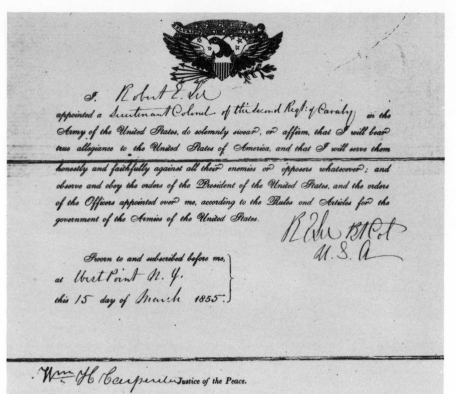

One object of permanent value to posterity came from the West Point experience—the portrait made by Robert Walter Weir, who had taught drawing at the Academy since 1834. It is the second portrait painted of Lee and is the only one that shows him as Superintendent of the Academy. His son Robert, however, did not care for the picture. He said of it: "To me, the expression of strength peculiar to his face is wanting, and the mouth fails to portray that sweetness of disposition so characteristic of his countenance. Still it was like him at that time. My father never could bear to have his picture taken, and there are no likenesses of him that really give his sweet expression. Sitting for a picture was such a serious business with him that he never could 'look pleasant.' "

The time Lee spent at West Point rounded out his training as an administrator. It also gave him experience in dealing with people—not only with cadets but with their parents, their instructors, and the ever-watchful high command in Washington. Some of this was to prove useful during the war; it was to be even more useful during the postwar years in Lexington, when he was president of Washington College. One thing that set Lee apart from—and above—most other men was his ability to learn from everything he did, and then, profiting from what he had learned, to go on to do better.

His work at West Point, more than anything else he had yet done, showed that he could handle a large-scale operation and run it well. Men who can do that are always scarce. And events were rapidly shaping up so that the need for them was going to be greater than ever.

When Lee started out to join his new cavalry regiment in April 1855, he left behind him those phases of his life in which he had been a working engineer or an army administrator. From now until Appomattox, except for a two-year respite at the end of the 1850s when he had to be at Arlington to settle family affairs, he was to be constantly in the field, spending most of the time in the saddle. He was now forty-eight years old.

ON THE TEXAS FRONTIER

Lee had fought actively in the field during the Mexican War, but only as an engineer who sometimes did reconnaissance work. He who had never commanded troops at any time in his career was now to test himself as a cavalry leader at a distant frontier post. He first saw his regiment in Louisville, Kentucky, where it was being assembled. The regiment that was then forming was to have a distinguished future as part of the Regular United States Army. It fought in the opening campaigns of the Civil War until August 1861, when it was renamed the Fifth Cavalry. As such, it then fought against Lee during all the Virginia campaigns right through to Appomattox. It must have been a bitter experience for him to see the men of his old regiment arrayed against him on one battlefield after another. After the war, the regiment made a name for itself in Indian fighting. Many of its former officers, notably George Armstrong Custer, who had started out as a green second lieutenant in the old Second during the summer of 1861, went on to win postwar fame in other regiments.

But in April 1855, the Second Cavalry was still untried. Its officers and men were soon sent to St. Louis where Lee, of course, must have been at home although he had not been there for fifteen years. Good horses, costing an average of $150 each, were purchased for the new regiment. The mounts were assigned to companies by color so all the grays, sorrels, bays, browns, and roans were grouped together. The men were armed with Colt's Navy revolvers and dragoon sabers. As an experiment, some squads carried the Springfield rifle-carbine, while one squadron had the shorter movable-stock carbine, and another the new breech-loading Perry carbine.

Orders arrived from Washington for the regiment to ride by easy marches from St. Louis to Fort Belknap in Texas, many hundreds of miles away. Before it started, however, both its colonel and its lieutenant colonel were ordered to go to Fort Leavenworth for court-martial service. Headquarters did not want to waste their higher officers' time waiting for a regiment to get ready and then ride across country on a two-month journey. Actually, Johnston and Lee were fortunate, for the long overland trek was made during an exceptionally bitter winter when the weather was so cold that 113 oxen belonging to a wagon train were frozen to death on the day the regiment finally reached Fort Belknap.

From Leavenworth Lee was sent to Fort Riley, Kansas, for additional court-martial duty. There he had a bit of luck, for he was ordered to go to

Carlisle, Pennsylvania, and then to West Point for still more courts-martial. The journey east gave him a chance to visit Arlington. When he left there in February 1856 to rejoin his rigiment, he was able to go by ship to Galveston. Then he went overland to San Antonio and Fort Mason to meet his regiment.

A few weeks after his arrival, Lee led two squadrons of the regiment to Camp Cooper. This new camp was a cheerless place, far out in the Texas wilderness. Everyone had to live in tents, for there were no buildings. Lee did not trust the Comanches. When the chief of their nearest camp came to pay a visit, the Colonel indicated that he would treat the Indians as friends so long as they remained friendly, but that he would not hesitate to deal with them as enemies if they broke their word. And when he visited the Indian camp, he did not like the way they lived nor did he admire the chief's wives who, he thought, made themselves hideous with paint and barbaric ornaments.

One of Lee's main duties at his new post was to explore the area to select a site for a new fort. He was often accompanied on these tours by a second lieutenant who had been one of his cadets at the Academy. This was John B. Hood of Kentucky, a young man who was to become a full general in the Confederate Army after he had received a crippling wound in his left arm at Gettysburg and had lost his right leg at Chickamauga. A plucky fighter, Hood was destined to be as unlucky in life as his riding companion was fortunate. Even in Texas, Hood soon got himself into a scrape with the Indians in which two of his men were killed and four wounded, while he himself had his left hand pinned to his saddle by an arrow.

One fine day when the two officers were riding together in the high prairies, Lee gave the younger man a bit of advice: "Never marry unless you can do so into a family which will enable your children to feel proud of both sides of the house." Hood said that he believed the Colonel "perhaps thought I might form an attachment for some of the country lasses and therefore imparted to me his correct and at the same time aristocratic views in regard to this very important step."

During the hot summer of 1856 Lee had to do more court-martial work at distant Ringold Barracks on the Mexican border. After his return to Camp Cooper, he wrote to Mrs. Lee on September 1 that she should ignore a petition which had been signed by a group of Virginians asking the President to make him a brigadier general. "You will be sure to be disappointed," he told her. "Nor is it right to indulge improper and useless hopes. It besides looks like presumption to expect it." He was right; the promotion never came.

Then he was off again for more court-martial duty at Fort Brown, also on the Mexican border. From there he wrote a letter of Christmas greetings to his family in Arlington. Two days later he wrote again. A ship had brought copies of President Franklin Pierce's annual message and the Report of the Secretary of War for him to read and ponder. Controversy over slavery stemming from the Kansas-Nebraska Act of 1854 and the consequent troubles in Kansas were then arousing much discussion. Lee said to his wife:

The views of the [President] of the systematic and progressive efforts of certain people of the North to interfere with and change the domestic institutions of the South are truthfully and faithfully expressed. The consequences of their plans and purposes are also clearly set forth, and they must also be aware that their object is both unlawful and entirely foreign to them and their duty; for which they are irresponsible and unaccountable; and can only be accomplished by them through the agency of a civil and servile war.

In this enlightened age, there are few I believe but what will acknowledge that slavery as an institution is a moral and political evil in any country. It

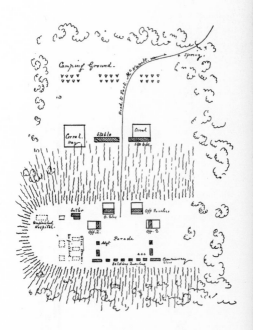

Fort Mason, Texas, in 1857.
From Robert E. Lee in Texas
by Carl Coke Rister.
With permission from the University of Oklahoma Press.

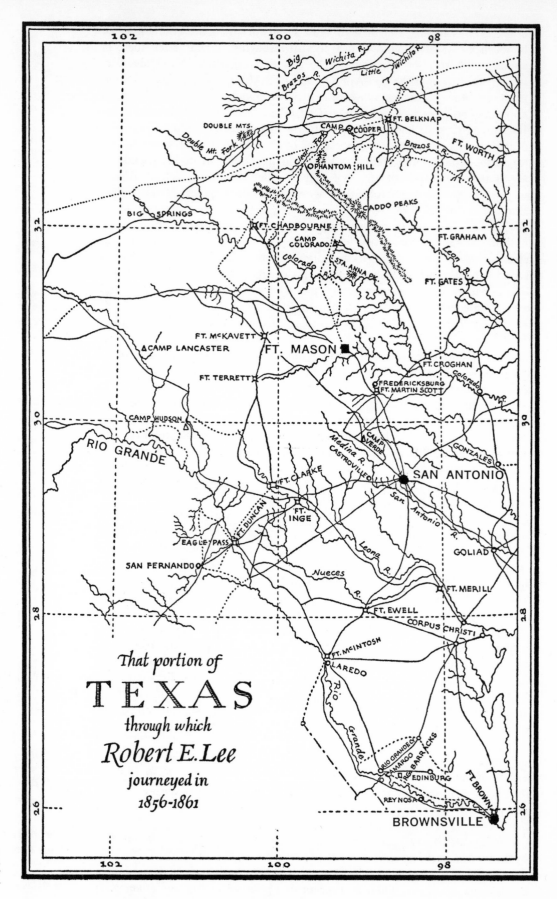

That portion of

TEXAS

through which

Robert E. Lee

journeyed in

1856-1861

is useless to expatiate on its disadvantages. I think it however a greater evil to the white than to the black race, and while my feelings are strongly enlisted in behalf of the latter, my sympathies are more strong for the former. The blacks are immeasurably better off here than in Africa, morally, socially, and physically. The painful discipline they are undergoing is necessary for their instruction as a race, and I hope will prepare and lead them to better things. How long their subjugation may be necessary is known and ordered by a wise Merciful Providence. Their emancipation will sooner result from the mild and melting influence of Christianity than the storms and tempests of fiery controversy. This influence though slow is sure. The doctrines and miracles of our Savior have required nearly two thousand years to convert but a small part of the human race, and even among Christian nations what gross errors still exist! While we see the course of the final abolition of human slavery is onward, and we give it the aid of our prayers and all justifiable means in our power, we must leave the progress as well as the result in his hands who sees the end; who chooses to work by slow influences; and with whom two thousand years are but as a single day.

Although the Abolitionist must know this, and must see that he has neither the right or power of operating except by moral means and suasion, and if he means well to the slave, he must not create angry feelings in the master; that although he may not approve the mode by which it pleases Providence to accomplish its purposes, the result will nevertheless be the same; that the reasons he gives for interference in what he has no concern holds good for every kind of interference with our neighbors when we disapprove their conduct; still I fear he will persevere in his evil course. Is it not strange that the descendants of those Pilgrim fathers who crossed the Atlantic to preserve their own freedom of opinion have always proved themselves intolerant of the spiritual liberty of others?

At this time, Lee's second son Rooney was at Harvard in the class that was to be graduated in 1858. Henry Adams, who was in the same class, admired Rooney for his natural habit of command. But the critical New Englander had only contempt for him as a scholar. Fortunately, the young Virginian had no ambitions to acquire higher learning. He wanted a career in the Army and left college in 1857 when he got a commission as a second lieutenant on the strength of a letter which General Scott addressed to Secretary of War John B. Floyd. In this letter Scott said: "I make this application mainly on the extraordinary merits of the father, the very best soldier that I ever saw in the field."

The "very best soldier's" long stay in Texas was ending. The last part of it was spent in San Antonio where he was summoned to replace Albert Sidney Johnston, who had been ordered to report to Washington to lead an expedition against the Mormons. One of the infantrymen who was to go with him was Rooney Lee.

News reached San Antonio that Washington Custis had died on October 10. Lee applied immediately for leave and was able to get away a few days later. He was badly needed in Arlington, for the death of its master had left the affairs of the estate in great confusion. And Custis' well-intentioned will was going to make matters difficult for the man who had to be its sole executor. Four executors had been named, but three of them could not serve, so the actual work had to be done by Lee. He had been given two months' leave of absence by the War Department, but more than two years were to pass before he had Arlington's affairs in good enough condition to request reinstatement to his command.

*The key to Arlington. Taken
by a Union soldier in 1863, it
was returned by him in 1930.*

INTERLUDE AT ARLINGTON

Lee had not seen Arlington for nearly two years. During that time matters had gotten worse there. Its aging owner, who had died at the age of seventy-seven, had let the place run down. Extensive repairs were now urgently needed. And Mrs. Lee had developed arthritis and was in pain much of the time. Her right arm was crippled, and she had difficulty walking. She was lonely, too, because most of her children were far away. Some of the girls were at boarding school, and the Army had sent Custis to California and Rooney to Texas.

Lee was known in the Army as a good administrator. Now he was to need all his ability for the long hard task that faced him. When he examined his late father-in-law's will, he found that the old gentleman had disposed of his estate in the kindest and most generous way, but his instructions for the distribution of his property were complicated. He had left Arlington to Mrs. Lee; after her death it was to become Custis Lee's property, since he was the eldest son and his grandfather's namesake.

The 4000-acre plantation on the Pamunkey River, known as the White House, was to go to Rooney. This had belonged to Martha Dandridge Custis at the time of her marriage to George Washington in 1759. The house in which the wedding ceremony had been performed had long since been demolished, but the family still cherished the old plantation for its association with Washington and his wife.

Robert E. Lee, Jr., the youngest son, was to get the Romancoke estate in King William County, a few miles north of the White House. He was so entranced by the prospect of being a farmer and leading the quiet life of a country gentleman that he resigned from the Army in 1859 and, except for the interruption of war, spent most of his time on his beloved farm.

The four girls were each to get $10,000 as a legacy. The money was to be raised by selling off certain tracts of land. Any deficiency needed to make

100

up the required amount was to come from revenues derived from the working of the White House and Romancoke estates. After everything was paid, the Custis slaves were to be set free; this had to be done within five years after the date of their late owner's death.

More than $10,000 of immediate debts had to be paid, but there was no ready cash to pay them. Arlington House had to be repaired and the land made to yield an income. It was obvious that the task would take not only money but time—much more time than the two months' leave already granted. Fortunately, General Scott was willing to extend one leave after another. Lee evidently considered resigning from the Army to devote himself entirely to the management of Arlington. In writing to his son Custis in February 1858, he said: "If you wished to resign and take this place [Arlington], and Rooney to get married and settle down at the White House, there would be no necessity for my leaving the Army."

Custis, with true Lee generosity, replied by sending his father a signed deed in which he relinquished all his right to Arlington and turned the place over to him. But his father, although touched by the offer, refused to accept the gift. He explained his refusal by saying: "Your dear grandfather distributed his property as he thought best, and it is proper that it should remain as he bestowed it. It will not prevent me from improving it to the best of my ability, or of making it as comfortable a home for your mother, sisters, and yourself as I can. I only wish I could do more than I shall have it in my power to do. I wish you had received my previous letter on this subject in time to have saved you the trouble of executing the deed you transmitted me. And indeed I also regret the expense you incurred, which I fear . . . is considerable, as I wish you to *save all* your money and invest it in some safe and lucrative way, that you may have the means to build up old Arlington and make it all we would wish to see it. The necessity I daily have for money has, I fear, made me parsimonious. In order that you may know the full intent of your grandfather's will, I enclose you a copy."

In the midst of all the difficulty Lee was having in connection with settling his father-in-law's estate and trying to put Arlington on a paying basis, the Army still required some of his time for courts-martial. He had made a name for himself in Army circles for doing this unpleasant and thankless work that called for true impartiality in rendering a just verdict. Fortunately, his assignments at this time were in reasonably nearby places so there were no long journeys to make.

A water color by Benson J. Lossing made on the scene in 1853

The problems of his family's health were always with the sorely troubled husband and father. A letter he wrote to Custis in May 1858 reveals his concern for his wife's suffering. "Your mother," he wrote, "has been taking the cold bath all winter, a doubtful experiment, but I have watched its effects carefully and anxiously, and really think it has been of service. It has apparently removed the swelling from her feet, ankles, etc., and relieved her of nearly all pain."

One of the main reasons for Lee's long absence from Army service was the Virginia court's delay in construing his late father-in-law's will, especially that part which called for the emancipation of the Custis slaves. Meanwhile, he was obliged to hire some of them out for wages. There was little need for their services in the Arlington area, so he had to send some of them to other parts of the state. This led to trouble, for a man and a woman ran away. When they were found and returned to Arlington, they were hired out in southern Virginia, where they could not so easily run away again. It cannot be said that Robert E. Lee never had enemies in the South, for two of his neighbors promptly wrote anonymous letters to Horace Greeley's New York *Tribune* giving lurid accounts of the affair. According to them, there were three fugitives, two men and a woman. Both letters were printed on the same day, June 24, 1859. The first letter, which is the more savage in its attack, was directed against both George Washington Parke Custis and Lee:

I live one mile from the plantation of George Washington P. Custis, now Col. Lee's, as Custis willed it to Lee. All the slaves on this estate, as I understand, were set free at the death of Custis, but are now held in bondage by Lee. I have inquired concerning the will, but can get no satisfaction. Custis had fifteen children by his slave women. I see his grandchildren every day; they are of a dark yellow. Last week three of the slaves ran away; an officer was sent after them, overtook them nine miles this side of Pennsylvania, and brought them back. Col. Lee ordered them whipped. They were two men and one woman. The officer whipped the two men, and said he would not whip the woman, and Col. Lee stripped her and whipped her himself. These are facts as I learn from near relatives of the men whipped. After being whipped, he sent them to Richmond and hired them out as good farm hands.

The second letter, dated two days later, made Lee out to be the villain:

It is known that the venerable George Washington Parke Custis died some two years ago; and the same papers that announced his death announced also the fact that on his deathbed he liberated his slaves. The will, for some reason, was never allowed any publicity, and the slaves themselves were cajoled along with the idea that some slight necessary arrangements were to be made, when they would all have their free papers. Finally they were told five years must elapse before they could go. Meantime they have been deprived of all means of making a little now and then for themselves, as they were allowed to do during Mr. Custis's life, have been kept harder at work than ever, and part of the time have been cut down to half a peck of unsifted meal a week for each person, without even their fish allowance. . . .

Some three or four weeks ago, three, more courageous than the rest, thinking their five years would never come to an end, came to the conclusion to leave for the North. They were most valuable servants, but they were never advertised, and there was no effort made to regain them which looks exceedingly as though Mr. Lee, the present proprietor, knew he had no lawful claim

Arlington in 1860. The Negro slaves are cutting the grass on the lawn by hand.

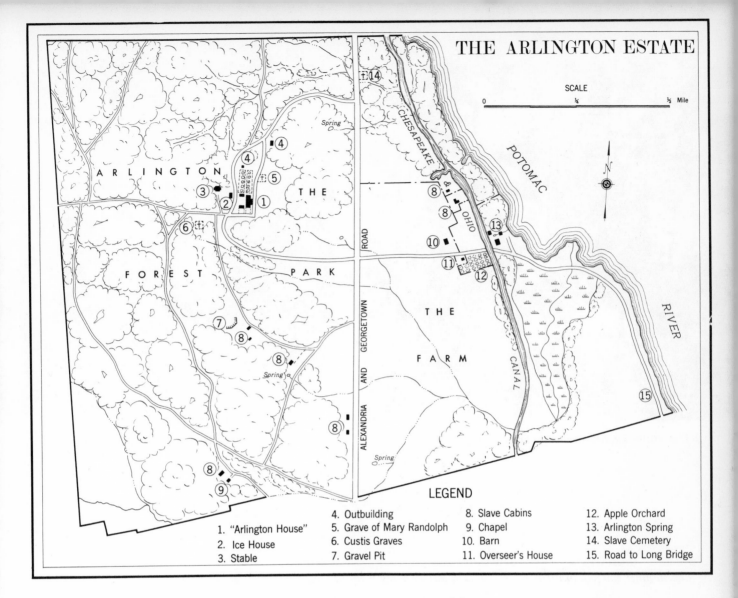

THE ARLINGTON ESTATE

SCALE

LEGEND

1. "Arlington House"
2. Ice House
3. Stable
4. Outbuilding
5. Grave of Mary Randolph
6. Custis Graves
7. Gravel Pit
8. Slave Cabins
9. Chapel
10. Barn
11. Overseer's House
12. Apple Orchard
13. Arlington Spring
14. Slave Cemetery
15. Road to Long Bridge

to them. They had not proceeded far before their progress was intercepted by some brute in human form, who suspected them to be fugitives and probably wished a reward. They were lodged in jail and frightened into telling where they had started from. Mr. Lee was forthwith acquainted with their whereabouts, when they were transported back, taken into a barn, stripped, and the men received thirty and nine lashes each from the hands of the slave-whipper, when he refused to whip the girl, and Mr. Lee himself administered the thirty and nine lashes to her. They were then sent to Richmond jail, where they are now lodged.

Next to Mount Vernon, we associate the Custis place with the "Father of this free country." Shall "Washington's body guard" be thus tampered with, and never a voice raised for such utter helplessness?

For those who knew Lee, the story was an obvious perversion of the truth. There was, however, no way of refuting it. He wrote to Custis to tell him that "the N. Y. *Tribune* has attacked me for my treatment of your grandfather's legacy, but I shall not reply. He has left me an unpleasant legacy."

And there the matter had to rest. The story, however, was to be revived and reprinted as wartime propaganda when the man who had been honored for his services during the Mexican War became the North's whipping boy after he sided with the South.

The winter kitchen in the basement of main house

The wine cellar in the basement of main house

ARLINGTON'S SERVICE AREAS

The summer kitchen in the north servants' quarters away from the main house

The children's playroom on the second floor

The school and sewing room

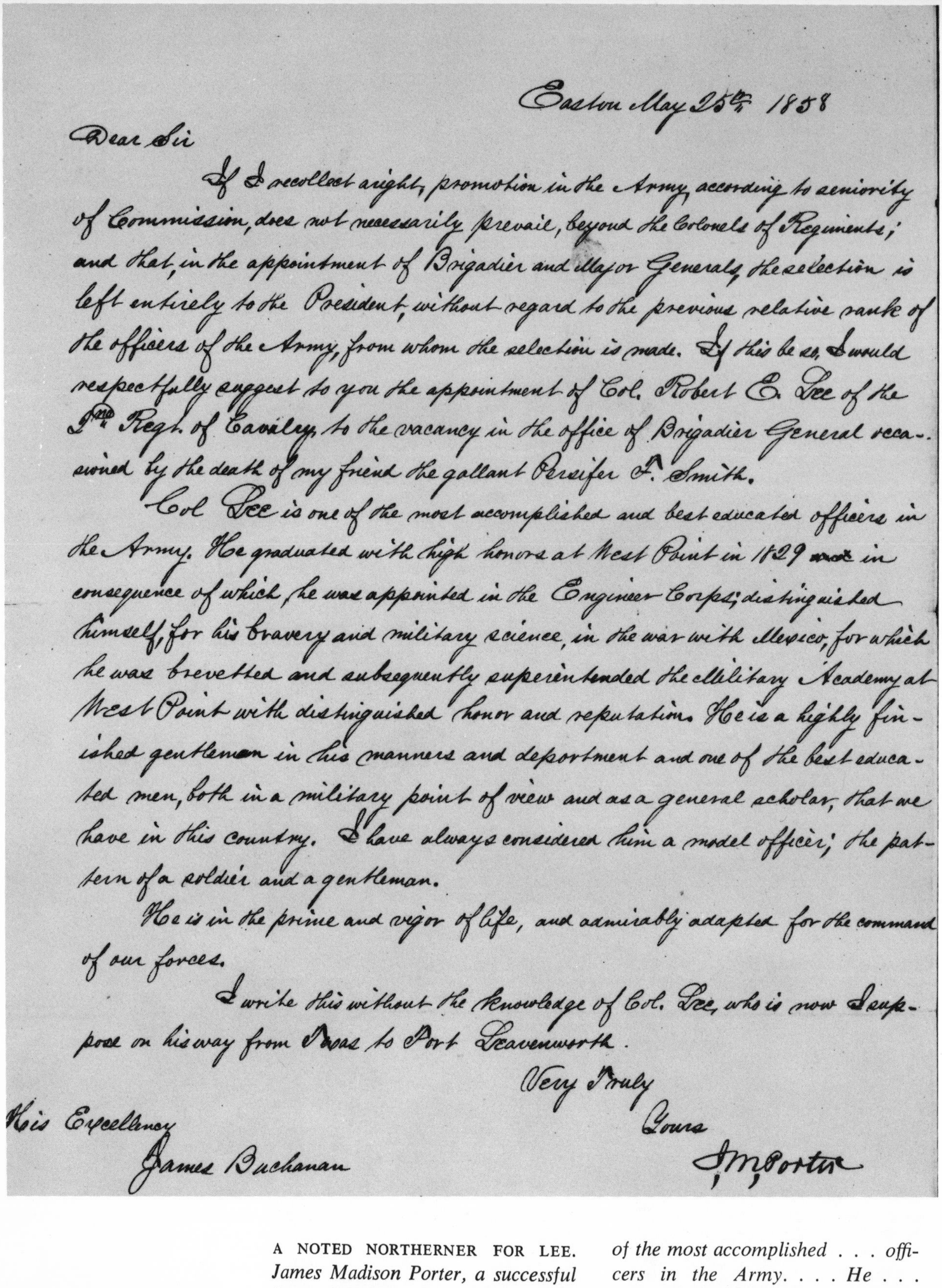

Easton May 25th 1858

Dear Sir

If I recollect aright, promotion in the Army, according to seniority of Commission, does not necessarily prevail, beyond the Colonels of Regiments; and that, in the appointment of Brigadier and Major Generals the selection is left entirely to the President, without regard to the previous relative rank of the officers of the Army, from whom the selection is made. If this be so, I would respectfully suggest to you the appointment of Col. Robert E. Lee of the 2nd Regt. of Cavalry, to the vacancy in the office of Brigadier General occasioned by the death of my friend the gallant Persifer F. Smith.

Col Lee is one of the most accomplished and best educated officers in the Army. He graduated with high honors at West Point in 1829 and in consequence of which, he was appointed in the Engineer Corps; distinguished himself, for his bravery and military science, in the war with Mexico, for which he was brevetted and subsequently superintended the Military Academy at West Point with distinguished honor and reputation. He is a highly finished gentleman in his manners and deportment and one of the best educated men, both in a military point of view and as a general scholar, that we have in this country. I have always considered him a model officer; the pattern of a soldier and a gentleman.

He is in the prime and vigor of life, and admirably adapted for the command of our forces.

I write this without the knowledge of Col. Lee, who is now I suppose on his way from Texas to Fort Leavenworth.

Very Truly
Yours
J M Porter

His Excellency
James Buchanan

A NOTED NORTHERNER FOR LEE. James Madison Porter, a successful Pennsylvania attorney and one of the founders of Lafayette College, wrote this unsolicited letter to President Buchanan, suggesting that he make Lee a brigadier general to replace his friend, the late General P. F. Smith. "Col. Lee," he wrote, "is one of the most accomplished . . . officers in the Army. . . . He . . . distinguished himself for his bravery and courage, in the war with Mexico . . . and subsequently superintended the Military Academy at West Point. . . . He is in the prime and vigor of life, and admirably adapted for the command of our forces."

Hartford Fire Insurance Company, of Hartford, Conn.

The estimated value of Personal Property, and of each Building to be insured, and the sum to be insured on each, must be stated separately. When Personal Property is situated in two or more Buildings, the value and amount to be insured in each must be stated separately. When insurance is wanted on Personal Property, the same description should be given of the Building containing the property, as if Insurance is wanted on the Building.

Application of *R. E. Lee, U. S. A.,*
for Insurance against loss or damage by fire by the **HARTFORD FIRE INSURANCE COMPANY**, in the sum of *Five Thousand, Eight Hundred* Dollars on the property specified: the value of the property being estimated by the Applicant.

	SUM TO BE INSURED.	VALUATION.
On *Dwelling House*	$5000	$20.000
On	$	$
On *Barn*	$800	$1200
On	$	$

The Applicant will answer the following questions, and sign the same, as a description of the premises on which the Insurance will be predicated.

1. BUILDING—Is it stone, brick, or wood? How many stories high? Where situated? When built? Which part occupied by Applicant?

2. WALLS—Are the division walls of brick? Are they entire? Do they rise above the roof?

3. ROOF—What is it covered with? Are the gutters stone, metal or wood? Is there a scuttle and stairs to it?

4. Are the stoves and apparatus for using fire properly secured, and will you engage to keep them so?

5. Do the pipes enter a chimney? And is it built from the ground? Do pipes pass one or more wood partitions or floors? If so, how secured?

6. What fuel is used? And how are ashes disposed of?

7. What material is used for lighting?

8. For what purpose is the building used? How many tenants?

9. Distance and materials of other buildings, within 100 feet of the one to be insured? And how occupied?

10. What other insurance is there upon the property, and at what office? Has this Company any other Insurance within 100 feet of this risk?

11. Is the property mortgaged? And to what amount? Is there any insurance by the mortgagee?

12. Is there any other party interested in the property?

13. Has the building a lightning rod? If so, is it on the old or new plan?

1. Dwelling of Brick, main building two stories high, and wings one story; In Alex^co, Va., built about the year 1820 - All occupied by applicant. The Barn is of brick, one story high, with a stone basement. 3 The main building of the Mansion House is covered with slate and the wings with gravel - 3 The Barn is cov^d with gravel. 3 The gutters are metal. 2 The division walls are of brick. 3 There is not a scuttle in the roof of the dwelling - 3 The Barn has a Cupola from wh. access to the roof is easy - 5 Pipes enter chimney - 5 Chimnies built from the ground. 5 No wood partitions - 4 Stoves and warming apparatus well secured 6 Wood & Coal are used for fuel - 6 Ashes are put out a safe distance - 7 Burning fluids, or candles, or Kerosene Oil, or Gas are permitted. 8 Dwelling House - one Tenant - 9 A one story brick Kitchen & a one story brick Store House, both cov^d. with wood. 9 The one standing West of the Dwelling on a line with the north line thereof, & the other on a line with the south line thereof, both distant 44 feet - 10 $5000. by the "Home" Insce. 10 No other risk within 100 feet. 10 No other Ins. on the Barn. 11 Property unencumbered. 13 Barn has a lightning rod. 13 Dwelling has... New plan. Barn has a cattle shed about 40 feet south east, and a waggon shed about 100 feet south otherwise detached.

And the said applicant hereby covenants and agrees to and with said Company, that the foregoing is a just, full and true exposition of all the facts and circumstances in regard to the condition, situation, value and risk of the property to be insured, so far as the same are known to the applicant and are material to the risk.

Dated *October 17* 185 *9.*

R. E. Lee .... *Applicant.*

For *1* year at *40* cents.
" *1* . at *80* [Make a diagram of the premises on the other side of this sheet]

"Arlington"

The desk in the office and study

LEE TAKES OUT FIRE INSURANCE FOR ARLINGTON. *Describing Arlington as a brick dwelling built about 1820 with a slate roof on the central part and gravel roof on the two wings, Lee insured the main house for $5000 against loss or damage by fire, although he valued it at $20,000. He also insured the barn, valued at $1200, for $800. The policy gives us a good idea of what the Arlington buildings were like at this time, but the most remarkable thing about it is its date, October 17, 1859. This means that Lee must have signed it early on the day he was summoned to Washington to suppress the John Brown insurrection at Harpers Ferry.*

OF BLOOD AND A PROPHECY
OF BLOOD

Now Robert Edward Lee, Virginian by ancestry and birth, professional Army officer, devoted husband and father, devout Christian, a slaveowner opposed to slavery, was to be drawn into the heart and center of the dreadful controversy that was tearing the nation apart. By a curious coincidence, his life had touched several of the momentous events which were to loom large when the history of slavery in America was written. He had been at Fort Monroe in August 1831 when troops marched out to suppress with a bloody hand the bloody Nat Turner slave insurrection. He had been in St. Louis in November 1837 when Elijah Lovejoy was killed by men who wanted to stop him from printing his antislavery newspaper. But so far, Lee had held himself aloof from the conflict. Now, as a matter of duty, he was to be plunged into it. Destiny had decreed that the man who was to play a leading role in the war that was less than a year and a half away was also to play a leading role in a violent prologue to that war. American history has few confrontations so dramatic as the one in which Robert E. Lee, commander of the future Confederate Army of Northern Virginia, stood face to face with John Brown, the fanatic enemy of slavery who was willing to give up his life for the cause for which he was fighting.

The War Department had been warned in August 1859 that the fierce old man, who had carried on a private war in Kansas against proslavery men trying to have that Territory admitted into the Union as a slave state, was planning to enter Virginia at Harpers Ferry to arm the slaves and stir up insurrection. The anonymous writer of the warning letter even told Secretary of War John B. Floyd that Brown had a man stationed in an armory which he erroneously described as being in Maryland. Harpers Ferry was then in Virginia. This led Floyd to believe that the entire letter was a fraud. He ignored it.

News of what was taking place at Harpers Ferry on Sunday, October 16, 1859, reached the War Department the next morning in the form of a telegram from the president of the Baltimore and Ohio Railroad. It said that Negroes and whites had seized the United States Armory and the railroad bridge. Garrett asked for troops to be sent on the next train.

Sitting in the War Department that rainy morning was one of Lee's former West Point cadets, Lieutenant J. E. B. Stuart, who was on leave after having been wounded in an Indian fight. During his convalescence, he had invented a device for detaching a saber quickly from a cavalryman's belt. A patent had been granted for this a few days before, and Stuart was waiting to see the Secretary of War about selling his device to the Department. When Garrett's telegram arrived, Stuart was asked to take a message to Colonel Lee in Arlington.

He renewed acquaintance with the man he had admired at West Point, rode back to the War Department with him, and volunteered to go on the mysterious expedition as his aide. Since there were no soldiers available in Washington, the War Department had sent a telegram to Fort Monroe ordering three companies of artillery to be dispatched from there. Meanwhile, 93 officers and men of the Marine Corps who were stationed at the Washington Navy Yard were pressed into service, put on a train, and shipped off to Harpers Ferry. A conference with the President and the Secretary of War delayed Lee and Stuart for so long that they were too late for the train which had taken the Marines. They went on a special train to Relay House where

J. E. B. Stuart, *sketched by Frank Vizetelly in 1863*

108

the Harpers Ferry line turned west. There they found that they had again missed the Marines, who had gone on to Harpers Ferry with four companies of volunteers from Baltimore. A locomotive came from that city to take Lee and Stuart to Sandy Point, a mile short of the besieged town. Lee telegraphed ahead to Lieutenant Israel Green, who was in charge of the Marines, to wait for him there. Then he sent a wire to the Secretary of War saying that "No reliable information has been received from Harpers Ferry. Rumour has swelled the number of the rioters to upwards of 500 men. The train from the West, due here at 2:30 P.M. has not yet arrived, and nothing is coming over the lines from Harpers Ferry."

The locomotive carrying the two Army officers pulled into Sandy Point some time before midnight. There Lee met Lieutenant Green, made a quick reconnaissance of the situation at Harpers Ferry, got what information he could from those who had witnessed or taken part in the fighting, and made his plans for the morning.

He had been able to learn only that a man calling himself Smith was the leader of a small band of insurrectionists who had taken refuge in a brick fire-engine house inside the Armory's gate; that they had with them some local citizens as hostages (among them was Colonel Lewis W. Washington, a great-grandnephew of the man who had meant so much in Lee's life); and that there were plenty of Government troops and state militia on hand. Lee therefore wired instructions not to send the artillery companies from Fort Monroe. From the information he gathered, he had good reason to believe that the leader of the insurrectionists was John Brown of Kansas fame. Jeb Stuart had seen the old antislavery fighter while on duty in the West. This was probably why Lee decided that Stuart was the best person to deliver a note to the men in the engine house demanding their surrender. He told them that it would be impossible for them to escape because the Armory was surrounded.

At sunrise, Lee asked the commanders of the militia if they wanted to make the attack. He was told that the citizen-soldiers had wives and children and should not be exposed to such risks, whereas the Marines were paid "for doing this kind of work." Lee then asked Lieutenant Green if he would like to have the honor. The Marine officer, who came from Vermont but who was to volunteer to fight for the Confederacy, took off his hat and thanked Lee for the privilege.

Twelve Marines were to make up the storming party; the others were to be drawn up in rank to impress the men in the engine house with their strength. They were all in full-dress uniform because someone at the Navy Yard had apparently been under the impression that they were being ordered

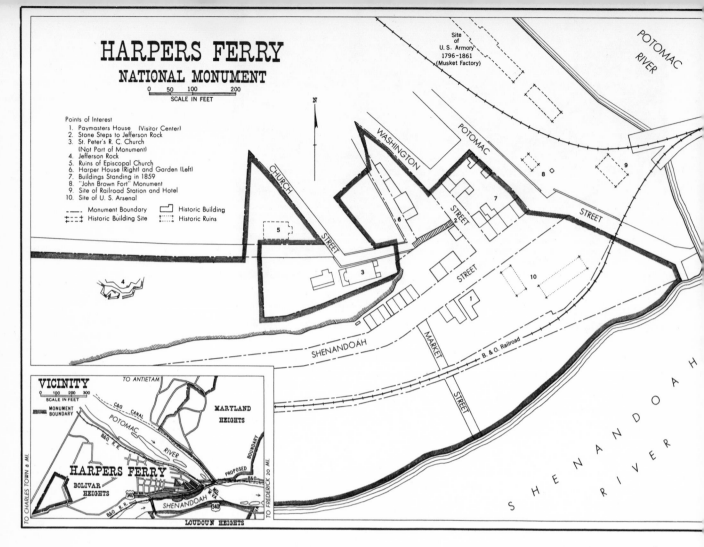

HARPERS FERRY
NATIONAL MONUMENT

0 50 100 200
SCALE IN FEET

Points of Interest
1. Paymasters House   (Visitor Center)
2. Stone Steps to Jefferson Rock
3. St. Peter's R. C. Church
   (Not Part of Monument)
4. Jefferson Rock
5. Ruins of Episcopal Church
6. Harper House (Right) and Garden (Left)
7. Buildings Standing in 1859
8. "John Brown Fort" Monument
9. Site of Railroad Station and Hotel
10. Site of U. S. Arsenal

Monument Boundary   Historic Building
Historic Building Site   Historic Ruins

VICINITY
0 100 200 300
SCALE IN FEET

JOHN BROWN

out for ceremonial purposes. Lee, in the civilian clothes he had been wearing when he was summoned to the War Department, took up a position about forty feet from the brick engine house.

Lieutenant Stuart then went into action. He describes the crucial moment in a letter to his mother: "I was deputed . . . to read . . . a demand to surrender immediately; and I was instructed to leave the door after . . . refusal, which was expected, and wave my cap; at which signal the storming party was to advance, batter open the doors, and capture the insurgents at the point of the bayonet. . . . I approached the door in the presence of perhaps two thousand spectators and told *Mr. Smith* that I had a communication for him from Colonel Lee. He opened the door about four inches and placed his body against the crack with a cocked carbine in his hand: hence his remark after his capture that he could have wiped me out like a mosquito. The parley was a long one. He presented his propositions in every possible shape and with admirable tact; but all amounted to this: that the only condition upon which he would surrender was that he and his party should be allowed to escape. Some of his prisoners begged me to ask Colonel Lee to come and see him. I told them he would never accede to any terms but those he had offered; and as soon as I could tear myself away from their importunities I left the door and waved my cap."

Stuart had immediately recognized the old man at the door as "Osawatomie Brown who had given . . . so much trouble in Kansas." He was the only person in that vast crowd who could have identified him.

Lee, in his official report to the Adjutant General, describes what hap-

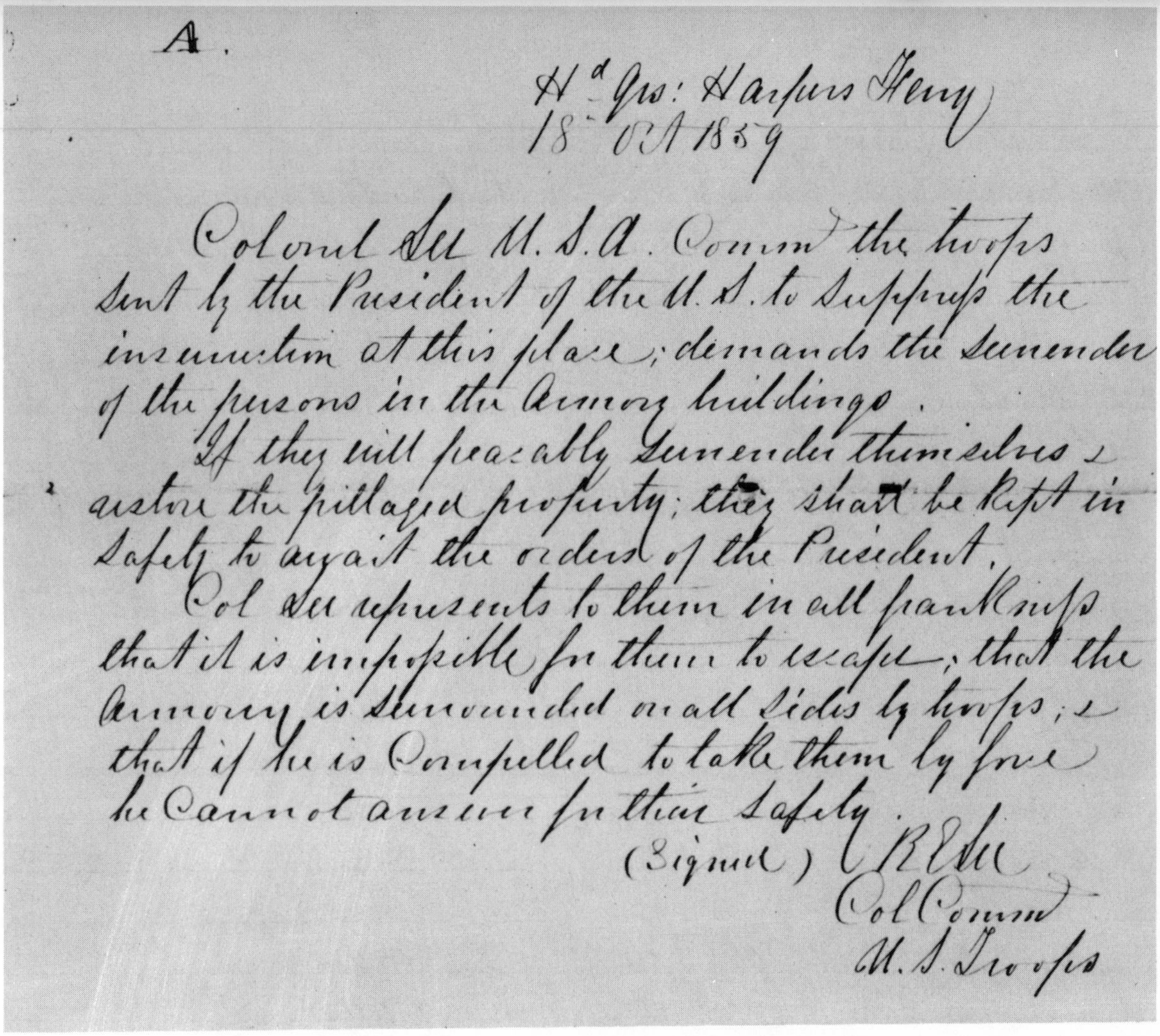

A.

Hd Qrs: Harpers Ferry
18 Oct 1859

Colonel Lee U.S.A. Comm'd the troops sent by the President of the U.S. to suppress the insurrection at this place; demands the surrender of the persons in the Armory buildings.

If they will peaceably surrender themselves & restore the pillaged property; they shall be kept in safety to await the orders of the President.

Col Lee represents to them in all frankness that it is impossible for them to escape; that the Armory is surrounded on all sides by troops; & that if he is compelled to take them by force he cannot answer for their safety.

(Signed) R E Lee
Col Comm'd
U.S. Troops

pened: "At the concerted signal the storming party moved quickly to the door and commenced the attack. The fire engines within the house had been placed by the besieged close to the doors. The doors were fastened by ropes, the spring of which prevented their being broken by the blows of the hammers. The men were therefore ordered to drop the hammers, and, with a portion of the reserve, to use as a battering ram a heavy ladder with which they dashed in a part of the door and gave admittance to the storming party. The fire of the insurgents up to this time had been harmless. At the threshold one Marine fell mortally wounded."

Lieutenant Green tells what took place inside the engine house when the Marines broke in: "The entrance was a ragged hole low down in the right hand door, the door being splintered and cracked some distance upward. I instantly stepped from my position in front of the stone abutment and entered the opening made by the ladder. At the time I did not stop to think of it, but upon reflection I should say that Brown had just emptied his carbine . . . and so I passed in safely. Getting to my feet, I ran to the right of the engine, which stood behind the door, passed quickly to the rear of the house, and came up between the two engines. The first person I saw was Colonel Lewis Washington, who was standing near the hose cart at the front of the engine house. On one knee, a few feet to the left, knelt a man with a carbine in his hand, just pulling the lever to reload."

Colonel Washington pointed out John Brown to Green. The lieutenant immediately attacked Brown with his light dress sword, beat him to his knees, and inflicted so many wounds on his head that they were at first

The Marines storm the engine house at Harpers Ferry

thought to be mortal. The living and the dying were then brought out of the engine house. The affair, Lee said in his report, was over in a few minutes.

John Brown's attempt to free the slaves had failed. Although he had five Negroes in his little band of twenty-one men and had impressed several into service when he took his hostages, not a single slave in the locality had voluntarily come to his aid. It would have been almost impossible for them to have done so, for the attempted insurrection had been so badly managed that it was over before he could send out a call for the slaves to rise. Now ten of his followers, including two of his sons, had been killed or mortally wounded in the raid. He and six others were to be executed; only five men got away.

About one o'clock in the afternoon, Governor Henry A. Wise of Virginia arrived at Harpers Ferry. He and a number of others interviewed John Brown, who had been carried into the paymaster's office in the Armory and placed on the floor. The New York *Herald* correspondent describes the prisoner: "Brown is . . . rather small-sized, with keen and restless gray eyes, and a grizzly beard and hair. He is a wiry, active man, and should the slightest chance for an escape be afforded, there is no doubt that he will yet give his captors much trouble. His hair is matted and tangled, and his face, hands and clothes all smouched and smeared with blood. Colonel Lee stated that he would exclude all visitors from the room if the wounded men were annoyed by them, but Brown said he was by no means annoyed; on the contrary he was glad to be able to make himself and his motives clearly understood."

Brown talked freely, too freely for the benefit of his friends and supporters, who were quickly identified when his papers were found. He had, strangely enough, made no attempt to destroy these incriminating documents. They were to set the South aflame when they were made public, for they showed clearly that Brown had not been alone in what might otherwise have seemed like a mad scheme to incite a slave insurrection singlehanded. Noted Northern men had supplied him with money and moral support. Many of them had only a vague idea of what he intended to do, for he was very secretive about his plans. And some of them had long been out of touch with him. But the South had no way of knowing this. Southerners learned only that such men as George L. Stearns, Samuel Gridley Howe, Theodore Parker, Thomas Wentworth Higginson, F. S. Sanborn (all from Massachusetts), and Gerrit Smith of New York had actively given aid to a man who had invaded Virginia with fire and sword; then they read in the newspapers that Henry David Thoreau and Ralph Waldo Emerson (also from Massachusetts) were openly praising John Brown. The prairie fire which had been lighted was to scorch the entire nation, destroying, maiming, and killing in the North and South alike.

Whenever John Brown spoke, he added fuel to the crackling flames by his astute and eloquent words. He may have been mad, as some said, but he did not speak like a madman. He spoke rather as one who knew that his life was already forfeit and who was determined to make it count for the cause he advocated so fervently. He knew he was worth more dead than alive, and he welcomed the idea that posterity would be his judge.

Colonel Lee sent the prisoners to nearby Charles Town under a Marine guard on October 19. That evening, when a report came through that a village a few miles from Harpers Ferry was being attacked by armed men, he had to lead a party of Marines there. The report proved to be false. Lee returned to the railroad station and boarded a late train for Washington, taking the Marines with him. He had his reports to file, and then he had to spend time serving on a board that dealt with the minutiae of military regulations.

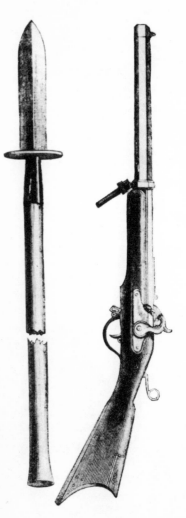

Swivel gun and pike used at Harpers Ferry

Inside the engine house. The hostages are at the left.

Interrogating the prisoners. The third figure from the left may be Colonel Lee. If so, this is his first published picture.

John Brown rides to the place of execution

. . . and ascends the gallows to be hanged

John Brown was brought to trial on October 25. A jury found him guilty on October 31, and on November 2 he was again brought into the courthouse to be sentenced. There was no doubt of what the sentence would be, but before pronouncing it, the judge, according to custom, asked whether the prisoner had anything to say. The doomed man then made a speech which exceeded in eloquence everything he had ever said before—and John Brown could speak with Old Testament fervor. The court, hushed and silent, listened to him. After he had finished, the judge sentenced him to death by hanging on December 2.

A few days before that date, and while the country was still in a state of great excitement over the trial and its disclosures, Lee was ordered to take command of four companies of soldiers who were being sent from Fort Monroe to Baltimore. They proceeded to Harpers Ferry, where they arrived on November 30 to act as a guard during the execution. Not only Regular Army troops but local militia, the Richmond Grays, and cadets from the Virginia Military Institute were being sent to Charles Town. There was no railroad in Lexington to bring the cadets north, but a wealthy stagecoach operator in Staunton donated a number of vehicles to take the boys to a railroad station where they could get a train to Washington and go from there to Harpers Ferry. With them went two howitzers in the charge of their instructor of artillery tactics, Thomas Jonathan Jackson. Also in Charles Town at this time was the young actor, John Wilkes Booth, who had come up from Richmond where he had temporarily enlisted with the Grays.

At 11 A.M. on December 2, the now-famous prisoner was led out of his cell, placed in a wagon to sit on his coffin, and driven to a field in which the gallows had been erected. Around it 1500 soldiers were drawn up in ranks to make a huge hollow square.

Jackson, who was a good observer, wrote to his wife that "Brown had his arms tied behind him, and ascended the scaffold with apparent cheerfulness. After reaching the top of the platform, he shook hands with several who were standing around him. The sheriff placed the rope around his neck, then threw a white cap over his head, and asked him if he wished to signal when all should be ready. He replied that it made no difference, provided he was not kept waiting too long. In this condition he stood for about ten minutes on the trapdoor, which was supported on one side by hinges and on the other . . . by a rope. Colonel Smith then announced to the sheriff 'all ready' . . . when the rope was cut by a single blow, and Brown fell through about five inches, . . . With the fall his arms, below the elbows, flew up horizontally, his hands clinched; and his arms gradually fell, but by spasmodic motions. There was very little motion of his person for several moments, and soon the wind blew his lifeless body to and fro."

While the body still swung in the wind, the artillery instructor, a deeply religious man, stood with his head bowed. He was saying a prayer for the soul of the man he had seen sent into eternity. Another V.M.I. instructor, although he too was moved by the sight, broke the silence by saying: "So perish all such enemies of Virginia! All such enemies of the Union! All such foes of the human race!" Lee's reactions to the death of John Brown are not known.

The man who had died had left a last message, a prophecy written on a slip of paper which he handed to someone as he left the jail. It read:

I John Brown am now quite certain *that the crimes of this* guilty *land: will never be purged* away; *but with Blood. I had* as I now think: vainly *flattered myself that without* very much *bloodshed; it might be done.*

The Lone Star flag
flies over the Alamo

FAREWELL TO THE OLD FLAG

John Brown's body was buried, but it did not rest easily in its grave. What he did had torn the country apart and was to divide it still further. The generations-old controversy over slavery now raged so furiously that Lee was probably glad when orders came for him to return to Texas. There he would be away from the overheated atmosphere of Washington, where the controversy was centered. Before he could go, however, he had to appear on January 10, 1860, before a Senate committee which was inquiring into "the late invasion and seizure of the public property at Harpers Ferry." He was asked only a few superficial questions. His testimony was very short, and it did not reveal anything new.

Then he went to New Orleans by train, arriving there on February 13. In a letter to Custis (who was working at the Engineer Bureau in Washington in order to be able to live at Arlington) Lee strikes the only comic note that appears in his life during these troubled times. A railroad journey was uncomfortable in those days. Travelers removed only their outer clothing even in the new sleeping cars which were then first being introduced. (It is unlikely that they were yet in use on the Washington-to-New Orleans run.) Lee writes from his hotel, where he had just opened his luggage: "Imagine my horror this morning when I found I had left my shaving brush and pants behind. The first I constantly leave, but my pants, my *new pants,* I cannot account for. I suppose they were overlooked [at Arlington]. I could hardly believe my eyes when I found them out of their accustomed place. Take care of them, or use them where they may be most convenient."

Lee arrived in San Antonio on February 19 to take command of the Department of Texas. Albert Sidney Johnston was away on the Utah expedition, so Lee was the highest-ranking officer in the state. An attempt was soon made to embroil him in a plot to organize a filibustering expedition against Mexico. The Governor of Texas, redoubtable Sam Houston, may have been sponsoring this. He favored the idea of a Mexican protectorate and had even proposed one to the United States Senate in 1858. Lee had met Houston at West Point during his cadet days when the famous frontiersman had been on the Board of Visitors. He admired the Texan and approved of the stand he was taking on preserving the Constitution and the Union, but he refused to be drawn into the Mexican adventure.

Needing immediate attention, however, was a man who was considered

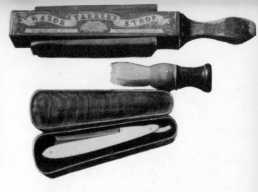

a hero in Mexico and a bandit in Texas. This was Juan Cortinas, who had raided border towns, fought with American troops and Texas Rangers, and had been so elusive whenever he stirred up trouble that Lee referred to him as "that myth Cortinas." The mythical Mexican had been defeated in a pitched battle before Lee arrived, yet he was still very real. When Lee started out in pursuit of him, he found that Cortinas had vanished across the border. A formal exchange of letters with the Mexican authorities followed, but nothing came of it.

After losing two months on this wild-goose chase, Lee returned to San Antonio where orders from the War Department involved him briefly in its experiment with the use of camels for desert warfare. About 75 had been imported from the Near East and had been quartered since 1857 at Camp Verde, 60 miles northeast of San Antonio. A group had been taken overland to California late that summer, and two trial trips had recently been made with them through the arid wastes of Texas. Lee reported favorably to the War Department on the camels' performance, but the war was soon to put an end to this experiment as it did to so many other things. For years to come, however, startled travelers were to see stray camels in desert areas all the way from Texas to California.

In the spring of 1860 Lee had become a grandfather, when Rooney's wife gave birth to a son whom they named after him. Modest as usual, the probably delighted grandfather wrote to the parents: "I wish I could offer him a more worthy name and a better example. He must elevate the first and make use of the latter to avoid the errors I have committed."

Lee was now fifty-three years old and had been in the Army twenty-two years. That spring he saw his friend Joseph Johnston appointed Quartermaster General with the rank and pay of a brigadier. He had been promoted over the heads of Lee and other officers who outranked him, and the aging lieutenant colonel isolated in Texas naturally felt slighted. But, as he said in a letter to Custis later that year, "My personal troubles sink into insignificance when I contemplate the condition of the country, and I feel as if I could easily lay down my life for its safety. But I also feel that would bring but little good."

Lee wrote these words on November 24, 1860, after news of the election of Abraham Lincoln had reached Texas. Reaction throughout the South to the idea of having a "Black Republican" President in office was violent, although some men like Governor Houston were urging a policy of moderation. But few people wanted to listen, and the man who had been the outstanding public figure in Texas was soon to be repudiated even by many who had supported him ever since he first held office during the early days of the former Republic.

Lee, stationed in Texas, was in a good position to see how the lower South was acting in the growing crisis. Writing to Custis on December 14, 1860, he said that seventy-year-old, Georgia-born General David E. Twiggs had been sent to Texas and had taken over command of the Department the previous day. Under the circumstances, Lee cannot have felt sorry to have been replaced. He then went on to say: "Feeling the aggressions of the North, resenting their denial of the equal rights of our citizens to the common territory of the commonwealth, etc., I am not pleased with the course of the 'Cotton States,' as they term themselves. In addition to their selfish, dictatorial bearing, the threats they throw out against the 'Border States,' as they call them, if they will not join them, argues little for the benefit or peace of Va. should she determine to coalesce with them. While I wish to do what is right, I am unwilling to do what is wrong, either at the bidding of the South or the North. One of their plans seems to be the renewal of the slave trade. That I am opposed to on every ground."

"My shaving brush," said Lee, "I constantly leave behind"

Governor Samuel Houston

General Twiggs surrenders to Texas troops in the Military Plaza of San Antonio, February 16, 1861

Four days after writing this letter, Lee left San Antonio to go to Fort Mason. News of the momentous events then taking place was slow to reach that isolated post. On December 20, South Carolina seceded; on December 26, Major Robert Anderson moved his garrison from untenable Fort Moultrie to Fort Sumter; on January 9, Mississippi seceded, and the *Star of the West* was fired on when she tried to come to the relief of Sumter; on January 10, Florida seceded; on January 11, Alabama seceded; on January 19, Georgia seceded; on January 26, Louisiana seceded—and then on February 1, Texas passed an ordinance of secession which had to be approved by the people on February 23. On January 23, 1861, in the midst of this crumbling of the Union, Lee wrote a letter that expressed his views on secession:

As far as I can judge by the papers, we are between a state of anarchy and civil war. . . . As an American citizen, I take great pride in my country, her prosperity and institutions, and would defend any state if her rights were invaded. But I can anticipate no greater calamity for the country than a dissolution of the Union. It would be an accumulation of all the evils we complain of, and I am willing to sacrifice everything but honor for its preservation. I hope, therefore, that all Constitutional means will be exhausted before there is a resort to force. Secession is nothing but revolution. The framers of our Constitution never exhausted so much labor, wisdom, and forbearance in its formation, and surrounded it with so many guards and securities if it was intended to be broken by every member of the Confederacy at will. It was intended for "perpetual union," so expressed in the Preamble, and for the establishment of a government, not a compact, which can only be dissolved by revolution, or the consent of all the people in convention assembled.

It is idle to talk of secession. Anarchy would have been established, and not a government, by Washington, Hamilton, Jefferson, Madison, and the other patriots of the Revolution. . . . Still, a Union that can only be maintained by swords and bayonets, and in which strife and civil war are to take the place of brotherly love and kindness, has no charm for me. I shall mourn for my country and for the welfare and progress of mankind. If the Union is dissolved and the Government disrupted, I shall return to my native state and share the miseries of my people, and save in defense will draw my sword on none.

During the tense month of February, while Texas waited for its ordinance of secession to be approved, Lee received orders to go to Washington to report to General Scott before April 1.

He left Fort Mason on February 13 and arrived in San Antonio three days later. The town was in the midst of an uprising, and the Lone Star flag had replaced the Stars and Stripes on the Alamo. Armed men patrolled the streets, some of them wearing strips of red flannel on their shoulders to identify them. Lee was told that Twiggs had surrendered all Federal property to the state of Texas that morning. "Has it come as soon as this?" he asked in evident surprise.

He went into the Read House and changed into civilian clothes before going out on the street again. A woman who was acquainted with him and who was staying in the same hotel said: "He returned at night and shut himself in his room, which was over mine, and I heard his footsteps through the night, and sometimes the murmur of his voice, as if he were praying. He remained at the hotel a week, and in conversations declared that the position he held was a neutral one."

Several Army men who knew Lee came to bid him farewell before he left. One of them wrote: "I have seldom seen a more distressed man. He said, 'When I get to Virginia I think the world will have one soldier less. I shall resign and go to planting corn.' " Another said that Lee had told him: "I still think . . . that my loyalty to Virginia ought to take precedence over that which is due to the Federal Government, and I shall so report myself at Washington. If Virginia stands by the old Union, so will I. But if she secedes (though I do not believe in secession as a Constitutional right, nor that there is a sufficient cause for revolution), then I will still follow my native state with my sword, and, if need be, with my life. . . . These are my principles, and I must follow them." And an officer to whom Lee wrote at this time quoted him as saying: "I fear the liberties of our country will be buried in the tomb of a great nation."

The views Lee expressed in San Antonio clearly sum up his attitude toward secession. They also indicate what he would do if Virginia seceded. The unhappy colonel sailed from Indianola on February 25, leaving behind him a wrecked and ruined Department, for Twiggs had turned over more than a million dollars' worth of Federal property to the Texans. Twiggs had also surrendered nineteen Army posts with 2328 men. Most of the troops were allowed to march out of the state, but 815 men were made prisoners, some of them for as long as two years.

It has been charged that Twiggs was sent to Texas by pro-Southern Secretary of War John B. Floyd because the local secessionists were uncertain of Lee. Bruce Catton, in *The Coming Fury,* makes this interesting point: "A few months earlier . . . Lee had been acting commander of the Department of Texas. If the secession crisis had come to a head then, or if Twiggs's return had been delayed past mid-winter, it would have been Lee and not Twiggs on whom the Texas commissioners would have made their demand for the surrender of Government property. Without any question, Lee would have given them a flat refusal—in which case it might easily have been Lee, and not Major Robert Anderson, who first received and returned the fire of the secessionists, with San Antonio, rather than Fort Sumter, as the scene of the fight that began a great war. Subsequent history could have been substantially different."

GENERAL DAVID E. TWIGGS

121

*Montgomery on February 8, 1861,
the day the Constitution of the
Confederate States of America
was adopted*

THE VIRGINIAN

The guns had not yet been fired, but the country was well advanced on the road to war when Lee landed in New Orleans on February 25. By that time, the Provisional Government of the Confederate States of America had been organized in Montgomery, Alabama, where delegates from the first six states to secede met on February 4. On February 9, Jefferson Davis was named Provisional President and Alexander H. Stephens Provisional Vice-President. They were inaugurated on February 18, and the new government began operating then. On February 23, the people of Texas approved the ordinance of secession by a large majority. And on March 1, the day Lee arrived home, General Twiggs was dismissed from the Army. The formal order charged him with "treachery to the flag of his country." This angered the old soldier, who felt that he had been powerless to do other than what he had done, for the War Department had given him neither instruction nor support.

The inauguration of Abraham Lincoln took place on March 4. The people at Arlington, with their unobstructed view of the city across the river, must have seen or heard some of the excitement that swept Washington that day. As soon as things quieted down, Lee went to the War Department to call on General Scott. What was said on this occasion is not known. They were both Virginians who knew the nation was waiting to see what they would do if and when their state seceded. In Scott's case, there was little doubt. Although born near Petersburg, he had been in the Army and in the North for so long that he did not feel the pull of his native soil to the extent that Lee did. Lee was Scott's favorite soldier, and he favored him as a father would a brilliant and talented son. He knew that he himself was too old—he was then nearly seventy-five—to take an active part in leading an army, and he apparently believed that if a large body of troops was raised, a show of force would prevent actual hostilities. Even in March 1861, few people in the North or South thought that the two sections would actually go to war. And even if they did, nearly everyone was quite certain that such a war would be very short, lasting only a few weeks or months at most. Scott may have tried to convince Lee that this was his great chance, that he would be the commander of an army that would never have to fight. No promises were made by either man, and the matter was allowed to rest during the tense days of March 1861 when the new administration's chief problem was Fort Sumter, where another Southerner, Kentucky-born Major Robert Anderson, was holding out.

JEFFERSON DAVIS, *President of
the Confederate States of America*

122

Twiggs's dismissal caused a vacancy in command that moved Lee up to a full colonelcy on March 28. (His commission was signed by Abraham Lincoln.) He also received an invitation from the Confederate Government in Montgomery to become a brigadier general in the army it was raising. Although he was probably flattered by the offer, he neither accepted nor refused it. As yet, he was not concerned with the new Confederacy. His immediate problem was to decide whether he owed allegiance to the Virginia of his ancestors or to the United States Army he had served all his life. It was evident that he would soon have to make a choice.

The problem, which was a major one for Lee and his contemporaries, is difficult for most modern Americans to understand, for swift transportation and communication have given the nation a close-knit unity which it lacked then. In Lee's time, many people still considered the states sovereign units joined together by a mutual compact that was only a few years older than Lee himself. And he had grown up in the shadow of the American Revolution in which his own father had fought. Washington and the men of the Revolution were very real to him even though they were of a previous generation. But vivid in his mind was the fact that the colonies had revolted against the mother country to found a new nation. And the people of that relatively new nation were still proud of their independence. Could the kind of act of separation that was justified in 1776 be wrong in 1861?

These were anxious days for Colonel Robert E. Lee, who was of the sixth generation of his family to live in Virginia. He was a grandfather, and his grandson was of the eighth generation. All around him, scattered across the tidewater country of Virginia were the broad acres, the homes, and the graves of his ancestors. The name Lee was part of the history and tradition of his state. He was so secure in his position in Southern society that he was one of the few who could afford to give voice to his opposition to slavery and secession. He stood between the past and the future. His mind looked forward, but his heart held him to what had been, to what still was, to what he felt might be perpetuated if the people of the South stood fast.

While he waited, the question was being decided for him in Charleston Harbor. There, on April 12, the guns gave the answer.

Major Anderson surrendered Fort Sumter on April 13 and evacuated it the next day. News of what was happening there ran through the country like an electric shock. On April 15, when President Lincoln called for 75,000 militiamen "to re-possess the forts, places, and property which have been seized from

General Scott's headquarters in Washington. A contemporary sketch.

Fort Sumter

the Union," the South knew that this would mean invasion of its territory. The upper Southern states reacted immediately to the proclamation. One after another, states that had been hesitating followed the lower South out of the Union. Virginia's new Governor, John Letcher, refused to send troops to answer Lincoln's call for militia. His reply was practically a declaration of war. Yet Letcher had opposed secession. On April 17, the Virginia Convention, meeting in secret session in Richmond, voted to secede. The people had to ratify the ordinance on May 23, but their approval seemed certain. Word of what had been decided at the secret meeting was not made public until late on April 18. On April 17 two messages arrived at Arlington for Lee. One asked him to call the next day on Francis P. Blair, Sr., whom he had known in St. Louis. The other was from General Scott, asking Lee to be at his office on the same day.

Lee rode into Washington on the eighteenth and went to the Blair house first. (It still stands on Pennsylvania Avenue across the street from the White House, of which it is now an adjunct.) Blair was the father of Postmaster General Montgomery Blair, a member of the Lincoln Cabinet. The only trustworthy account of what happened at that meeting was written in 1868 by Lee himself in a letter to Reverdy Johnson, Maryland Senator and attorney. In it Lee said: "I never intimated to any one that I desired the command of the United States Army; nor did I ever have a conversation with but one gentleman, Mr. Francis Preston Blair, on the subject, which was at his invitation, and, as I understood, at the instance of President Lincoln. After listening to his remarks, I declined the offer he made me, to take command of the army that was to be brought into the field; stating, as candidly and as courteously

HARPER'S WEEKLY
A JOURNAL OF CIVILIZATION

Vol. V.—No. 227.]   NEW YORK, SATURDAY, MAY 4, 1861.

Harper's Weekly *shows the women of Charleston watching the bombardment of Fort Sumter*

as I could that, though opposed to secession and deprecating war, I could take no part in an invasion of the Southern states."

Lee then went across the street to the old War Department Building to tell General Scott about his interview with Blair. Scott is said to have told his protégé that he was making a mistake but that if he insisted on standing by Virginia, he should resign from the Army at once.

Lee visited his elder brother, Sydney Smith, who was in Washington facing the same problem as an officer of the United States Navy. The two brothers apparently expected to consult each other again before making any final decision, but events were moving too swiftly to permit that. Lee then left Washington to ride back to Arlington. He was not to see the city again until long after the war was over.

The next morning, April 19, Lee rode into Alexandria, where he found the town boiling with excitement about the news from Richmond. It was public knowledge now that Virginia had seceded. When Lee entered the Stabler-Leadbeater Apothecary shop to pay a bill, he was asked what he thought of the state's decision. The pharmacist, evidently aware of the fact that the colonel's reply might be of historic importance, recorded Lee's words in his ledger alongside the notice of payment. They were: "I must say that I am one of those dull creatures that cannot see the good of secession."

The "dull creature," who was going through the worst day of his life while he watched his neighbors rejoice over what he thought was a national tragedy, returned to Arlington. The isolated house must have seemed like an island of peace in the midst of the hysteria that was gripping the nation. Lee spent the rest of the day there. He would have preferred to postpone making a decision until May 23 to be sure the people of the state would ratify the ordinance of secession, but he knew they would almost surely do so. And he knew that he could not wait until then. The letter to his brother which he must have been shaping in his mind at this time indicates how clearly he understood his predicament. His conversation with General Scott evidently had straightened him out on that.

According to Mrs. Lee, he asked to be left alone that evening. He went upstairs and paced the bedroom for some time. She heard him fall to his knees and pray for divine guidance. It was well after midnight when he came down to show her two letters he had just written. One, to Secretary of War Simon Cameron, was a brief formal note which read:

Sir—I have the honour to tender the resignation of my Commission as Colonel of the 1st Regt of Cavalry.

The other, addressed to his friend and superior officer, General Scott, was more detailed:

Arlington, Virginia, April 20, 1861
General: Since my interview with you on the 18th inst. I have felt that I ought no longer to retain my commission in the Army. I therefore tender my resignation, which I request you will recommend for acceptance. It would have been presented at once but for the struggle it has cost me to separate myself from a service to which I have devoted the best years of my life and all the ability I possessed.

During the whole of that time—more than a quarter of a century—I have experienced nothing but kindness from my superiors and a most cordial friendship from my comrades. To no one, General, have I been as much indebted as to yourself for uniform kindness and consideration, and it has always been my ardent desire to merit your approbation. I shall carry to the grave the most

126

grateful recollections of your kind consideration, and your name and fame shall always be dear to me.

Save in the defense of my native state, I never desire again to draw my sword.

Be pleased to accept my most earnest wishes for the continuance of your happiness and prosperity, and believe me, most truly yours,

R. E. LEE

The two letters were sent to Washington the next morning. The numerous endorsements on the back of the official letter of resignation show that it was circulated through the War Department for several days, but Cameron's signature, the date April 25, and the single word *Accepted* made it final. After thirty-two years of service, Robert E. Lee's career in the United States Army had come to an end. He had made the answer which Douglas Southall Freeman said he was born to make.

That morning Lee wrote to his brother in Washington and to his sister in Baltimore. He had to explain to Sidney Smith what he had done without consulting him. To him he wrote:

Arlington, Virginia, April 20, 1860
My Dear Brother Smith: The question which was the subject of my earnest consultation with you on the 18th inst. has in my own mind been decided. . . . I concluded to resign and sent in my resignation this morning. I wished to wait till the Ordinance of Secession should be acted on by the people of Virginia; but war seems to have commenced, and I am liable at any time to be ordered on duty which I could not conscientiously perform. To save me from such a position, and to prevent the necessity of resigning under orders, I had to act at once and before I could see you again on the subject, as I had wished. I am now a private citizen, and have no other ambition than to remain at home. . . .

His sister Ann had married a pro-Union man and their son was in the United States Army. In his letter to her, Lee said:

With all my devotion to the Union and the feeling of loyalty and duty of an American citizen, I have not been able to make up my mind to raise my hand against my relatives, my children, my home. I have therefore resigned my commission in the Army, and save in defense of my native State (with the sincere hope that my poor services may never be needed), I hope I may never be called on to draw my sword. I know you will blame me; but you must think as kindly of me as you can and believe that I have endeavored to do what I

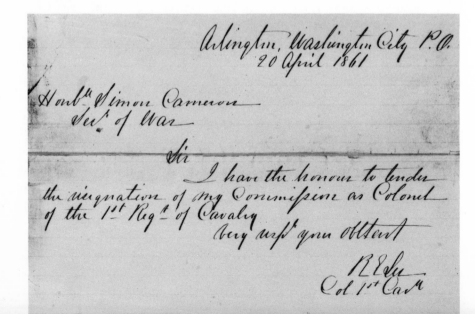

*Lee's letter of resignation
from the United States Army*

Lee never parted with the shoulder eagles that indicated his rank in the United States Army

thought right. To show you the feeling and struggle it has cost me, I send you a copy of my letter of resignation. . . .

Lee had now explained his actions to those who, he thought, required explanation. He was, of course, attacked then and for many years afterward for resigning from the Army which had educated and employed him all his adult life. In the North he was called a turncoat and a traitor. Oddly enough, however, he was never made an object of ridicule as Jefferson Davis and other highly placed Confederates often were. One could easily collect a book of caricatures of Davis, but Lee was never regarded as a comic figure even by Northerners who denounced him. Yet, as the war went on, Lee became at least as well known as Davis. Better able, perhaps, to judge Lee's actions than any American observer is an Englishman who, like Lee, was a general and an educator—Major-General Sir Frederick Maurice. In his book on Lee as a soldier he said: "Lee fought as a man who acts on conviction. . . . There have been critics of his career who, while expressing every sympathy with him in the terrible situation in which he was placed in April 1861, have been unable to explain . . . his breach of his oath as a regular officer of the Union and his enthusiasm for a cause which, as they say, he must have known to be based on slavery. As to the first of these criticisms, I would say that Lee did not break his military oath. He resigned his commission, and the acceptance of that resignation released him from that obligation. It is true . . . that he went to Richmond before the formal notification that he had ceased to be an officer of the Army of the United States reached him. He assumed that his resignation would be accepted . . . for in the United States it was recognized that in the event of civil strife the State should permit those in its service who had family ties with the participants in a rebellion to obtain release from service if they so desired. To act otherwise and to force men to fight those near and dear to them would be to make military service an unendurable tyranny. This implicit right to resignation does not relieve those who act upon it from the pains and penalties attaching to them as rebel citizens, but does absolve them from the charge of having broken a military oath. The fact that the authorities at Washington accepted Lee's resignation and also accepted wholesale resignations of other regular officers who were of Southern blood shows that this was so.

"Those who maintain that Lee must consciously have been fighting for the maintenance of slavery would make of him a casuist. My reading of his character is different. . . . Lee was not a politically minded man. . . . He could not follow political developments to their conclusion. . . . He could not foresee the outcome of the struggle between those who advocated limitation and those who pressed for the extension of slavery. . . . In 1861 abolition was the creed of a comparatively small number in the North. The Lee I see was essentially a simple-minded man with a keen sense of duty and a perfect trust in God's providence. His nature was not such as to make him eager to investigate the complexities of involved political questions, and his military training was calculated to strengthen his natural distaste for such investigations. . . . He regarded the Union as a great possession, but only so long as it was a free association of free states."

With his future still unsettled, Lee attended services in Alexandria's Christ Church that Sunday. A letter had come to him from a Judge Robertson, an outspoken elderly man who, like Lee, had opposed secession up to the last minute, and then had decided to stand by his native state. Robertson wanted Lee to accompany him to Richmond on Monday to meet Governor Letcher. There was no doubt what such a meeting would mean. Lee sent a note to

128

Robertson saying that he would be at the railroad station in Alexandria in the morning.

Sunday, April 21, 1861, was the last full day Lee was ever to spend in Arlington. He must have known that the place might be forever lost to him, for it stood on the border between the North and the South. It would be occupied by Union troops when they entered Virginia—and there was every reason to believe they would soon do so.

At this crucial moment in his life, Lee was fifty-four years old, in excellent health. His hair was graying, but his mustache was still black. His face was smooth-shaven; the beard with which he is so often associated had not yet been grown.

When he arose early on Monday to meet Judge Robertson, Lee had only nine and a half years to live. But those were to be the great years of his life. All that had gone before was preparation; fulfillment was just beginning.

The day was a glorious one with the sky clear and the weather unusually warm for April. Arlington was at its best on that spring morning, a dear and heartbreaking place to leave. The man who was going to Richmond was never to set foot in his beloved home again.

The Capitol, Richmond

The train to Richmond passed through a peaceful countryside which had yet to hear the sound of war. It carried Lee through a part of the state that had been wilderness when his ancestors first settled in Virginia. But civilization had long since moved westward, and the land was now covered by farms, villages, and good-sized towns. When Lee arrived in Richmond, he entered a city with which he had had little previous contact.

With a normal population of 40,000 (which was to triple during the war), Richmond was already overcrowded. The capital of the Confederacy was still at Montgomery, but Virginia's secession had brought hordes of people to the state capital. One of its citizens said that "Our beautiful city presents the appearance of an armed camp. . . . Every train pours in its multitude of volunteers, but I am not as much surprised at the number as at the apparent discipline of the country companies. Some of them really march like regulars, and with their stalwart forms, dark fierce countenances, and the red-coated Negro fifers and drummers in front, present quite a picturesque as well as most warlike aspect. But the war spirit is not confined to the men. . . . The ladies are not only preparing comforts for the soldiers, but arming and practising themselves. Companies of boys . . . from ten to fourteen years of age, fully armed and well-drilled, are preparing for the fray."

There was much excitement in Richmond on the day of Lee's arrival. The United States Armory at Harpers Ferry had been burned by Federal officials on the night of April 18 in an effort to keep it from falling into the hands of the Virginia militia who had gone there to seize it. And on April 20, ships and supplies at the Norfolk Navy Yard had been put to the torch for the same reason. Reports were coming in that a great many weapons, much ammunition, and—most important of all—some machinery had been saved in both places.

The sword of Robert E. Lee

The South would need all she could get, for she had few factories to make munitions of war.

And the day before Lee's arrival, Richmond had been thrown into a panic when word was received that the USS *Pawnee* was steaming up the James to shell the city. The report was false, as was one circulated in the North at the same time that Virginians were assembling a large force to seize Fort Monroe.

Lee registered at the Spotswood House on Main at Eighth Street, only a few hundred feet from the Capitol and the Governor's Mansion. Then he went to call on Letcher, who told him that he had been recommended for the newly created position of "commander of the military and naval forces of Virginia."

When Lee agreed to accept the post, Letcher offered his name to the Convention which was still in session. It gave unanimous approval to the Governor's choice, and before the day of his arrival in Richmond was over, Lee found himself a major general in command of all the state's armed forces. Virginia had not yet joined the Confederacy, so she was still an independent unit with the right to have her own army and navy. This rather odd situation was to last until June 8, when her armed forces were transferred to the Confederacy. Lee was a Virginia major general for just forty-seven days.

The next morning he moved into a temporary office, where he was soon called upon by a committee which wanted to take him to the Capitol to be formally notified of his appointment. He was given a standing ovation when he entered the room where the Convention was meeting. He was presented to its members as Major General Lee and a long speech of praise was then made. It probably embarrassed the always-modest man who cared little about rhetoric or fine phrases. He replied to it in just three courteous sentences.

After the ceremony was over, he received a note from Alexander Stephens, Vice-President of the Confederacy, who had come to Richmond the day before. He was there to invite Virginia to join the Confederate States of America, and he was afraid that Lee might block the move because it would reduce his rank to that of brigadier general, the highest grade the new government could then offer. Lee told him that he wanted to see the alliance formed and would certainly not stand in its way because of his own official rank or personal position. Stephens said of him that "I was wonderfully taken with Lee in our first interview. I saw him put to the test that tries character. He came out of the crucible, pure and refined gold."

On April 25, the Convention ratified an agreement which would put all the military operations of the state under control of the Confederate government. But that government was far away in Montgomery. Lee had to face the immediate problem of organizing an armed force for the defense of a state that was just across the Potomac from the Federal capital.

President Lincoln's proclamation of April 15, which called for 75,000 militia and ordered Congress to convene in special session on July 4, also commanded those who were in revolt against the national government "to disperse and retire peaceably . . . within twenty days." This meant that Federal forces could not be used against the South until May 5.

In Richmond, Lee worked hard to organize the defenses of Virginia. Indefensible, however, were Arlington and Alexandria, for they were too close to Washington to be held. He knew that his own home would soon be occupied by Union troops, and he was greatly concerned about his wife, who was still at Arlington. He wrote to her on April 26 and again on April 30, urging her to leave and send the silver, the portraits, and the Washington relics to a safe place. In the second letter he said: "Where to go is the difficulty. When the war commences no place will be exempt in my opinion, and indeed all the avenues into the state will be the scene of military operations. Tell Custis

Statue marking the place in the Virginia State Capitol where Lee accepted command of the armed forces of Virginia on April 23, 1861

to consider the question. He is a discreet person. . . . I wrote to Robert that I could not consent to take . . . young men from their colleges and put them in the ranks at the beginning of a war when they are not wanted and when there were men enough for the purpose. The war may last 10 years. Where are our ranks to be filled from then?"

Lee was also concerned about salvaging the war material found at Harpers Ferry and at the Norfolk Navy Yard when Virginia militia seized those places. Colonel Talcott, whom Lee had known at Fort Monroe when he brought Mary Custis there as his bride, was now the state engineer. Lee gave him a free hand to use guns from Norfolk to fortify the river banks in order to prevent the Federal Navy from steaming up to Richmond. He then turned his attention to Harpers Ferry.

The V.M.I. cadets had come up from Lexington to help defend the state capital. With them was their instructor in artillery tactics, Major Thomas Jonathan Jackson. Lee undoubtedly remembered him from the Mexican War. When Governor Letcher asked the convention to give Jackson a commission as colonel of infantry so he could take command of the troops at Harpers Ferry, Lee approved the choice and wrote out the orders for the new colonel to proceed to that post. Gunmaking machinery which had escaped the fire at the Armory was to be shipped to Richmond.

The deadline of May 5 passed, but the Federal forces made no move to enter Virginia. Since Lee thought that his wife had left Arlington, he addressed a letter to her at his cousin's home, Ravensworth. He was then surprised to receive a letter from her dated May 9 at Arlington. He replied immediately: "I am glad to hear that you are at peace and enjoying the sweet weather and beautiful flowers. You had better complete your arrangements and retire further from the scene of war. It may burst upon you at any time. It is sad to think of the devastation, if not ruin it may bring upon a spot so endeared to us. But God's will be done. We must be resigned."

Time was running out for the Lees' ownership of Arlington. On May 12, Mrs. Lee wrote: "This is a lovely morning. I never saw the country more beautiful, perfectly radiant. The yellow jessamine in full bloom and perfuming

THOMAS JONATHAN JACKSON
drawn from life in 1861

all the air, but a deathlike stillness prevails everywhere; you hear no sounds from Washington."

But the beating of drums in Washington was soon to be plainly audible in Arlington. And she had word that Union troops would start marching across the Potomac River bridges at any moment. On May 14, she left the house in which she had spent most of her life and moved to Ravensworth. It was to be the first of many stops she was to make during the next few years as she went from place to place to keep out of the hurrying armies' way.

On May 23, Virginia approved the ordinance of secession. Before the dawn of the next day, the Federal Army made its long-threatened move. Some 13,000 Union soldiers crossed the Potomac by ship or by the three bridges. The USS *Pawnee* went to Alexandria, where the few Confederate troops still left in the town quickly withdrew. It was there that young Elmer Ellsworth was killed by the proprietor of the Marshall House when he tried to haul down a Confederate flag flying defiantly from a flagstaff on the roof. Ellsworth was the first Union officer to die in the war that was now beginning to drench the land with blood. John Brown's prophecy was less than 18 months old, but it was already becoming true.

On that same day, Major General Charles W. Sandford of the New York Militia entered the grounds of Arlington. In his report he said: "Finding the mansion vacated by the family, I stated to some of the servants left there that had the family remained I would have established a guard for their security from annoyance; but, in consequence of their absence, that I would, by occupying it myself, be responsible for the perfect care and security of the house and everything in and about it." Entrenchments were dug the next day, and on the twenty-sixth, troops went into camp at the rear of the house.

On May 21 the Confederate government decided to move from Montgomery to Richmond, and the cumbersome business of transferring personnel and records began. Jefferson Davis arrived in Richmond on May 29. Troops from other Southern states were being sent to Virginia because it seemed likely that the first Union attacks would be aimed at that northernmost state to secede. In May and early June there was some friction between officers in the Virginia armed forces and those in command of the regiments which were pouring into the state.

On May 14, the Confederate Congress confirmed the nominations of Joseph E. Johnston, and Robert E. Lee as brigadier generals in the Confederate Army. Lee still had to carry on the work of building Virginia's defenses, and he continued to sign his mail as major general of the Virginia Forces until May 24.

When Jefferson Davis arrived in Richmond, Lee was away on a tour of inspection of Manassas, where the vital railroad junction made that area essential to the state's defenses. He was back again in Richmond on May 30 and was present the next day at a conference between President Davis and General Beauregard.

Lee knew Davis fairly well and was on excellent terms with him. Davis and Beauregard had already had differences of opinion, and were destined to have more. But when Davis heard Lee's analysis of the situation at Manassas, he immediately decided to put Beauregard in command of that area. This was fortunate for the Creole general, because the victorious outcome of the battle that was soon to take place at Manassas would greatly enhance his reputation. At this time, Lee's usual good luck deserted him. He was now to go from one frustrating experience to another. And then, exactly one year later, he would assume command of the troops which he was to make world-famous as the almost invincible Army of Northern Virginia.

This photograph, a retouched copy of the one by Brady on page 88, has a uniform and VA painted in to represent Lee as a Virginia general. It was distributed early in 1861, starting in Baltimore.

132

But no man can know his fate. Lee went calmly about his business, doing what he thought had to be done. Early in June he visited the batteries that were being built on the James and York rivers. His journey took him to the White House plantation, where he saw Rooney's family and caught a brief glimpse of Rooney himself at the railroad station.

On his return to Richmond, he formally turned over command of Virginia's military and naval forces to the Confederate government. This was on June 8. The next day he wrote to Mrs. Lee: "I do not know what my position will be. I should like to retire to private life if I could be with you and the children, but if I can be of any service to the State or her cause, I must continue."

On June 15, he wrote a long report to Governor Letcher, informing him of what had been accomplished up to June 8, when the state's preparations for defense were transferred to the Confederate government. In this report he said that more than 35,000 troops had been raised and fairly well provided with arms which included 115 pieces of field artillery. He also gave details of the naval preparations and river defenses.

After that there was very little for Lee to do. But hostilities were beginning. On June 10, Confederate and Union troops clashed at Big Bethel. It was a minor affair, but it created much excitement in Richmond. So did the Union raid on Romney on June 13.

During the next few weeks Lee marked time, although he was often consulted by President Davis for advice on military matters. With good cause he wrote to his wife on June 24 that his "movements were very uncertain." But he was still hoping for service in the field.

Meanwhile, Richmond's streets were thronged with soldiers from Georgia in homemade jackets, with Maryland Zouaves brightly clad in blue and orange, with long-haired Texas horsemen in Western costumes, and with a motley assortment of volunteers dressed in all sorts of military clothing from the

United States Volunteers digging trenches on Arlington Heights in May 1861

drabbest and most practical kind to garments more suitable for a masquerade ball.

John Beauchamp Jones, in his day-by-day account of wartime Richmond entitled *A Rebel War Clerk's Diary,* gives a vivid picture of one regiment that was attracting much attention: "The ladies are postponing all engagements until their lovers have fought the Yankees. . . . They go in crowds to the fairground where the 1st S. C. Vols. are encamped, showering upon them their smiles and all the delicacies the city affords. They wine them and cake them— and they deserve it. They are just from taking Fort Sumter and have won historic distinction. I was introduced to several of the privates by their captain, who told me they were worth from $100,000 to half a million dollars each. . . . These rich young men were dressed in coarse gray homespun! We have the best horsemen and the best marksmen in the world."

Another group of wealthy young men was the famed Battalion of Washington Artillery from New Orleans. But most of the volunteers arriving in Richmond were not as well off as these. Some had no arms or ammunition, evidently expecting Virginia to supply them. But the state's modern weapons had already been distributed, and only ancient flintlock muskets were available. Lee had to write to the Governor of Georgia, politely suggesting that his state send arms as well as men.

Weapons were scarce in those early days, but volunteers came to Richmond with wagonloads of unnecessary things which they were to discard as soon as they went into battle.

While this display of martial ardor was going on in the streets and public places, the men who had to direct the Army's efforts went quietly about their business of preparing the troops for combat. Mechanics' Hall now housed the War Department; Lee had an office on the top floor of that hastily converted building.

Early in July, word began to reach the Confederate capital that the Washington government was marshaling a huge army under the command of General Irvin McDowell and that it would soon move against the Confederate forces at Manassas. A few days later, Richmond papers carried accounts of a young Union general's successful operations in the western part of Virginia. His name was George Brinton McClellan, and what he was doing caused much concern at Confederate headquarters, for the people in forty western counties had voted against secession and were setting up the new state of West Virginia.

But what was happening at Manassas was nearer home. On July 16, Davis got a secret message from a female spy in Washington that McDowell's troops were starting to move south. The next day, word came from Beauregard that his outposts were under attack and that he was falling back to a creek called Bull Run. He urged that reinforcements be sent quickly. Jackson's 2500 men were ordered in from the Valley.

It was evident that matters were building up to a climax at Manassas. Lee wanted desperately to be there, but Davis "thought it more important" that he stay in Richmond. On Sunday, July 21, Davis went to Manassas by special train. When he arrived there, the battle was already far advanced, and at first it seemed to be a Confederate defeat. Then it became known that the Federal forces had been routed and that Jackson had been one of the heroes of the day. (It was in this battle that he got the name Stonewall.) Davis telegraphed his wife: "We have won a glorious though dear-bought victory."

Lee witnessed the celebration in Richmond and watched the troops return, but he had played no part in the battle. He wrote to Mary to say that he was "mortified" at his absence, but there was no help for it. He was a general without a command.

Troops of the Virginia Cavalry, 1861

134

VIRGINIA VOLUNTEERS OF **1861**

They carry back bright to the coiner the mintage of man,
The lads that will die in their glory and never be old.
—*A. E. Housman*

vid Mead, *Dunwiddie Troops, 3rd Virginia Cavalry*

John Worth, *Richmond Howitzer Battalion*

arles A. Pace, *18th Virginia Infantry, Danville Blues*

J. T. Jobson, *Company G, 9th Virginia Infantry*

THE CONFEDERATE GENERAL

The situation in western Virginia had worsened even before Manassas was fought; General Robert S. Garnett, the Confederate officer in command there, had been killed on July 13. He was the first general to die in battle, and his loss was a serious one, especially since he had to be replaced by a wrangling lot of less able officers.

Acting on verbal instructions from Davis, Lee left Richmond by train on July 28 and arrived in Staunton that evening. He was not to be in charge of the troops in Western Virginia, but was supposed by some feat of diplomacy or legerdemain to coordinate the activities of the local commanders. At Staunton he met some of the troops who had been with Garnett and saw how disastrous their defeat had been.

Lee rode west into the mountains in what was to be one of the wettest summers ever seen in that isolated hill country. With him went Lieutenant Colonel John A. Washington and young Captain Walter H. Taylor, who was to be Lee's assistant adjutant general until the end of the war. Their first stop was at Monterey, headquarters of Brigadier H. R. Jackson. More of Garnett's former troops were here; those still effective were strung out through the mountains for miles. Most of the others were wet, tired, and dejected; many were ill with measles and diarrhea.

From Monterey, Lee went to Huntersville to see General W. W. Loring, a one-armed veteran of the Mexican War. There he discovered that rivalry among the minor Confederate generals was holding up the campaign. He saw plainly that Loring should move into action immediately but showed no sign of doing so. Lee now made a serious error. Instead of using his higher rank to order the troops to advance, he decided to humor the hesitant Loring. On August 5, he issued special Orders No. 239—which assigned three more regiments to Loring. This bolstered that general's self-esteem and annoyed his rivals, but did not start his army moving. Even Douglas Southall Freeman, who has often been criticized for being too adulatory in his biographical treatment of Lee, said of this:

All his life Lee had lived with gentle people, where kindly sentiments and consideration for the feelings of others were part of noblesse oblige. *In that atmosphere he was expansive, cheerful, buoyant even, no matter what happened. . . . Now that he encountered surliness and jealousy, it repelled him, embarrassed him, and well-nigh bewildered him. Detesting a quarrel as undignified and unworthy of a gentleman, he showed himself willing . . . to go to almost any length, within the bounds of honor, to avoid a clash. In others this might have been a virtue; in him it was a positive weakness, the first serious weakness he had ever displayed as a soldier. It was a weakness that was to be apparent more than once and had to be combated, deliberately or subconsciously. His personal humility and his exaggerated sense of his obligations as a man and a Christian were to make him submit to a certain measure of intellectual bullying by those of his associates who were sour and self-opinionated. The more inconsiderate such people were of him, the more considerate he was of them, and the more forbearant, up to the point where his patience failed and his temper broke bounds. Then he would freeze men quickly in the cold depths of his wrath. . . . There was always a question whether Lee . . . would conquer his inordinate amiability or would permit his campaigns to be marred or his battles to be lost by it. . . . It became necessary to ask, for two years and more, whether his judgment as a soldier or his consideration as a gentleman dominated his acts.*

136

Lee left Huntersville on August 6 to go farther into the mountain wilderness. Some rain had fallen every day since he left Staunton, and it continued to fall. Nevertheless, he wrote cheerful letters to his wife, commenting on the beauty of the mountains and their wealth of timber. After leaving Huntersville, he had met his son Rooney. He wrote to Mary: "He is very well and very active, and as yet the war has not reduced him much. He dined with me yesterday and preserves his fine appetite. Today he is out reconnoitering and has the full benefit of this fine rain. I fear he is without his overcoat, as I do not recollect seeing it on his saddle. I told you he had been promoted to a major in cavalry and is the commanding cavalry officer on this line at present. He is as sanguine, cheerful, and hearty as ever."

Lee and his little party now spent days exploring the mountains, trying to find a practicable route to the Federal camps. Meanwhile, the rain never ceased; it soaked the woods until every tree dripped water. As August advanced, the weather grew so cold that the troops had to build fires to keep warm.

On August 29, Lee wrote to his daughters: "It rains here all the time, literally. There has not been sunshine enough since my arrival to dry my

This photograph, taken by Mathew B. Brady in Richmond after the war was over, shows the three men who began their Civil War careers in the Virginia mountains in 1861. Walter Taylor is at left; R. E. Lee in center; Rooney Lee at right.

137

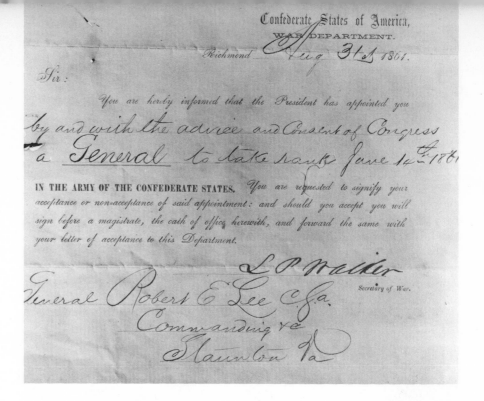

*The North takes notice of Lee.
Harper's* Weekly *ran this
engraved portrait on August 24, 1861.
It was drawn from the retouched picture
shown on page 132.*

clothes. . . . But the worst of the rain is that the ground has become so saturated with water that the constant travel on the roads have made them almost impassable, so that I cannot get up sufficient supplies for the troops to move. It is raining now. Has been all day, last night, day before, and day before that. . . . It is quite cool, too. I have on all my winter clothes and am writing in my overcoat. All the clouds seem to concentrate over this ridge . . . and . . . give us rain."

Two days after writing this letter, Lee's commission as a full general in the Confederate Army was confirmed in Richmond. It had been authorized on May 13. It is ironic that this honor should have come to him when he was nearing the very bottom of his career.

Early in September the weather cleared, and the patient exploring of the area began to yield results. A way was at last found to cross the tangled ravines and steep slopes to attack the Federals on Cheat Mountain. Lee drew up plans for his first Civil War battle. His orders, which were to be issued under Loring's name, called for an assault on September 12. While preparing for it, Lee received a disturbing letter from his wife. He replied on September 9: "As to the reports which you say are afloat about our separation I know nothing. Anyone that can reason must see its necessity under present circumstances. They can only exist in the imaginations of a few. So give them no heed. We both know it cannot be otherwise and must, therefore, be content. As to the vile slanders . . . with which you say the papers abound, why concern ourselves? I do not see them and would not mind them. They are inserted for no good intention, you may be sure. . . . I do not recollect the letter to you or even the part that you wish to publish. I only know I never write private letters for the public eye, and suppose what I said was for your own perusal. I am content to take no notice of the slanders you speak of but to let them die out. Everybody is slandered, even the good. How should I escape?"

Meanwhile, the brief interlude of fair weather ended and the rains set in again. Constant dampness spoiled rations and made gunpowder hard to ignite. But the attack was scheduled, and it had to go on.

Lee first saw action against Union troops on September 11, when the Confederates drove them back at Conrad's Mill. The next morning, after an-

138

other terrible night of rain, he looked down from the heights to see the Federal camp far below. He waited expectantly for the sound of firing on the crest of the mountain, where the attack on a blockhouse was to be the signal for a general assault. It never came. Instead, the worried general heard scattered shots along a watercourse farther down the slopes. He hurried there and narrowly missed running into a Federal cavalry patrol that was dashing through the woods.

He went on to visit the various Confederate regiments and talk to their commanders. Everywhere he found them despondent. The men were too wet, too tired, too hungry to fight, the officers said. The morning drifted away inconclusively. By afternoon, Lee knew that his chance for surprise, for a spirited attack, or for any kind of action that day was gone.

Next morning, Lee's son Rooney and his friend Colonel John A. Washington were fired on by Union pickets whose bullets instantly killed the colonel and wounded Rooney's mount. The youth leaped on the dead man's horse and brought word of the tragedy back to camp. The grief-stricken Lee had to write to the family of the slain officer. It was the first of many such letters.

Lee soon learned what had gone wrong with the attack on the mountain. Federal prisoners taken early that morning had talked the Confederate commander in charge of the front-line troops into believing that the crest was heavily fortified and strongly held. He had called off the assault. Lee's first Civil War battle had come to an end without ever having been fought. He now had to listen to his subordinate generals wrangle about making further attacks.

October came, and winter was drawing near. Confederate and Union troops in the mountains had reached a stalemate. Lee himself now believed that nothing conclusive could be done and that to bring on a battle at this time would unnecessarily cost the lives of five or six hundred men.

On October 24, an overwhelming number of votes were cast in the western counties of Virginia to form the state of West Virginia, which was to remain in the Union. Even if Lee had won a military victory, the new state could not have been held for the Confederacy.

Six days later, he turned his horse eastward and headed toward Richmond. He came back wearing a gray beard he had grown during his three

The kind of mountain country in which Lee's first Civil War campaign was fought

Fort Pulaski late in 1861

months in the wilderness. On October 31, he arrived in the Confederate capital to report failure. The possibility of success had been slight, and the entire campaign was not important, but Lee was not used to defeat. He felt the sting keenly.

For the first time, he met public criticism. The Richmond newspapers were caustic. One of them called him "Granny Lee." His nephew Fitzhugh Lee, writing later about this period in his uncle's life, said: "Men apparently wise shook their heads and said he had been overrated as a soldier; that he relied upon a 'showy presence' and a 'historic name,' and that he was 'too tender of blood' and leaned too much to the engineer side of a military question, preferring rather to dig intrenchments than to fight."

Fortunately, Lee had a firm supporter in Jefferson Davis. Lee had no apologies or excuses to make to the President. Davis said: "He came back, carrying the heavy weight of defeat, and unappreciated by the people whom he served. . . . Yet, through all this, with a magnanimity rarely equalled, he stood in silence, without defending himself or allowing others to defend him, for he was unwilling to offend any one who was wearing a sword and striking blows for the Confederacy."

The Richmond government had known for some time that a huge Federal naval expedition was fitting out at Fort Monroe. On November 1, it learned that the ships had sailed and that Port Royal, South Carolina, was their destination. Since a smaller expedition had captured the forts at Hatteras Inlet in August, much concern was felt about the safety of the Confederacy's Atlantic ports, which were essential to the conduct of the war. Only by bringing in arms from Europe could the South hope to equip her fighting forces.

Lee was Davis' choice for defensive work along the coast, and on November 5 orders were issued creating the new military department of South Carolina, Georgia, and East Florida, with Lee as its head. After his failure in western Virginia, Lee's stock had fallen so low that Davis had to write letters to the state governors to justify his appointment.

Lee left Richmond the next day and arrived at Coosawhatchie just as the Federal fleet captured Forts Walker and Beauregard at the entrance to Port Royal Sound. Troops landed from the ships were occupying Beaufort. The now-unlucky general had been given another impossible assignment, for, as events of the next few weeks were to show, the Atlantic coast of the Confederacy could not be defended except at a few strongly held places like Charleston and Wilmington.

Lee went to Savannah to revisit the scene of his first assignment as an Army Engineer—Cockspur Island, where he had helped to build Fort Pulaski.

During his visit, the first blockade-runner owned by the Confederate Government arrived in the Savannah River on November 13. Among other munitions and supplies, the *Fingal* had on board 9000 Enfield rifles, of which Lee was to get half to arm the troops in South Carolina and Georgia. The remaining 4500 were to be sent to General Joseph Johnston in Nashville.

Lee now obtained the only good thing that ever came from his ill-fated campaign in western Virginia. While there, he had greatly admired a gray horse named Jeff Davis. This animal was now brought to South Carolina by his owner's brother. When Lee saw the horse again, he purchased him for $200 and renamed him Traveller. He was to be Lee's favorite mount for the rest of his life.

Lee moved rapidly from one place to another along the 300 miles of seacoast for which he was responsible. Since he believed that only a few well-fortified coastal entrances could be held, he ordered the outlying minor defenses to be abandoned. On November 10, troops and guns were removed from Tybee Island near Fort Pulaski. Two weeks later, Federal ships landed men and guns on Tybee. Lee was still convinced that the Savannah River could not be forced and said so in a report written when the Federals moved in. Actually, he was right. Federal batteries on Tybee went into action in April and in two days reduced massive Fort Pulaski to rubble. After that, Federal troops occupied Cockspur Island for the rest of the war. But Savannah did not fall until December 21, 1864, when William Tecumseh Sherman took the city after having marched across the interior of Georgia.

Lee was in Charleston in mid-December when a disastrous fire swept the city. And he was there on the first anniversary of South Carolina's secession, December 20. On that day the Union Navy brought in old ships loaded with stone and sank them in one of the harbor's three entrance channels in an unsuccessful effort to bottle up the port.

Then came the first Christmas of the war. Lee's daughters had visited Stratford the month before, and their letters stirred up old memories. When he wrote to his wife on Christmas Day, he mentioned regretfully the two fine houses which had meant so much to him: "As to our old home [Arlington], if not destroyed, it will be difficult ever to be recognized. Even if the enemy had wished to preserve it, it would almost have been impossible. With the number of troops encamped around it . . . it is vain to think of its being in a habitable condition. I fear books, furniture, and the relics of Mount Vernon will be gone. It is better to make up our minds to a general loss. They cannot take away the remembrances of the spot and the memories of those that to us rendered it sacred. That will remain to us as long as life will last, and that we can preserve. In the absence of a home, I wish I could purchase Stratford. That is the only other place that I could go to now accessible to us that would inspire me with feelings of pleasure and local love. You and the girls could remain there in quiet. It is a poor place, but we could make enough cornbread and bacon for our support, and the girls could weave us clothes. I wonder if it is for sale and at how much. Ask Fitzhugh to try and find out when he gets to Fredericksburg."

He also alluded to the *Trent* case, which came near bringing on a war between England and the United States when a Union warship took the Confederate Commissioners Mason and Slidell off the British mail steamer *Trent* which they had boarded in Havana, Cuba. Many Southerners were hoping that the incident would bring England's armed might to their assistance, but Lee had no illusions about such a possibility. He said: "You must not build your hopes on peace on account of the United States going into a war with England. She will be very loath to do that, notwithstanding the bluster of the

Lee on Traveller.
A photograph made after the war.

141

*The bachelors' mess
at 707 East Franklin Street,
Richmond, as it looked
during the war*

*The Franklin Street house
as it appears today*

Northern papers. Her rulers are not entirely mad, and if they find England is in earnest and that war or a restitution of their captives must be the consequence, they will adopt the latter. We must make up our minds to fight our battles and win our independence alone. No one will help us." He was right. Under the threat of war, the United States government backed down and offered to return the two Commissioners. They were put aboard a British warship on January 1.

In another Christmas letter, addressed to one of his daughters, Lee said: "Having distributed such poor Christmas gifts as I had to those around me, I have been looking for something for you. Trifles even are hard to get these war times, and you must not therefore expect more. I have sent you what I thought most useful . . . and hope it [a gift of money] will be of some service. . . . I send you some sweet violets that I gathered for you this morning while covered with dense white frost, whose crystals glittered in the bright sun like diamonds and formed a brooch of rare beauty and sweetness which could not be fabricated by the expenditure of a world of money. May God guard and preserve you for me, my dear daughter! Among the calamities of war, the hardest to bear, perhaps, is the separation of families and friends. . . . In my absence from you I have thought of you very often, and regretted I could do nothing for your comfort. Your old home, if not destroyed by our enemies, has been so desecrated that I cannot bear to think of it. I should have preferred it to have been wiped from the earth, its beautiful hill sunk, and its sacred trees buried, rather than to have been degraded by the presence of those who revel in the ill they do for their own selfish purposes. You see what a poor sinner I am, and how unworthy to possess what was given me; for that reason it has been

142

taken away. I pray for a better spirit, and that the hearts of our enemies may be changed."

Lee had been given the use of the John Stewart house at 707 East Franklin Street, which he occupied while in Richmond. Late in December his son Custis, who was working as Jefferson Davis' aide-de-camp, said that he and some other young officers wanted to set up a bachelors' mess in this house. Lee encouraged the idea and wrote: "If you can get pleasant people to join in taking the house, it would certainly be more agreeable for you to live there than at a hotel, but I know how expensive a bachelors' mess is . . . unless there is someone who will attend to it and conduct it economically. If you can make the arrangement, however, do so, and I will pay my share."

In the same letter (December 29), Lee had more to say about the *Trent* case. After again predicting its outcome, he told Custis: "We must make up our minds to fight our battles ourselves. Expect to receive aid from no one. Make every necessary sacrifice of comfort, money, and labour to bring the war to a successful issue and then we will succeed. The cry is too much for help. I am mortified to hear it. We want no aid. We want to be true to ourselves, to be prudent, just, fair, and bold. I am dreadfully disappointed at the spirit here. They have all of a sudden realized the asperities of war, in what they must encounter, and do not seem to be prepared for it. If I only had some veteran troops to take the brunt, they would soon rally and be inspired with the great principle for which we are contending."

The eventful year 1861 was now ending. It had been, by far, the worst of Lee's life. But the new year was to give him his great chance.

*General Lee's camp chest
and mess equipment*

143

THE BIRTH OF AN ARMY

The year 1862 began badly for the Confederacy. On February 6, Fort Henry in Tennessee was captured by Federal gunboats; then, ten days later, nearby Fort Donelson was taken by troops under the command of a young West Pointer who had fought with Lee in the Mexican War. Ulysses S. Grant's climb to fame began when he demanded and got unconditional surrender of the garrison. And on February 8, a combined Union attack captured Roanoke Island, a strategically located naval base in the North Carolina sounds. Coming after Hatteras, it showed that the Federal Government was making a concerted effort to gain control of the Atlantic coast.

Lee was in Savannah when Roanoke Island was attacked. In January he had been on Cumberland Island where his father had been buried in 1818. He wrote to Mary about his visit to the grave: "The spot is marked by a plain marble slab. . . . The family have moved into the interior of Georgia, leaving only a few servants and a white gardener on the place. The garden was beautiful, enclosed by the finest hedge I have ever seen. . . . The orange trees were small, and the orange grove . . . had been destroyed by an insect that has proved fatal to the orange on the coast of Georgia and Florida. There was a fine grove of olives. . . . The garden was filled with roses and beautiful vines, the names of which I do not know. Among them was the tomato vine in full bearing with the ripe fruit on it. There has as yet been no frost in that region of country this winter. I went in the dining room and parlour, in which the furniture still remained. In the latter room hung the portraits of Mr. John and James King, father and uncle of Mrs. N[ightingale] rabid abolitionists, with a bad likeness of Gen'l Green[e], and a handsome print of Florence Nightingale and some landscapes. There also hung over the mantle a representation of Gen'l Green[e]. . . . The house has never been finished, but is a fine, large one and beautifully located. A magnificent grove of live oaks envelops the road from the landing to the house."

After the loss of the two forts in Tennessee, the Confederate War Department began to recall troops from the more indefensible points along the Atlantic coast to send them farther inland where they were badly needed. This was in line with Lee's own thinking, for he saw clearly that exposed positions could not be held against a determined attack. But it meant that there was less and less for him to do and that whatever he did might go for nothing. He was probably not sorry to receive a telegram from Davis on March 2 calling him back to Richmond.

He arrived just in time to learn that Johnston was evacuating the Confederate lines at Manassas. But this was quickly forgotten on March 8, when the city celebrated the destruction of two Federal men-of-war at Hampton Roads by the *Virginia*. This was the formidable ironclad which had been built on the hull of the former USS *Merrimack* after that burned-out ship had been salvaged from the wreckage the Federals had made of the Norfolk Navy Yard when they abandoned it in April 1861. But the rejoicing was short-lived, for the next day John Ericsson's little "cheesebox on a raft" arrived in Hampton Roads to defend the rest of the Union fleet. The heavy guns on both ships exchanged shot after shot without doing much damage to their seemingly invulnerable armor. The encounter was a draw, but the *Virginia* lost her chance to destroy the Federal fleet in Hampton Roads. Simultaneous with this came news from the West that the battle of Pea Ridge, Arkansas, was no Confederate victory even though Union casualties were much greater.

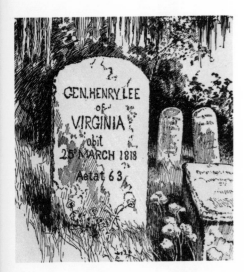

The grave of "Light-Horse" Harry Lee at Dungeness

Lee had returned to Richmond when reverses in the field made it necessary to reorganize the President's Cabinet. A new Secretary of War was to be appointed, and there were many good reasons to believe that Lee would get the post. But Jefferson Davis was convinced that one military expert (himself) was enough for his Cabinet, so he chose a civilian. On March 13, Lee was "assigned to duty at the seat of government . . . under the direction of the President." Commenting on this to his wife the next day, Lee said: "It will give me great pleasure to do everything I can to relieve him and serve the country, but I do not see either advantage or pleasure in my duties."

Lee's life was being further complicated by the fact that his son Robert had left school and had made up his mind to join the Rockbridge Artillery. They had seen so little of one another during the last six years that the young lad admitted that he was "somewhat in awe" of the illustrious general who was his father. Lee, always the soul of patience in handling family matters, took the time to outfit his son as a private. Robert, Jr., wrote of this: "I think it worthy of note that the son of the commanding general enlisting as a private in his army was not thought to be anything remarkable or unusual. Neither my mother, my family, my friends, nor myself expected any other course, and I do not suppose it ever occurred to my father to think of giving me an office, which he could easily have done. I know it never occurred to me, nor did I ever hear, at that time or afterwards, from anyone that I might have been entitled to better rank than that of a private because of my father's prominence in Virginia and in the Confederacy." With his father's blessing, the new soldier then went off to join Stonewall Jackson in the Valley.

Meanwhile, news from the various fronts continued to be bad. On March 14, the Union Navy followed up its capture of Roanoke Island by taking over New Bern, thus strengthening its position in the North Carolina sounds. And on the same day, Federal troops occupied New Madrid on the upper Mississippi River.

Late in March, the Confederate high command knew that McClellan's troops were assembling in great numbers at Fort Monroe, but they could not yet tell whether they were to be used against Norfolk or Richmond. While plans were being made to hold them off whichever way they went, more disheartening news arrived from the West. During a brilliant first-day battle on April 6 at Shiloh, Tennessee, General Albert Sidney Johnston had been mortally wounded. The next morning, the increasingly formidable Grant rallied his troops and recovered the ground lost the day before. Casualties were high on both sides; nothing was gained by either. And then, the day after Shiloh, fortified Island No. 10 on the upper Mississippi River was occupied by the Federals. Two of the forts on which Lee had worked, Pulaski and Macon, were also lost as Union forces extended their efforts to gain more bases along the Atlantic coast. Worst of all, however, was the capture of New Orleans, the South's largest city, which was taken by Farragut's fleet late in April. Federal occupation of that vital port closed the lower Mississippi to the Confederacy for the duration of the war. In order to meet the realities of the situation, the Confederate Government passed a draft law on April 16.

The disasters which were taking place many hundreds of miles from Richmond, serious as they were, did not disturb the Confederate capital as much as what was happening on the Peninsula near Yorktown. It was now evident that McClellan's goal was not Norfolk but Richmond, and General Joseph E. Johnston, who was in charge of the defense of the Peninsula, indicated that he was going to move his men out of the Yorktown area and form new lines closer to the city. Almost everyone in the government was opposed to the idea, but Johnston was stubborn, and there was little doubt that he

This photograph, taken in 1862, is probably the first to show Lee with a beard. The beard, unfortunately, has been retouched to darken the graying hair. The signature indicates that the picture was once the property of Mary Custis Lee.

145

McClellan's army on the march up the Peninsula

would do exactly what he said he would do. On May 1 he sent a telegram to Davis saying that he was going to abandon the Confederate defenses at Yorktown.

He evacuated Yorktown on the night of May 3–4. A brief rearguard battle was fought at Williamsburg on the fifth, but the Army fell back toward Richmond to take up new defensive positions outside the city. T. C. DeLeon describes the troops as they struggled through the muddy roads leading to the capital: "Hungry and worn, the men struggled through it [the mud] day after day—bearing their all on their backs, unable to halt for cooking; and frequently stopped to labor on a broken-down battery, or a mired wagon. Discipline naturally relaxed. It was impossible to keep the weary and half-starved men to regular routine. They straggled into Richmond muddy—dispirited— exhausted; and, throwing themselves on cellar doors and sidewalks, slept heavily, regardless of curious starers that collected around every group."

Norfolk also had to be abandoned. The navy yard was again set on fire after Federal troops took possession of the city on May 10. The big ironclad *Virginia* no longer had a base. Lee urged Johnston to run her into Yorktown to destroy Federal gunboats and transports there, but this was not done. An attempt was made to lighten her draft so she could be taken up the James, but this was found impracticable. She was blown up on May 11 to save her from capture.

Richmond was now exposed to possible attack from Union gunboats that might steam up the James to shell the city. People began leaving, and for a few days it looked as though the Confederate capital might fall into McClellan's slow but eager hands. A Cabinet meeting was held to discuss the possibility of moving the seat of government to some other place. The archives were packed up and boxes marked "War Dept., Columbia, S.C." were stacked in the halls, ready for shipment. When Lee was summoned to give his opinion about retiring to the interior, he showed visible signs of emotion and said: "Richmond must not be given up; it shall not be given up!"

Frantic efforts were made to strengthen the fortifications on the high banks of the James at Drewry's Bluff, seven miles below the city. Big guns were rushed to the spot, pilings were driven into the river bottom, and ships were sunk in the channel to serve as obstructions. On May 15, a Federal fleet,

GENERAL GEORGE B. MCCLELLAN

146

which included the heavily armored *Monitor,* came up the river. When the guns on shore poured shot and shell into the ships, the sound of their firing could clearly be heard in Richmond. Both Lee and Davis rode down to watch the battle. It did not last long, for the *Monitor* could not elevate her guns high enough to reach the batteries on the bluff, and the less well-armored vessels could not withstand the plunging fire from the Confederate guns. Slowly and sullenly, the badly battered Federal fleet steamed downriver. It was not to get past the Drewry's Bluff batteries until the end of the war.

The Chickahominy River as it looks today

The only good news received in Richmond during these gloomy days came from Jackson in the Valley. He had been defeated in his first encounter with Federal troops at Kernstown on March 23, but he had had one victory after another since. And what he was doing in the Shenandoah was weakening McClellan, for Union troops had to be sent there to cope with the redoubtable Jackson. When he beat Banks at Front Royal and Winchester on May 23 and 25, Washington was exposed to attack. More Federals had to be hurried to the Valley, depriving McClellan of the reinforcements he insisted he needed. Lee played a vital part in encouraging and guiding Jackson. The man who had earned the name Stonewall at First Manassas was then still relatively unknown and untried. Lee's support at headquarters was of great help to him. Together they took some pressure off Richmond by making Lincoln and Stanton believe that Washington was in immediate danger.

But the threat against Richmond grew worse as McClellan's army of more than 100,000 men advanced up the Peninsula. And when his troops overran the country, many civilians left their homes to go elsewhere. Among them was Mrs. Lee. Before departing from the White House, where she had been staying with Rooney's wife, Charlotte, she pinned this note to the door:

Northern soldiers, who profess to reverence Washington, forbear to desecrate the home of his first married life, the property of his wife, now owned by her descendants.

A Granddaughter of Mrs. Washington

On May 16, McClellan took over the White House estate for use as his headquarters. During the three days he remained there he lived in a tent and did not permit the house or its grounds to be occupied. He visited the church in which George and Martha Washington were married more than a century before, and, alone for a few moments, knelt down at the chancel to pray that he might serve his country as well as Washington did. Despite his reverence for the first President, however, McClellan did not hesitate to set up an enormous supply base on the historic plantation.

As McClellan got nearer and nearer to Richmond, prices rose daily in the threatened city. Scarcity of goods and dwindling confidence in Confederate currency sent coffee to $1.50 a pound, tea to $10, and shoes to $15 and $30 a pair. Prices were to go much higher. Huge stores of supplies had been destroyed when Yorktown was evacuated. Hungry citizens now regretfully remembered the great quantity of meat that had to be burned when the the army started its march up the Peninsula.

Dismal as their prospects were that spring, the Confederates had one factor working in their favor. The weather was helping them. Heavy rains swelled the streams and flooded the wide swamps around the Chickahominy River, which was Richmond's best natural defense. When McClellan's troops arrived at its shores, they found all the bridges except one at Mechanicsville either purposely destroyed or swept away by the flood waters.

Since the Federal army was straddling the river, its engineers had to build

GENERAL JOSEPH E. JOHNSTON

The uniform Lee wore as a Confederate general

bridges in order to move troops from one side to the other as needed. But high water and soft swampy ground delayed construction. On May 30, a violent rainstorm began and continued throughout the night. As a result of the downpour, the level of the streams rose even higher to paralyze the movements of the Federal army. Since Johnston had only about half as many troops as McClellan did, the chances were greater than that careful general would ordinarily take. But he had to strike before reinforcements arrived to increase the odds against him. He got ready to move on May 31. The battle which was fought on that day is called Four Oaks in the North and Seven Pines in the South. Lee had no part in it, but it was to mark a turning point in his career.

Fighting, which was supposed to begin in the morning, did not actually get under way until after noon. Then the wet swamps rang with musket fire and echoed with the deep boom of cannon. In some places, the water was so high that the troops had to wade waist-deep through it. And the Federals were putting up more resistance than had been expected. Late in the afternoon it became evident that the outcome of the battle could not be decided that day. The men in the field were ordered to stay where they were and sleep on their arms.

Lee had wanted desperately to play an active part in the fighting and had volunteered his service to Johnston the day before. But his old friend from West Point and Mexico had been vague. He had suggested that Lee ride out on the field and said that he hoped he could send in some much-needed reinforcements. As a result, Lee and Davis both witnessed the battle. Toward sunset, they must have felt that it had been poorly managed. Casualties were heavy, especially among officers, and gains had been small.

Then a courier hurried up in the gathering dusk to tell them that Johnston had been wounded—perhaps fatally.

The senior officer on the field was General Gustavus W. Smith, a younger man than Johnston or Lee. He had been ill and was showing the strain of battle. Nevertheless, Smith was in command, and they would have to see what he would do.

Before long, litter-bearers carrying Johnston approached. As the suffering but still-conscious general was about to be put into an ambulance, Davis dismounted to speak to him. He described the occasion in a letter to his wife: "He opened his eyes, smiled, and gave me his hand, said he did not know how seriously he was hurt but feared a fragment of shell had injured his spine. It was probably a shell loaded with musket balls, as there appears to be a wound of a ball in his shoulder ranging down toward the lungs. . . . His breathing was labored, but he was free from fever and seemed unshaken in his nervous system."

The ambulance drove away to take Johnston to Richmond. Smith soon appeared, and Davis and Lee tried to find out from him what his plans were for the next day. Although Smith was known for his coolness in battle, he now seemed distraught. His answers were uncertain; so were his plans.

Davis and Lee rode on in the darkness. What they discussed on that memorable ride is not known. Only Davis left any account of the historic evening, and he wrote that in the stiff and colorless prose of his *Rise and Fall of the Confederate Government*. There he said (vol. II, p. 130): "When riding from the field of battle with General Robert E. Lee . . . I informed him that he would be assigned to the command of the army . . . and that he could make his preparations as soon as he reached his quarters, as I should send the order to him as soon as I arrived at mine."

With those words, the general who had yet to fight a Civil War battle or even to have direct command of troops was precipitated into the midst of

148

things. With no preparation, Lee had to take over an army that was still involved in a half-finished battle. Then he had to cope with McClellan's big force which was now only a few miles from Richmond and in full fighting trim.

Union troops bury their dead and burn their dead horses after the Battle of Seven Pines

When the order from Davis arrived, Lee found that his new command was only "to interfere temporarily" with the general service to which he had been assigned and that it was limited to the armies of eastern Virginia and North Carolina. He also discovered that his appointment was far from popular. The Richmond *Examiner,* remembering his failure in western Virginia in 1861, now called him "evacuating Lee, who has never risked a single battle with the invader." The Richmond *Whig* was also hostile. And in the Army itself, there was opposition from those who did not know the new commander. So far as the public was concerned, Lee was merely another staff officer and not a celebrated fighter like Beauregard or Johnston.

Smith was still in command of troops on the field, but as the battle continued for the second day he showed signs of nervous collapse and soon began to develop a partial physical paralysis that may have been psychogenic. He had suffered a similar attack the year before. When Lee met him that day, Davis was with the quickly deposed general and had already told him that Lee was to take over the Army.

Lee now had much reorganization work to do, so he was probably not sorry when the rains again came in to give both armies a respite. His plans matured quickly. He wrote to Davis on June 5, correctly predicting that McClellan would now take position after position under the cover of his heavy guns. Lee proposed that the Confederate Army be put to work digging entrenchments even though he knew that "our people are opposed to work . . . all ridicule and resist it." But to work he put them, making himself so disliked that he was called "the King of Spades." But his thoughts ran far ahead of merely building defenses. "To reinforce Jackson strongly," he said, "would change the character of the war." Troops should be sent to Jackson from other Southern states. And while holding Richmond, Lee was going to "endeavor to make a diversion to bring McClellan out."

General Lee's field glasses

The Confederacy had at last found a general who could see the over-all picture and plan offensive as well as defensive action. How well the new commander would carry out his ideas had yet to be proved. The odds were heavily against him.

149

"A Bayonet Charge at Seven Pines"
by Winslow Homer.
Harper's Weekly *sent young*
Homer, who was unquestionably
the most talented artist to make
on-the-spot sketches of the war,
to Yorktown to cover the Peninsular
campaign. This spirited wood engraving
appeared on July 12, 1862.

151

THE ARMY OF NORTHERN VIRGINIA BEGINS ITS CAREER

When Lee assumed command on June 1, he issued Special Orders No. 22. In this document he called his troops the Army of Northern Virginia. He had used the term before, but never in official orders. Nor did the name have any formal standing; it was Lee's own creation.

June 10 brought word that Rooney's two-year-old son had died. And on that day Mrs. Lee came to Richmond after having been passed through the lines and treated with great courtesy by General McClellan. Her husband was not in town when she arrived, but when they did meet it was the first time they had seen each other since they had parted at Arlington nearly fourteen months before. Mrs. Lee had aged considerably and was so crippled by arthritis that she could hardly walk.

Jackson's victories in the Valley at Cross Keys and Port Republic on June 8 and 9 made the Federal Government cancel orders for 50,000 men to go to McClellan's aid. This left a large body of Union troops stranded on the north side of the Chickahominy where they had confidently been expecting reinforcements to join them. Fears for the safety of Washington were, as usual, dominating Northern military movements.

Lee now put into effect his plan for attack. On June 11 he sent an order to Jeb Stuart instructing him to take about 1000 cavalrymen and locate the right wing of McClellan's army. The expedition started out the next morning. With it went Rooney Lee and his cousin Fitz Lee. The raiding party did more than was expected of it, for once Stuart got going there was no stopping him. He rode 150 miles around McClellan's army, capturing prisoners and destroying Federal property as he went. When he returned on June 15, he had the information Lee needed.

The next day, Lee wrote to Jackson asking him to bring his 18,000 men to Richmond to take part in a massive assault on McClellan's army. Troop movements would have to be kept secret in order to be effective. Then, after starting this part of his plan in motion, Lee rode out of the city to make a reconnaissance of Fitz John Porter's position on the north side of the Chickahominy. When he spoke to Colonel A. L. Long about the Union soldiers he saw there, he referred to them as "those people." The derogatory words were becoming his customary way of describing the men and officers who had

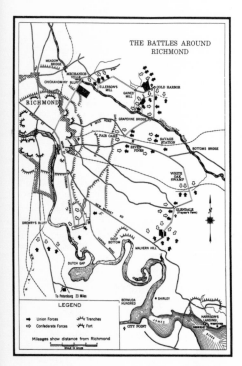

MAP OF SEVEN DAYS BATTLE

152

once been his friends but who were now his enemies. The phrase enabled him to depersonalize them, make them faceless, and reduce them to blue-clad, bloodless automatons that could be knocked down like so many toy soldiers.

His own image of himself was evidently changing at this time. On June 22, he—who had been called "the handsomest man in the Army"—wrote to his wife: "I have the same handsome hat which surmounts my gray head . . . and shields my ugly face, which is masked by a white beard as stiff and wiry as the teeth of a card. In fact, an uglier person you have never seen, and so unattractive is it to our enemies that they shoot at it whenever visible to them." Then, with sudden tenderness he added: "But though age with its snow has whitened my head, and its frosts have stiffened my limbs, my heart, you well know, is not frozen to you, and summer returns when I see you."

The armies were now gathering for the all-out attack that was to drive McClellan from the gates of Richmond. The plan for the campaign was a good one. But one thing went wrong. The always-dependable Jackson was late. A combination of circumstances had delayed him so that he was not on hand to take any part in the fighting on June 26, the date he had set for his army to arrive.

Lee's grand strategy for the Seven Days Battles was well conceived, but both he and Jackson were new at handling large masses of men. And Lee's staff was inexperienced, officers and men were still untrained, maps were poor, much uncertainty prevailed, and mistakes were made. Nevertheless, at Gaines' Mill on the second day, the Federals were driven back to the south side of the Chickahominy. The fighting went on, day after day—at Savage's Station on June 29, at Frayser's Farm on June 30, and then at Malvern Hill on July 1. Federal artillery and guns on ships in the river made the last day a costly one. But McClellan's hold on Richmond was broken, even though his army had not been destroyed. His troops were now at Harrison's Landing on the James, where they were protected by the Federal fleet. The cost of the campaign had been high—20,614 killed, wounded, and missing for the Confederates compared to 15,849 for the Federals. But even so hostile a critic as British General J. F. C. Fuller could say: "Lee deserved well of his countrymen, for it was he and he alone who saved Richmond. His conceptions were brilliant, his executions faulty and unnecessarily costly. This was due to the lack of co-operation between his subordinate commanders."

But Seven Days had been their first battle under Lee. His subordinates learned quickly, and with their help he made his newly named Army of

Confederate artilleryman, Rockingham Battery

*Stuart and his cavalry,
sketched in the field
by Frank Vizetelly*

*One of Jackson's "Foot-Cavalry"
on the way to Second Manassas*

Northern Virginia into a finely tempered weapon. Meanwhile, he and Jackson were the heroes of the day. They had broken the long series of Confederate defeats and had given the South new hope. After Forts Henry and Donelson, Pea Ridge, Shiloh, and New Orleans, the Seven Days Battles looked very good. They seemed even better when it became known that a change was being made in the Union command. John Pope was being brought in from the West to take charge of the new Army of Virginia which was to consist of the units defending Washington and the Valley.

Pope antagonized his new command when he addressed the troops on July 14. He compared the Eastern armies unfavorably with those of the West, implying that the Eastern soldiers were always on the defensive while the Western fighters sought out the enemy to attack them. He made himself even more unpopular with the Confederates by issuing orders that placed civilians in war areas in great jeopardy.

Another shift of command in the Union Army which showed that McClellan's stock was rapidly depreciating in Washington was the appointment of General Henry W. Halleck as Lincoln's military adviser. He, too, had been brought from the West. Halleck was so well informed in military affairs that he was called "Old Brains," but he was so confused and so dilatory in putting his ideas into action that his new exalted position was to be more of an asset to Richmond than to Washington.

The major problem now facing both armies was to bring them back to strength. This was easy for the North to do since it had a far greater population than the South. A call for 300,000 more Union volunteers had gone out on July 1, and a bounty was being offered for enlistment. But the men who had died in the defense of Richmond could not be replaced. The odds against the Confederacy, already great, were now increasing. But Lee, realizing that time was against him, began to plan on taking the offensive against the growing might of the Federal Army. First Manassas and the battles around Richmond had been defensive. Now, for the first time, the Confederates in the Eastern theater of war would launch a major attack.

154

The situation was an extraordinary one, for the Federal Army was widely separated; McClellan's big force was still on the Peninsula; Burnside had some troops at Fort Monroe; and Pope, who remained in Washington until the end of the month, was assembling nearly 50,000 men north of Culpeper. If these armies were brought together, they would have more than twice as many troops as Lee had at his disposal.

Despite the fact that Jackson had not done particularly well in the Seven Days Battles, Lee chose him to spearhead the attack on Pope. After a council of war in Davis' home in Richmond on July 13, the three leaders emerged from the house. A Confederate captain who saw them wrote: "Lee was elegantly dressed in full uniform, sword and sash, spotless boots, beautiful spurs and [was] by far the most magnificent man I ever saw. The highest type of the Cavalier class to which by blood and rearing he belongs. Jackson, on the other hand, was a typical Roundhead. He was poorly dressed . . . though his clothes were made of good material. His cap was . . . pulled down over one eye, much stained by weather and without insignia. His coat was closely buttoned up to his chin and had upon the collar the stars and wreath of a general. His shoulders were stooped and one shoulder was lower than the other, and his coat showed signs of much exposure."

Jackson rode northwest to Gordonsville to set up his headquarters there. When Lee sent him reinforcements later in the month, he had about 24,000 men in his command. On August 7, his spies informed him that Pope was heading south toward Culpeper. Jackson went north to meet him, ran into the advance of his army at Cedar Mountain on the ninth, and won a quick victory which startled the North.

Meanwhile, Lee was pinned down near Richmond keeping watch on McClellan. Instinct told him that the army on the Peninsula was no longer a threat, but he had to wait until he could be sure. On August 13, matters came to a head. Lee knew that Burnside had taken about 12,000 troops from Fort Monroe to Fredericksburg. Now he learned that this force had gone on from there to join Pope. And on the same day a deserter brought word that McClellan had abandoned the Peninsula and was moving men and supplies by ship to the Potomac.

After sending Longstreet with ten brigades to Jackson, Lee left Richmond on August 15, bound for Gordonsville. On the way, he passed Hickory Hill, where his wife was staying in the country, but it was early morning, and she was asleep, so he did not see her. He soon met Jackson and went into conference with him, Longstreet, and Stuart. Together they planned the whirlwind campaign that was to be known as Second Manassas because its climactic battle was fought on the same ground as the first.

SECOND MANASSAS

Lee's plans were necessarily fluid at this time, but one thing was certain: he had to attack Pope before McClellan's troops could arrive. Then the plans he drew up for such an attack were accidentally betrayed when one of Stuart's officers was captured while carrying a letter giving the details to Stuart. And Stuart himself was nearly taken prisoner by Federal cavalry at Verdiersville. He got away, but without his cloak and famous plumed hat.

When Pope read the captured battle plans, he pulled his army back to the north side of the Rappahannock. Lee went toward him, crossing the Rapidan on August 20, but he then lost two days trying to pass the closely guarded Rappahannock. On the twenty-second, Stuart got permission to ride around Pope's army to raid the railroad behind it and bring back information.

MAJOR GENERAL JOHN POPE, *photographed early in the war*

155

Jackson's men pillaging Union supplies at Manassas Junction. Note canned food.

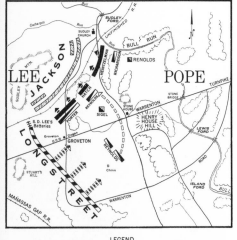

MAP OF SECOND MANASSAS

Rooney Lee was with Stuart when his hard-riding troopers hit Catlett's Station in the midst of a thunderstorm. The raid was a complete success, for among other booty, Stuart got Pope's best uniform, his personal baggage, and —most important of all—his papers. Both Lee and Pope now knew each other's plans, an extraordinary circumstance in warfare.

But Lee acted first. Breaking an accepted rule of tactics, he divided his army, and on August 25 sent Jackson and Stuart on a long swing west of Pope's widely spread forces to come east again through Thoroughfare Gap to attack Manassas Junction. Jackson's "foot cavalry" marched more than fifty miles through the mountains. When they reached Bristoe Station they were between Pope's army and Washington. News of their whereabouts got to the Federals when a locomotive engineer dashed through them under fire to run his train to the Alexandria terminal. Union authorities there notified the War Department that the dreaded Confederates were only 26 miles from the capital. Before anything could be done about it, Jackson's hungry men fell upon the rich Federal stores at Manassas Junction on August 27 and had a great feast.

Lee and Longstreet were following the route Jackson had taken and were a day's march behind him. On the morning of the twenty-seventh, Lee was riding far ahead of the column, attended only by a few officers. Suddenly a quartermaster galloped back, shouting that Federal cavalry were coming up the road. The officers spread out to protect their commander. Then the Union horsemen approached, stopped, and thinking that the Confederates were the head of a long column turned around and rode off. It was a narrow escape for Lee—and at a crucial time.

At 3 A.M. on August 28, Jackson moved from Manassas Junction to Groveton. Later that day, Lee was approaching Thoroughfare Gap. When the first troops entered the pass, shots were heard. A Federal division (Rickett's) was posted there to stop them. The rocky walls of the gorge sent back resounding echoes. One observer said that "a gun fired in its depths gave forth roars fit to bring down the skies." Lee rode up to the top of a hill west of the Gap to examine the terrain with his field glasses. John Esten Cooke, who was with him, said that he "was vividly impressed by the air of unmoved calmness which marked his countenance and demeanor. Nothing in the expression of his face, and no hurried movement, indicated excitement or anxiety. Here, as on many other occasions, Lee impressed the writer as an individual gifted with the most surprising faculty of remaining cool and unaffected in the midst of circumstances calculated to arouse the most phlegmatic. After reconnoitering for some moments without moving, he closed his glass slowly, as though he were buried in reflection, and deliberating at his leisure, and, walking back slowly to his horse, mounted and rode down the hill.''

Lee then used the trick he had learned at Cerro Gordo in 1847. Troops were sent north of the Gap to attack the Federals in the rear. Their strength was found to be small, and they were quickly driven away. The Confederate columns poured through the gap. On the afternoon of the next day they joined Jackson's troops, already under heavy attack in the hills west of the fought-over field of First Manassas. When Longstreet's men went into position at Jackson's right, the Army of Northern Virginia, which had been dangerously split apart for three days, was together again.

The great fighting team of Lee, Jackson, and Longstreet was about to startle the world with a series of brilliant campaigns that would hold off the much more powerful Federal army for eight long months. Jackson's and Longstreet's lines stretched for more than four miles along an unfinished railroad embankment and cut that ran from Sudley Church to the old Warrenton–Alexandria Road. Pope had trouble locating his elusive Confederate opponents. Now he knew where they were, although he did not learn until hours after the arrival of Longstreet's men that they, too, were facing him.

The battle on August 29 and 30 brought out the difference between Jackson and Longstreet. Jackson was all fire and dash and eagerness to attack. Longstreet was a brave fighter, but he was slow and cautious, unwilling to take chances unless he knew the odds and could calculate the probable results. Lee himself was more like Jackson than Longstreet, but the three men made a superb team, for Longstreet's caution balanced the other two men's willingness to take risks.

On the twenty-ninth, Lee got a sample of Longstreet's reluctance to move until he felt sure that the moment was ripe for attack. Several times that day, Lee suggested that Longstreet advance, because the Federals were concentrating their fire on Jackson's section of the line. When Longstreet demurred, Lee was obviously disappointed, but he believed in giving his generals a free hand. Not until the next afternoon, when Jackson's men had long been under heavy fire, did Longstreet move. Then, sensing the exact moment (as did Lee), he sent his men into action. It was like striking a shaky structure that has already begun to totter. When the Confederates swept across the field, the Federals, in a curious re-enactment of the battle that had been fought there thirteen months before, broke and ran. And they fled down the same roads and crossed the same bridges that McDowell's men had used the year before.

When a doctor who had just returned from a tour of the corpse-strewn battlefield told Jackson, "General, this day has been won by nothing but stark and stern fighting," the God-fearing commander replied: "No, it has been won by nothing but the blessing and protection of Providence."

Robert, Jr., had fought with Jackson's artillery at Manassas. On the second day, after long and continuous action, the cannoneers were ordered to cease firing and were leaning on their guns when Robert saw his father ride up. The general reined in Traveller about fifteen feet away but paid no attention to the gunners. Robert asked his captain to present him to his father. The boy had not had a chance to wash for four days; his clothes were ragged and stained with red dust, and his face and hands were black with powder. The captain said: "General, here is someone who wants to speak to you."

Lee, seeing a powder-stained artilleryman standing with sponge-staff in hand, said: "Well, my man, what can I do for you?"

His son replied: "Why, General, don't you know me?" Robert reported

Lee watching the fighting at Thorofare Gap. From a drawing made by A. R. Waud.

THOMAS JONATHAN JACKSON

157

that his father was amused at his appearance and was glad to see him safe and well.

On August 31, Lee was slightly injured by an accident. It had been raining, and he was dressed in clumsy rubber clothing. Traveller shied while Lee was dismounted. In trying to reach for the bridle, the general tripped and fell, landing on his hands, breaking a small bone in one of them and spraining the other. A surgeon had to put both hands in splints. For some time, Lee could not use the reins and had to be carried around in an army ambulance, much to his annoyance.

Jackson swept on to Chantilly where both Federal commanders, Phil Kearny and I. I. Stevens, were killed on September 1. After Chantilly, Halleck ordered the Union forces to fall back to the defenses of Alexandria and Washington. The Second Manassas campaign was over. Like the first one fought on that field, it was a complete victory for the Confederates. But the cost for both armies was high. Of the 73,000 Federals engaged, 14,462 were killed, wounded, or missing, while 9474 of the 55,000 Confederates were casualties.

Pope was removed from command immediately after Chantilly. The British biographer of Jackson, Colonel G. F. R. Henderson, says of the discredited Union commander: "As a tactician Pope was incapable. As a strategist he lacked imagination, except in his dispatches. His horizon was limited, and he measured the capacity of his adversaries by his own. . . . He had no conception that his adversaries would cheerfully accept great risks to achieve great ends; he had never dreamt of a general who would deliberately divide his army, or of one who would make 56 miles in two marches."

LEE INVADES MARYLAND

Lincoln reluctantly put McClellan back in command, first of the defenses of Washington and then of Pope's forces, which were merged into the Army of the Potomac. Most of the Cabinet opposed the idea of giving power to McClellan again, but the President had offered the post to Burnside, who had refused it, and now, with the Confederates almost at the gates of Washington, someone had to take firm control of the Army.

But Lee's troops were in no condition to storm the Federal capital. Thinned out by fighting, hungry, short of shoes and ammunition, they now needed supplies more than anything else. It was late in the summer, and corn was ripe on the stalks. They could subsist on that and find plenty of it wherever they went. The time was propitious for an invasion of Maryland, Lee told Davis on September 3. The Army was not properly equipped for such a move, but it could not afford to remain idle. A bold invasion of the North would draw the Union Army away from Richmond. Ammunition could be forwarded to the Confederates while they were on the way. And march they did, starting out on the day Lee wrote to Davis. The blood was hardly dry on the wounds of those who were well enough to go along when the columns swung north. About 55,000 Confederates crossed the Potomac on September 5 and 6 and then trudged through the rich Maryland farm country that had yet to experience the horrors of war.

Maryland was a Southern state which had been held to the Union, many believed, by force. It was also thought that the Marylanders would now rise and come to the assistance of their fellow Southerners. But the state's well-fed farmers and prosperous shopkeepers took one look at Lee's ragged and shoeless veterans and decided that they wanted nothing to do with them. On September 7, Lee wrote to Davis that despite "individual expressions of kindness . . . and general sympathy" he did not anticipate any general uprising of the people.

A Confederate sharpshooter

158

The next day he drew up a printed circular which told the people of Maryland why the Army had come; it also said that it would help them regain their rights. The same day he wrote a letter to Davis which does not sound like Lee. It is the only instance of his departing from the role of professional soldier. In it he suggested that "the Government of the Confederate States . . . propose to that of the United States the recognition of our independence." One of Lee's newfound Maryland friends may have persuaded him to write this political message. And Lee, eager to end an internecine war which was painful to him, may have been willing to break a lifetime of reticence on such affairs to speak out on this occasion. Nothing came of his suggestion, and he never ventured into politics again.

The entire world was watching the Confederacy's struggle for existence at this time, and there was a good chance that European nations would have recognized the Richmond government if the invasion of Maryland had been successful. But luck, which had been with Lee at Manassas, was beginning to turn against him at this time. His plan of action was daring and original. Knowing that ammunition and supplies had to be sent up the Shenandoah Valley to reach him en route, he had to make sure that the Federal forces at Harpers Ferry and Martinsburg were driven out. To accomplish this, he divided his army into four parts. Longstreet and D. H. Hill were to make a drive on Hagerstown; Jackson was to swing around in a wide circle through Williamsport and Martinsburg to approach Harpers Ferry from the west, while McLaws and Walker were to come in from the east to occupy the heights along the Potomac that overlook the former Federal arsenal. Meanwhile, Stuart's cavalry was to screen these well-coordinated movements from Federal observation by staying between the Confederate and Union armies. It was an elaborate and well-conceived plan, but an accident, like the two before Manassas, revealed the details to the Federals. Copies of the intended troop movements were sent to division commanders on September 9 (Special Order No. 191). An extra one of these, wrapped around three cigars and addressed to D. H. Hill, was found by the Federals on the thirteenth when they occupied the camp which Hill's men had just vacated. It was immediately given to McClellan and was

Stuart's cavalry on their way to the Potomac in the campaign to invade Maryland. Sketched near Poolesville by A. R. Waud.

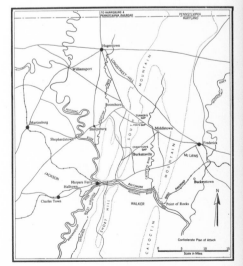

Lee's plan for invading Maryland

159

This photograph, taken by Alexander Gardner while the Battle of Antietam was in progress, was long believed to show the smoke of the guns (at right). Recent research, however, indicates that it was taken near McClellan's headquarters, where there was no fighting. The Union artillery at the left is not engaged, and the men at the right are sitting on the ground.

identified as authentic. He made use of the information, but characteristically did not begin to move until the next day.

Even so, he moved fast enough to make trouble for Lee. With McClellan in pursuit, the three passes over South Mountain had to be defended. Intensive attacks in the narrow gaps enabled the Federals to break through. At 8 P.M. on September 14, Lee was ready to abandon the campaign. He started to order his commanders to return to Virginia. A conference with Longstreet, D. H. Hill, and John B. Hood confirmed him in this decision. Then a courier arrived with the news that Jackson expected Harpers Ferry to surrender the next day. At 11:15 P.M. Lee countermanded the orders to retreat. The various armies were to converge on Sharpsburg, a village between the Potomac River and Antietam Creek where there was a long ridge that could be defended.

Harpers Ferry fell the next day just as Jackson had predicted. About 12,000 prisoners, 13,000 arms, 73 guns, and hundreds of wagons were taken with it. Leaving A. P. Hill's division behind to settle details of the surrender, Jackson hurried north to meet Lee.

That same morning, Longstreet at Sharpsburg saw "the blue uniforms of the Federals . . . among the trees that crowned the heights on the eastern bank of the Antietam. The number increased, and larger and larger grew the field of blue until it seemed to stretch as far as the eye could see, and from the tops of the mountains down to the edges of the stream gathered the great army of McClellan. It was an awe-inspiring spectacle as this grand force settled down in sight of the Confederates."

More Union troops kept arriving on the field on the sixteenth, which was a gray and somber-looking day. Only the occasional bark of artillery indicated that the men in gray and in blue were enemies. The Confederates began the shooting, but the Union gunners did most of it, for they had shot and powder to spare, while the Confederates had to conserve theirs for the close-up work which they knew would soon come.

Jackson rode into Sharpsburg shortly after noon and went into a council of war at Lee's headquarters. The situation was discouraging, for the odds were heavily against them. Neither Lee nor McClellan knew just how many troops the other had, but records show that there were about 87,000 well-equipped men in the Army of the Potomac against 41,000 poorly outfitted, foot-weary soldiers in the Army of Northern Virginia. Yet neither Lee nor Jackson seemed disturbed; they were used to fighting against odds.

On the afternoon of the sixteenth, 12,000 Federals commanded by Hooker crossed Antietam Creek north of Sharpsburg. Foreseeing that the first Union attack would come from that direction, Lee had placed Jackson and Hood there. A brief attempt was made to get the Union assault under way before dark, but a halt had to be called when darkness set in. At midnight Hooker was reinforced by Mansfield, while Sumner's 2nd Corps was brought up later.

There was mist over the field at dawn, but the sun drove it away as the Union assault began. Hooker and Mansfield sent their troops in in a great wave of blue which struck the Confederate lines and kept going through two patches of wood into a 30-acre field of ripe corn. When Union canister blasted the field, "every stalk of corn . . . was cut as closely as could have been done with a knife." And the Confederates who had been concealed in the green leaves went down, falling in rows just as they had stood in ranks. But Union casualties were also high. Among them was General Mansfield, mortally wounded.

Then, after a lull, Sumner's troops attacked. Jackson was waiting for Sedgwick's division with his men hidden behind rock outcroppings at the edge of the North Woods. They slaughtered the Union troops and badly wounded Sedgwick himself. The left of Sumner's line hit D. H. Hill's troops, who were strung out along a sunken road that received the name "Bloody Lane" because Confederate corpses were strewn so thickly there that they covered the soil beneath them.

Action then switched to the southern end of the field when Burnside's blue-clad troops tried to cross Antietam Creek on a stone bridge that acted like a bottleneck as masses of men crowded into its narrow roadway. Yet the stream could easily have been forded—and eventually was. When Burnside's troops reached the outskirts of Sharpsburg, it looked as though they would sweep everything before them. But A. P. Hill's division appeared at the crucial moment to save the day. They had come up from Harpers Ferry after marching more than seventeen miles in seven hours. After they stopped the Union onslaught, the fighting ceased. The day had been the bloodiest of the war, with heavy casualties on both sides.

The Confederate commanders met at Lee's headquarters during the night. They expected the Union attack to be continued in the morning, but McClellan had had enough. Neither army had won a victory; neither was in condition to fight any more. The Confederates quickly withdrew to Virginia. McClellan, much criticized for not pursuing them, was removed from command and replaced by Burnside. Lee's attempt to invade the North had failed, yet he was to try again at Gettysburg less than a year later.

Both armies, bled white by the terrible battle (called Antietam in the North and Sharpsburg in the South), rested for weeks while they tried to rebuild their strength. Many stragglers returned to Lee's army, and the new conscription laws helped to fill the ranks. Lee reorganized the command with Jackson and Longstreet as lieutenant generals, each in charge of a corps of four divisions. By late autumn the Army had about 78,000 men—more than it had had for the invasion of Maryland when Lee started north with only 55,000 men.

Lee's hands, hurt in the accidental fall at Second Manassas, were slow in healing. He was not able to hold a pen until mid-October. And on the twentieth of that month, his beloved daughter Annie died in North Carolina at the age of twenty-three.

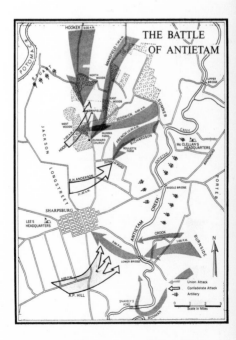

THE BATTLE OF ANTIETAM

Fredericksburg as seen from the Union side. From a drawing by A. R. Waud.

FREDERICKSBURG

Winter was setting in, and it seemed unlikely that there would be any serious fighting until spring. Bad roads and weather made the movements of large bodies of troops so difficult that the armies ordinarily went into hibernation. But the Army of the Potomac's new general was being pushed into action by the high command in Washington. Ambrose E. Burnside had not wanted his new post with its enormous responsibilities, nor did he feel qualified for it. Although he had been trained at West Point, he was not suited for command decisions. Well-intentioned, able enough in non-military fields, he was hopelessly outmatched by the great Lee, Jackson, Stuart and Longstreet team which was now at the height of its powers.

Lee would have been content to spend the winter at the North Anna River, about halfway between Fredericksburg and Richmond, but his scouts informed him that the Federals were crossing the Potomac and moving southward. This was before Burnside took command. On October 28, Lee again divided his army, sent Jackson to guard the Valley, and went to Culpeper with Longstreet. There he learned that Burnside had replaced McClellan on November 9. Lee alerted Jackson and awaited developments. When he was told on the seventeenth that Union forces were advancing on Fredericksburg and that several Federal warships were in nearby Aquia Creek, he started moving troops to the Rappahannock. It was not impossible that the Federals might be planning to fight a winter battle, especially with a new commander in charge.

When Lee arrived at Fredericksburg on November 20, the advance guard of the Army of the Potomac was already in camp on the heights along the Rappahannock's north shore. The pleasant little city on the south shore was between the two armies. The Federals were threatening to shell the town and

162

were advising its civilians to leave their homes. Most of them were evacuated on the twenty-second in a rainstorm.

Days passed while the Federals did nothing. Lee did not know it, but Burnside was awaiting the arrival of pontoon boats which he needed to bridge the river. A combination of stupidity, error, poor coordination, red tape, and bad weather was delaying them. On November 29 Jackson, summoned from the Valley, rode into Fredericksburg in the midst of a snowstorm. The war's only major battle to be fought in dead of winter was now rapidly shaping up.

An understanding of the setting is essential for following the action. According to Burnside's battle plan, artillery would be massed on the ridge north of the river. Under the protection of its fire, engineers would build pontoon bridges at each end of Fredericksburg, plus three more about a mile downstream. Troops would cross on these to assault the Confederates, some of whom were concealed in buildings along the shore while thousands more were stretched out in a long line on the heights behind the town. The Confederate position was so strong that only a commander with a vast army and practically inexhaustible supplies would even think of assaulting it. Burnside had both. He also had so little imagination that he was apparently unable to foresee what would happen to his men.

During these troubled days of waiting to find out what the Federals would do, Lee received word that his infant granddaughter had died. She was the second child Rooney and Charlotte had lost, and the personal tragedy of her death, coming at this time, deeply disturbed the general who was about to watch thousands of men die on the shores of the Rappahannock.

A heavy mist settled on the river during the night of December 10–11. Masked by the white fog, Federal engineers were busily at work long before dawn trying to get their pontoons in place. Downstream the work was fairly easy, and there they made rapid progress. But the bridges under construction at either end of the town had to be built under the deadly fire of Barksdale's Mississippians. Man after man was picked off by their rifles, and as the mist began to thin, work on the pontoons became even more dangerous.

About 10 A.M. nearly 150 Federal guns on the north shore went into action. They sent thousands of shots crashing into the town to tear buildings apart and set them on fire. Smoke from these fires was added to the mist hanging over the river to impair visibility still further. But the heavy bombardment had little effect on Barksdale's men, who were hidden in cellars or rifle pits. Finally, about sixty Union soldiers were put into one of the pontoon boats and rowed quickly across the river to establish a bridgehead. Others soon followed. They spread through the streets to drive Barksdale's sharpshooters out. It took hours of house-to-house fighting to clear the town, and night set in before the job was done. Meanwhile, the pontoon bridges were completed and were ready for the main body of troops to cross. No attempt to put the men on the Fredericksburg side was made until the next morning (December 12), when another heavy mist concealed their movements. It took a whole day to get the vast host across.

Troops were still passing over the bridges when December 13 dawned chill and damp with another heavy mist. More than 80,000 Union soldiers were now assembled on the south shore, ready for attack. About 78,000 Confederates awaited them on the heights beyond the town.

Lee had already inspected most of the 7-mile line with more than 300 pieces of artillery in place. After another hurried tour with Jackson, he took a position on a hill south of Marye's Heights, where Longstreet's men were waiting along a sunken road behind a stone wall. Still farther south, Jackson's troops were stretched out for miles, the last of them just hurried into line.

GENERAL AMBROSE E. BURNSIDE

163

Jackson, who was ordinarily careless about dress, appeared that morning in a fine uniform. "It was some of my friend Stuart's doings," he muttered when teased about it.

About 10 A.M., the sun began to drive away the mist. The Confederates were soon able to get their first glimpse of the mighty army on the plain below them. Bronze cannon and bayonets flashed in the sunlight as thousands of men marched slowly forward in ranks with regimental flags flying. The first attack was on Jackson's line, where Stuart's cavalry was covering the far right. His artillery commander, young Major John Pelham, ran two guns forward to fire down the length of the advancing Federal line. Union artillery replied, knocking out one of his guns. He shifted the other from place to place as soon as the Union gunners got his range. Stuart finally had to order him back. Lee, watching from the hilltop, said admiringly "It is glorious to see such courage in one so young" and called him "the gallant Pelham" in his report.

The Federal lines pressed on until they were within range of Jackson's artillery posted along the ridge. Then the Confederate guns spoke out, sending down shot and shell that blasted holes in the Union ranks. The blue lines broke and reformed and broke again. After heavy losses, the Federals found a wooded swamp, now frozen over, through which they could attack. By using this, they broke through the Confederates' front line and threatened to keep going. Early's division came up to plug the gap. The blue flood reversed itself and began flowing back through the frozen swamp. It was at this moment that Lee, watching the scene from his observation post on the hill, said: "It is well that war is so terrible—we should grow too fond of it!"

To his left, where Longstreet's men were posted on the steep slopes of Marye's Hill, the Federals were having a bad time. They had come through the town and had tried to attack the troops behind the stone wall halfway up the heights. The Confederate ranks were four or five deep there with the men in the rear loading and passing rifles to the front to be fired with the rapid efficiency of a machine gun. Their firepower mowed down the advancing blue-coats until the ground was literally covered with their bodies. Confederate rifles along the stone wall and Confederate batteries higher up the hill poured deadly fire into wave after wave of blue. To send more men into that smoothly working, death-dealing machine was senseless—but they were sent. And they died, row on row.

The heavy Federal guns across the river hurled shot and shell into the Confederates on the ridge behind Fredericksburg. One of their massive shells buried itself in the soil near the spot where Lee was standing, but it did not explode. And later in the day, a big Parrott gun burst into pieces about fifty feet away from him. One of the huge slabs of iron rose into the air and landed on the ground just beyond him.

The short winter day ended early, and with it the terrible slaughter ceased. The wounded cried out untended all through the night, and in the cold black sky above them the shimmering curtains of aurora borealis burned away the darkness. Dawn was long in coming. When it did come, most of the Union Army had withdrawn to the river and was in no condition to renew the attack. The next day, when it marched back over the river, it left behind 12,653 casualties—more than twice as many as the Confederates' 5377. Fredericksburg had been Lee's easiest battle. He was now at the peak of his career. The noted British military historian, Sir Frederick Maurice, writing in 1925, said: "Lee's campaigns of 1862 are . . . supreme in conception, and have not been surpassed, as examples of strategy . . . by any other commander in history."

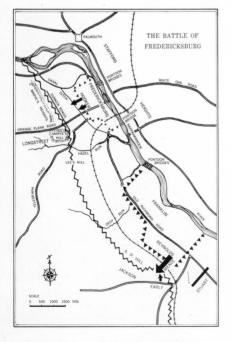

MAP OF FREDERICKSBURG

Building a pontoon bridge under fire as Union batteries (at right) drive sharpshooters from Fredericksburg

Confederates hold Marye's Hill against a massed Union assault

The Union bombardment of Fredericksburg as seen from the Confederate side

THIS MORTAL FRAME

The year 1863 was to be a turning point for Lee and the Confederacy. It began well for both, although the winter was so severe that Lee often commented on it in letters to his family. Early in February he said: "We are in a liquid state. . . . Up to our knees in mud, and what is worse, on short rations for men and beasts. This keeps me miserable. I am willing to starve myself but cannot bear my men or horses to be pinched." Later that month he wrote: "We have mud up to our eyes."

Burnside, too, was struggling with the mud. On January 20 he made an ill-advised attempt to put his army across the Rappahannock again, this time by using routes about eight miles west of Fredericksburg. Rain set in during the night and kept falling heavily for the next two days. Men, animals, wagons, and artillery floundered so helplessly in the mud that the expedition had to be called off. (It became known as the Mud March.) This fiasco finished Burnside; he was replaced by Joseph Hooker on January 26. The Army of the Potomac was having trouble with its commanders. And "Fighting Joe" Hooker, aggressive and ambitious, was to prove no abler than his predecessors.

On March 9, when there was a promise of spring in the air, Lee wrote to his wife: "As for my health, I suppose I shall never be better." This was an ironic but sadly true prediction, for in less than two weeks he was to meet a major threat to his well-being. He went on to say: "Old age and sorrow are wearing me away, and constant anxiety and labour, day and night, leave me but little repose." To add to his troubles at this time, young Major John Pelham, whose brilliant artillery work at Fredericksburg had endeared him to Lee, was mortally wounded on March 17 in a minor battle at Kelly's Ford.

Soon after this, Lee received a copy of the *Illustrated London News* containing portraits of him and Jackson engraved from sketches which that paper's artist correspondent, Frank Vizetelly, had made in the field. The accompanying text, reprinted from the *Times,* said that "General Lee . . . wears his years well and strikes you as the incarnation of health and endurance." Lee sent the paper to his wife on March 21 with this amused comment: "I send you . . . a likeness of your husband that has come from beyond the big water. He is a hard-favoured man and has a very rickety position on his pins. I hope his beard will please you, for the artist seems to have laid himself out on that. We are poor judges of ourselves, and I cannot therefore pronounce as to his success. But I can say that in his portrait of Gen'l Jackson he has failed to give his fine candid and frank expression, so charming to see and so attractive to the beholder."

A few days later, Lee's health suddenly took a turn for the worse. On March 27 he said in a letter to Mrs. Lee: "I have felt so unwell . . . as not to be able to go anywhere. I have been suffering from a heavy cold which I hope is passing away. The weather has been wretched." He wrote to her again on April 5 to say: "I am suffering with a bad cold as I told you, and was threatened, the doctors thought, with some malady which must be dreadful if it resembles its name, but which I have forgot." The doctors had ordered him to be taken to a private house near Fredericksburg where he could rest in a comfortable bed and be kept warm.

Lee may have forgotten the name of his malady, but his description of

Britain sees Lee on June 4, 1864, when this engraved portrait appeared there

THE "BOOTED-AND-SPURRED" PORTRAIT OF 1863

This photograph, the finest of Lee as a soldier, was taken in the Richmond studio of Minnis and Cowell some time in 1863, when Lee was fifty-six. A wood engraving of it was published in The Illustrated London News *on June 4, 1864. Harper's* Weekly *printed a poorer copy on July 2, 1864.*

The London paper called Lee "one of the greatest soldiers of this age." Harper's, after admitting that Lee was "unquestionably a consummate master of the art of war," wrote unfavorably about him—as was to be expected. Both articles said that Lee was plain in dress, and that he wore an ordinary black felt hat with a narrow strip of gold around it, with a brigadier's coat that had three stars on the collar.

Lee and Jackson sketched in the field by Frank Vizetelly. These engraved portraits appeared in The Illustrated London News *on February 14, 1863.*

its symptoms give us a good idea of what it was. In the same letter he wrote: "I have not been so very sick, though have suffered a good deal of pain in my chest, back, and arms. It came on in paroxysms. . . . But they have passed off, I hope. Some fever remains, and I am enjoying the sensation of a complete saturation of my system with quinine. The doctors are very attentive and kind and have examined my lungs, heart, circulation, etc. I believe they pronounce me tolerable sound. They have been tapping me all over like an old steam boiler before condemning it."

The pain in the chest, back, and arms, his subsequent medical history, and the manner of his death twelve years later indicate that Lee had probably had a mild heart attack during the fourth week of March 1863. Douglas Southall Freeman in *R. E. Lee* (Appendix IV–7 to the fourth volume) gives the pertinent medical details and a diagnosis of the case by a modern doctor. Medical science in 1863 was not far enough advanced for the Army surgeons who attended Lee to know just what was wrong, but they did call it an "inflammation of the heart-sac"—which at least defined the location of the ailment.

At Chancellorsville, now less than a month away, the head of the Army of Northern Virginia was still a sick man, although his illness did not affect his skill as a commander in that well-fought battle. Yet for him to have to undergo the hardships of an active campaign at that time was asking for trouble. He was lucky to survive the experience, for he was then in as much danger of dying from his own internal disabilities as he was from bullets and shells.

But there was no putting off the contest, because Hooker was eager to prove his prowess against the Confederate leadership that had beaten his predecessors. And the Army of the Potomac, now built up to a fighting strength of more than 130,000 men, was considerably larger than its Confederate opponent, for Longstreet had been called away with two of his divisions to defend the area near Suffolk, Virginia. The populous North could

168

ROBERT EDMUND LEE,

COMMANDER-IN-CHIEF OF THE CONFEDERATE FORCES.

[W. B. CAMPBELL, Engraver.] [FROM A PHOTOGRAPH BY REES, TAKEN TEN YEARS AGO.]

The Southern Illustrated News, *published in Richmond during part of the war, devotes the cover of its January 17, 1863, issue to a portrait of Lee engraved locally from a photograph "taken ten years ago" as it candidly admits. Below, a later issue uses a more recent portrait of "Virginia's greatest living son."*

easily raise more troops, but the South was running out of able-bodied men and horses. The Army of Northern Virginia at this time numbered about 60,000. Lee was up against the greatest odds he had faced in any major battle.

When Lincoln appointed Hooker, he had many reservations about him as a top commander, reservations which he expressed to Hooker in a remarkably frank letter. He criticized him for having secretly worked against Burnside at Fredericksburg; he also said he knew that Hooker had stated that the country needed a dictator. After reminding the new commander that "only those generals who gain successes can set up dictators," Lincoln said he would risk the dictatorship. And in closing, he warned Hooker to beware of rashness. At Chancellorsville, oddly enough, rashness was what Hooker lacked most. He could have used some of it there.

Lee had only a few weeks to recover as well as he could from the most debilitating ailment that had ever struck him. Neither he nor his doctors, of course, knew that his heart had been permanently injured. On April 19 he told his wife: "I am feeble and worthless and can do but little." Five days later, however, he said that his health was improving. But he also said: "I can write to no one and feel oppressed by what I have to undergo for the first time in my life."

By his own testimony, he was in no condition to fight a great battle in a confusing terrain against a resolute force that outnumbered him so greatly. Longstreet was still away on April 29, when Hooker's army began crossing the Rappahannock as Burnside's had done less than five months before. This time, however, the crossings were made at points above and below Fredericksburg. That war-torn little city was again to see some of the fighting, but the heart of the conflict was to be about eight miles west near a large country house owned by the Chancellor family.

The October 17, 1863, issue

*The last council of war
between Lee and Jackson
on the night of May 1, 1863*

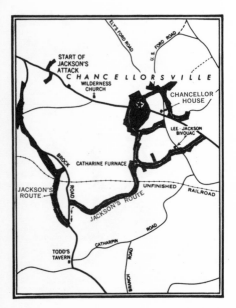

MAP OF CHANCELLORSVILLE

CHANCELLORSVILLE

Hooker's battle plan was a good one. The plans of most of the commanders of the Army of the Potomac usually were. Their failure came from faulty execution. Hooker's main force was to go around Lee's army to the west and then swing back to fall upon it from that direction. Meanwhile, a smaller body under General John Sedgwick was to cross the Rappahannock below Fredericksburg and make a diversionary attack in the east. Some troops were to remain in reserve so they could be sent in wherever they were most needed.

Starting on April 27, three corps of the Union Army marched northwest while Sedgwick's two corps went southeast. The next morning, the Confederates holding Fredericksburg could see Sedgwick's men building pontoon bridges below the town. Troops crossed on these and took shelter under the high banks on the south side where they were protected against artillery fire.

Early on the twenty-ninth, Jackson's scouts brought him word that large numbers of Federal troops were crossing the Rappahannock much farther west under cover of a morning fog. Lee had left the house where he had stayed while ill and had spent the night in a field tent. He was awake when a courier from Jackson arrived. He greeted the officer cheerfully and said: "I thought I heard firing and was beginning to think it was about time one of you young fellows would be here to tell me what it was all about." He then told the courier that he would meet Jackson at the front.

Longstreet was miles away in Suffolk with two of his divisions, and it was unlikely that he could be brought back in time to take part in a battle that was rapidly shaping up. It was obvious that Hooker was not going to repeat Burnside's error of concentrating everything on a frontal attack on Fredricksburg's strongly held heights. Since it was still too soon for Lee to figure out just what Hooker was trying to do, he watched and waited.

Stuart's scouts kept him informed of the Union Army's movements west of Fredericksburg. It soon became evident that the various Federal units were marching east on roads that would converge at Chancellorsville. After a brief recurrence of his illness on the morning of April 30, Lee was able to concentrate his attention on the Chancellorsville area. He had sent R. H. Anderson there; he now ordered him to build breastworks in the woods. The war was becoming sophisticated; this was the first time Lee had built field defenses before a battle. The day of sending men out to fight in solid ranks without any kind of protection was passing. Lee spent the next morning near Fredricksburg watching Sedgwick's movements and then rode toward Chancellorsville, where he met Jackson. Both expected the Union Army, with which they had already exchanged shots, to make a determined assault on the thinly held Confederate lines. To their surprise, it did not. For some inexplicable reason, "Fighting" Joe Hooker had lost his nerve. He ordered his forward-moving columns to halt, decided to take up a defensive position, built elaborate field fortifications in the thick forests of the Wilderness, and waited for the Confederates to attack.

Nothing could have suited Lee and Jackson better. They met on the night of May 1–2 and planned the next day's action. Fitzhugh Lee's scouts had found out that the far right of the Federal lines could be attacked from the west and north because its works faced south. To do so meant a long march through the narrow roads of the Wilderness. Seated on Union Army cracker boxes, Jackson and Lee did their mapwork during the night. With the help of a local resident, Jackson found a route which would take him where he wanted to go.

At dawn, Jackson's whole corps was ready to move out. He was to have 26,000 men while Lee held the entrenched position east of Chancellorsville with 17,000. The two generals talked to each other for a few moments before Jackson rode off. It was their last meeting.

To distract attention from Jackson's column as it went silently through the woods near the Federal lines, Lee's troops opened fire with artillery and muskets. Nevertheless, Jackson's movements were noticed by the Federals, who even fired a few cannon shots at the half-hidden column. But the Union high command assumed that the troops they saw in the woods were being withdrawn from the front and did not heed the warning. Union General Daniel E. Sickles, however, finally got permission to "harass" Jackson's slowly moving troops. Sickles had many defects as a commander, but willingness to fight was not one of them. The attack he launched hit the rear of Jackson's long column, which was annoying, but it did not impede the progress of the main body of troops.

Late in the afternoon Lee received discouraging news from Fredericksburg. Through a mistake in orders, all but one Confederate brigade had been removed from the strong positions there, leaving them open to attack by Sedgwick. Fortunately for Lee, Sedgwick had not noticed the withdrawal even though his balloonists were observing the field. Confederate troops were hurried back to reoccupy their former positions.

Between five and six o'clock, Lee heard the sound of firing in the west which told him that Jackson was beginning his assault. Lee instantly sent the troops in his area into action in order to keep the Federals busy there. For hours the dense woods and occasional clearings around Chancellorsville echoed with the sound of war. The sky darkened as night set in, and the moon, only a day short of being full, rose early to shine down on thickets and glades where the fury of battle was still raging. It did not quiet down until midnight. Then Lee tried to get some sleep, lying on the ground under a waterproof cloth to do so. He was not allowed to rest for long. Some time after 2 A.M. he was awakened by the sound of voices which must have been tense with excitement. Jackson's signal officer had come in from the front. Lee questioned him eagerly. All had gone well. The troops had attacked and had swept back the surprised Federal line. There was no doubt that it was a great victory. But— and then the truth came out. Jackson had been seriously wounded in the dark by shots fired by his own men. The signal officer had been at his side, had witnessed the dreadful scene. The general was still alive, but he had been hit

Jackson photographed two weeks before his death

GENERAL JOSEPH HOOKER

171

Lee and Jackson meet at dawn on May 2, 1862. A painting by E. P. F. Julio

Jackson is fatally wounded by his own men

by three bullets, one of which had struck the right hand, while the other two had badly damaged the left arm. One bullet had passed through the hand while the other had shattered the large bone in the upper arm and had severed the main artery. (While Lee was being told this, a surgeon was amputating Jackson's left arm. The patient, mercifully under chloroform, felt nothing and was having a brief respite from pain.)

Lee, who had seen countless battle wounds, was visibly disturbed. Jackson was not merely a soldier, or even a top general; he was the man on whom Lee depended most. That Jackson, the superb and seemingly invincible commander, might die was unthinkable. Lee's subsequent actions show that he tried to put such a thought out of his mind. But it was there to plague him and could not be dismissed.

At 3 A.M. he wrote to Stuart, telling him that "it is necessary that the glorious victory thus far achieved be prosecuted with the utmost vigor, and the enemy given no time to rally. . . . Endeavor, therefore, to dispossess them of Chancellorsville, which will permit the union of the whole [Confederate] army."

When Stuart went into action before sunrise, Lee rode quickly toward the area where the fighting was at its thickest. He sat on his horse watching the desperate effort being made to unite the two wings of his army. With him was a military observer from Germany. To him Lee spoke about the need for educating the young Southerners who survived the war. Freeman says of this prophetic conversation: "It may have been at this bloody moment that he sowed the seeds that were later to ripen into the resolution to devote his own life after the war to the education of youth. The Orange plank road pointed the way to Lexington."

172

About 9 A.M., while Hooker was standing on the porch of the Chancellor House, a solid shot from a Confederate gun hit the pillar against which he was leaning, knocking him down and stunning him. His subordinates hoped that this would put him out of the battle, but it did not. He recovered sufficiently to supervise what he was best at—a hasty withdrawal from the field.

The two separated wings of the Confederate Army now came together with wild cries of victory. United, they swept on to drive the Federals from the ground around the Chancellor house. Lee rode across the battlestrewn field toward the big mansion which was now in flames. His troops cheered him as he went. At this moment Lee and the Army of Northern Virginia were at the top of their careers. After this there were to be no more clear-cut victories, no more decisive defeats of the enemy. Ahead were Gettysburg with its inconclusive ending, the bitter series of stand-off battles with Grant, and then the long last march to Appomattox.

But the day was not yet done, nor was the fighting yet over. Sedgwick's engineers had built another pontoon bridge across the river during the previous night over which troops had crossed to reoccupy Fredericksburg. The Union forces in and around that town now greatly outnumbered the few Confederates left there. All morning long they attacked Marye's Heights again. But the Confederate lines, which had been so strong there during the battle on December 13, were now too thin to hold. During the middle of the day, the Federals broke through and swept on toward Chancellorsville. That afternoon and the next day (May 4) more fighting took place. The Federals were finally forced back to the river, where they withdrew to the northern side. The Battle of Chancellorsville was over. It was a Confederate victory, but again the price that had to be paid was high—13,000 casualties against 17,000 for the Union. And Stonewall Jackson was in critical condition with his chances for recovery getting worse every hour.

When a shell hit Confederate caissons on Marye's Heights on May 3, it left these shattered remains of horses and ammunition boxes

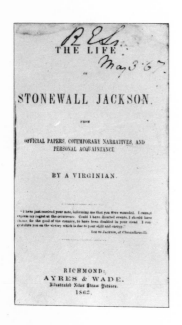

Stonewall Jackson's death mask

THE DEATH OF STONEWALL JACKSON. While Lee was still near the Chancellor house, a courier rode up with a congratulatory message which Jackson had dictated as soon as he came out of the chloroform. By this time, Lee must have known how seriously Jackson had been hurt. His aide, Charles Marshall, said that he would never forget the look of pain and anguish upon Lee's face at this moment of reminder. He dictated his reply to Marshall: "General: I have just received your note, informing me that you were wounded. I cannot express my regret at the occurrence. Could I have directed events, I should have chosen for the good of the country to be disabled in your stead. I congratulate you upon the victory, which is due to your skill and energy."

On May 4, Jackson was taken in an ambulance to Guiney's Station, 25 miles away. There he was housed in a small cottage on the Chandler farm whose owners had been his hosts before. Lee sent a verbal message to him: "Give him my affectionate regards, and tell him to make haste and get well, and come back to me as soon as he can. He has lost his left arm; but I have lost my right arm."

At first the patient seemed to be on the road to recovery, but he awoke during the night of May 6–7 complaining of nausea. In the morning the surgeon found symptoms of pneumonia. After that the wounded man's condition grew steadily worse. Morphia was administered, but mounting fever sent the ailing man into occasional lapses of delirium and incoherence.

On May 7, Jackson's wife arrived from Richmond. She was appalled by what she saw. Everything that could be done was done, but the dying man sank deeper toward death.

May 10 was Sunday, a clear and pleasant day. The devout Jackson had always wanted to die on Sunday, and before this one was over he was to be granted his wish. He was coherent at times. During one such period he said that he wanted to be buried in Lexington. When he was told that the army was praying for him, he smiled and said: "Thank God. They are very kind to me."

During the early part of the quiet Sunday afternoon he was unconscious much of the time. Evidently he was refighting old battles and reviewing the scenes of recent conflict, for he suddenly spoke out of his delirium: "Order A. P. Hill to prepare for action! Pass the infantry to the front! Tell Major Hawks——" Then he was silent for a while. At quarter after three he came out of his dreams of battle to say in a normal voice: "Let us cross over the river and rest under the shade of the trees." They were his last words.

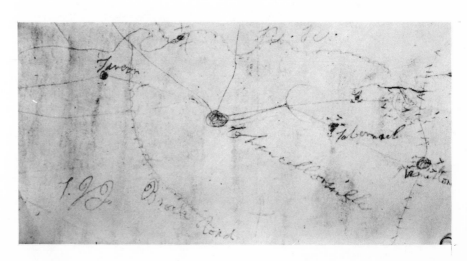

Jackson's map of Chancellorsville

LEE INVADES THE NORTH
FOR THE SECOND TIME

THE GETTYSBURG CAMPAIGN

Although Lee was heartbroken at the death of his chief lieutenant, the urgency of war gave him little time for mourning. With Jackson gone, the Army of Northern Virginia had to be reorganized. Under the new setup there were three corps of three divisions each. The First Corps was under Longstreet; the Second under Richard Ewell; and the Third under A. P. Hill. It seems odd that the loss of one general could make so much difference to an army, but it did. And, although no one then understood the true nature of the illness Lee had experienced in March, it was to have a permanent effect upon him, slowing him down and making him tire more easily until his damaged heart finally ceased beating seven years later.

Much of the dash and daring had gone out of the Army of Northern Virginia even though it still had the irrepressible Jeb Stuart to lead its cavalry. But he would never again have Jackson to side with him in a council of war when decisions had to be made to take unusual risks. Gettysburg was to test the new army, and Gettysburg was now only a little more than six weeks away.

The second invasion of the North was undertaken because of a complicated situation that then faced Richmond. For the first time, Lee was now confronted by the rising fame of a Union soldier whose career had been peripheral to his in the Mexican War. Ulysses S. Grant was threatening Vicksburg, which was the key to the control of the Mississippi River. Because of pressing need for more troops to defend the western city, Secretary of War Seddon wanted to send Pickett's division there. This would strip Lee's forces at a time when the Union Army was being built back to strength on the north side of the Rappahannock and was sure to attack again.

Lee went to Richmond on May 14 to consult with Jefferson Davis. J. B. Jones, the observant clerk in the War Department, noted that Lee "looked thinner and a little pale"—probably as a result of his heart attack in March. At the conference, which lasted for three days, Lee was more than ordinarily persuasive. He proposed an invasion of the North, this time with the rich farm country of Pennsylvania as its immediate goal. If he was successful, he could then go on to Baltimore, Washington, Philadelphia—perhaps even to New York. Such a campaign would have a tremendous psychological effect on the war-weary Northern people. It might even induce European countries to grant recognition to the Confederacy. And pressure would be taken off Vicksburg by a spectacular attack on Pennsylvania. Lee got what he wanted, and Pickett's men stayed with the Army of Northern Virginia.

During this short stay in Richmond, Lee spent an evening visiting Mrs. Archibald Cary and her beautiful daughter, Constance. The young girl wrote a vivid account of the Confederate general: "I recall . . . the superb figure of our hero . . . saying a few last words as he swung his military cape around his shoulders. It did not need my fervid imagination to think him the most noble looking mortal I had ever seen. As he swept off his hat for a second and final farewell, he bent down and kissed me as he often did the girls he had known from their childhood. At that time General Lee was literally the idol of the Confederacy. . . . We felt, as he left us and walked off up the quiet leafy street in the moonlight, that we had been honored as by more than royalty."

GENERAL A. P. HILL

GENERAL RICHARD S. EWELL

Stuart's cavalry raids a Union wagon train near Rockville, Maryland, on the way to Gettysburg

This was Lee just before he rode off to invade the North for the second time. Confident of his troops' often-proved fighting ability, doubtless encouraged by the fact that he had persuaded the President and his Cabinet to approve his plan (only Regan of Texas opposed it), and hopeful that the next few weeks would see him firmly established in untouched areas far beyond Mason and Dixon's line, Lee must have been looking forward to the early summer days when the weather would be at its best and crops would be ripening in the fields to feed his men.

On June 3, Confederate troops started moving west and then north to go down the Shenandoah Valley toward Maryland and Pennsylvania. While the infantry marched, Jeb Stuart held a grand review of nearly 10,000 cavalrymen near Brandy Station on June 5. It was an impressive ceremony with much daring horsemanship and firing of cannon followed by a ball on the greensward that night, but Lee was not present. When he arrived later, another review was staged for him on June 8. This was a quieter affair, for the general suggested that the horses be spared as much as possible for the coming campaign.

It was just as well that they were, for the next morning Pleasanton's mounted men attacked at dawn. The cavalry battle which then took place was the world's last major engagement to be fought by men on horses using swords and pistols as weapons. There had been no rain for days, and clouds of dust swirled around the cavalrymen as steel clashed on steel under the bright warm sun along the ridge called Fleetwood Heights.

Union casualties at Brandy Station were greater than Confederate, but the Yankee cavalrymen fought well that day and earned more respect as a foe than they had ever received before. Among the wounded was Rooney Lee, whose leg was badly gashed. His father saw him taken from the field and wrote to his mother to report that "neither the bone or artery . . . is injured. He is young and healthy, and I trust will soon be up again."

For days the Confederate columns kept marching north. Stuart was to screen their movements from Federal observation. Lee started off to join the main army on June 17 and crossed the Pennsylvania border on the twenty-sixth. On his way to Chambersburg, a minor but memorable incident took place. As the troops passed a large house, a number of well-dressed pro-Union women stood watching them go by. In front of them was a young girl defiantly waving a small American flag. When Lee rode by, she looked at him, lowered the flag, and said aloud: "Oh, I wish he was ours!" No greater tribute could be paid to the commander of an invading army.

GENERAL JAMES LONGSTREET

176

That night Lee set up camp in a little woods east of Chambersburg. Beyond it was the Cashtown Gap, which led to a small town named Gettysburg. No one in either army knew that a great battle was soon to be fought there.

On the night of the twenty-eighth, a scout brought word that the Federal Army had crossed the Potomac. He also said that there was a rumor that Hooker had been replaced by a new commander, General George Gordon Meade.

Lee had not heard from Stuart, so he had no firm information about the movements of his opponents. His cavalry leader had gone off on a wide swing around the Union forces and had been still further diverted by a chance to capture 125 wagons filled with supplies. It was a rich haul, but Stuart's absence reprived Lee of vital information.

Acting on what he had learned, however, Lee issued orders for his far-flung troops to come together with Cashtown as their rendezvous. Ewell was at Carlisle on his way to Harrisburg; Early was at York, east of Gettysburg; and other Confederate units had not yet reached Chambersburg. The twenty-ninth was spent in reshuffling troops; so was the thirtieth.

On that day, Lieutenant Colonel J. A. L. Fremantle, a British observer, was introduced to Lee. He described the commander as he appeared to him on the eve of the great battle: "General Lee is, almost without exception, the handsomest man of his age I ever saw. He is fifty-six years old, tall, broad-shouldered, very well made, well set up—a thorough soldier in appearance; and his manners are most courteous and full of dignity. He is a perfect gentleman in every respect. I imagine no man has so few enemies, or is so universally esteemed. . . . He has none of the small vices, such as smoking, drinking, chewing, or swearing, and his bitterest enemy never accused him of any of the greater ones. He generally wears a well-worn long gray jacket, a high black felt hat, and blue trousers tucked into his Wellington boots. I never saw him carry arms; and the only mark of his military rank are the three stars on his collar. He rides a handsome horse, which is extremely well-groomed. He himself is very neat in his dress and person, and in the most arduous marches he always looks smart and clean. . . . I believe he has never slept in a house since he had commanded the Virginian army, and he invariably declines all offers of hospitality, for fear the person offering it may afterwards get into trouble for having sheltered the Rebel General." Even this stranger from abroad had heard about Lee's one weakness as a soldier. "His only faults, so far as I can learn," Fremantle wrote, "arise from his excessive amiability."

And on the thirtieth, a Confederate brigade which was marching from Cashtown to Gettysburg in the hope of obtaining some much-needed shoes, stopped about a mile short of the town. Upon seeing Union cavalry through their field glasses, the officers ordered the men to return to Cashtown. The armies had made contact.

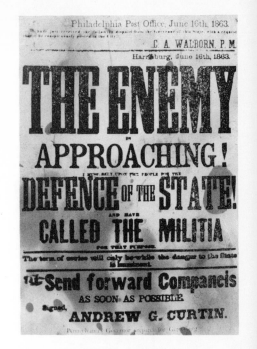

A poster issued on June 10 by Pennsylvania's Governor Curtin urging the people to come to the defense of the state

The little crossroads town of Gettysburg as the Confederates saw it on the morning of July 1. The Chambersburg Pike is at the right.

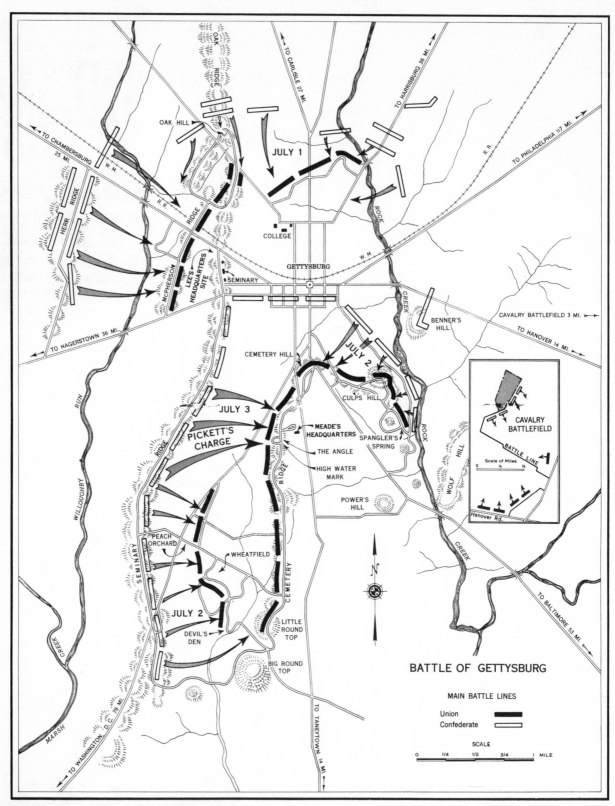

MAP OF BATTLE OF GETTYSBURG

On July 1, at 5 A.M. Confederate infantry and artillery started out on the Cashtown–Gettysburg road but were stopped three miles west of the town by Union cavalry, who fired at them as they approached. The battle, which Lee had not wanted to bring on at this time or place, had begun. Both armies were still in the dark about each other's strength and disposition of forces. They were soon to find out.

All morning long, Confederate and Union armies fought in the area west and north of the town, and the Federals were having the better of it, for some of their dismounted cavalry were using the new eight-shot Spencer repeating carbines, and they also received support from fresh troops. The picture changed during the early afternoon when more Confederates appeared north of the town. Now the Federals were outnumbered. Step by step, they were driven back until they were retreating through the streets of Gettysburg. Those who avoided capture and survived the grueling experience reached Cemetery Hill, a good defensible position south of the town.

Lee arrived on the field about 3 P.M. and saw the headlong rout of the Union troops. He gave orders to Ewell to attack Cemetery Hill, but Ewell waited for more troops to arrive. By dawn, the Federals there and on nearby Culp's Hill had strengthened their positions, and as reinforcements came in had extended their line to the south along Cemetery Ridge. Lee's first opportunity to win a decisive victory at Gettysburg was lost.

Lee was also having trouble with Longstreet. That slow and cautious general, dedicated to the idea of fighting a war of offensive strategy and defensive tactics in Pennsylvania, had suggested on the afternoon of July 1 that the army swing around the Federals, get between them and Washington, find a strong position, and wait for them to attack as they had at Fredericksburg. But Lee would have none of Longstreet's plan. He wanted to launch an attack before his opponents' entire army could arrive. His subordinates, however, were the ones who had to translate his battle plans into action, and he gave them wide powers of discretion.

On July 1, Confederate victory had been left hanging inconclusively in the air. Lee tried to force a conclusion on July 2. He ordered a simultaneous attack on the two ends of the Union line which was now stretched out in the shape of a giant fishhook on Cemetery Hill and Ridge. Ewell was to hit the north end while Longstreet was to strike the south; both were to begin their assault early in the morning. Longstreet was to start first, while Ewell was to send his men in as soon as he heard Longstreet's guns. For many reasons, a few of them good, the attack did not get started until midafternoon.

This was the day of the bloody battles in the Peach Orchard and the Wheatfield, the day of the struggle for Little Round Top from which Longstreet's artillery could have shelled the entire length of the Union lines if his guns could be brought up there, but fierce Union resistance prevented that. And on this day Confederate attacks on East Cemetery and Culp's Hill went far into the night. All either failed or were inconclusive. Night fell on a field where the Federals, badly battered, still held their well-protected positions.

And on July 2 Stuart at last arrived, too late to be of much use. During the afternoon attack, Colonel Fremantle, the British observer, climbed up a tree to get a good view of the field. Below him was Lee sitting on a tree stump talking to members of his staff. Near them a Confederate band was playing polkas and waltzes at the height of the artillery fire. Fremantle noted that "during the whole time the firing continued, he [Lee] only sent one message and only received one report. It is evidently his system to arrange the plan thoroughly with the three corps commanders and then leave to them the duty of modifying and carrying it out to the best of their abilities." This

GENERAL GEORGE G. MEADE

Confederate Vedette

179

method, with an eager fighter like Jackson, had been a great success. With more cautious men like Longstreet and Ewell, it was not working out well.

And on that crucial day, Lee himself was not at his best. He was ill again, not with a heart ailment, but with the ever-present scourge of the Civil War that affected privates and generals alike. W. W. Blackford, who was on Stuart's staff, was sent to Lee's headquarters during the evening. When he saw that Lee "walked . . . as if he was weak and in pain," he asked one of his officers what was wrong and was told that "General Lee was suffering . . . from an attack of diarrhea." The veteran Blackford understood how serious this could be and commented sympathetically: "We all know the desperately weakening power of severe diarrhea. . . . Who in such condition would not be afflicted in vigor of both mind and body, and will this not account for several things which were behind time, or not pushed forward as they should have been the 3rd of July?"

Many things went wrong on the third and last day of the battle, and Lee learned that Jackson could not be replaced. The high command of the Army of Northern Virginia was now overbalanced with caution. Lee, whom Harry Heth called the most aggressive man in the Army—and he hid not except Jackson—now had to depend upon subordinates who did not agree with his insistence upon taking the offensive. Longstreet, his second in command, was to give him the most trouble. And it was Longstreet who, years later in his book *From Manassas to Appomattox* (1896), said about Lee at Gettysburg: "That he was excited and off his balance was evident on the afternoon of the 1st, and he labored under that oppression until enough blood was shed to appease him." In all the literature on Lee, this statement is the most malicious.

There is some dispute as to whether or not Lee had given orders the night before for Longstreet to attack on the morning of July 3. Lee says that he did; Longstreet, writing after Lee was dead, said that he did not. But Lee's orders for Ewell to begin the day by attacking the northern end of the Union line were obeyed, and as Lee rode out at sunrise to meet Longstreet he could hear the sound of firing around Culp's Hill and Spangler's Spring where Ewell's troops were fighting.

At the early-morning conference, Longstreet again suggested that his corps swing around the end of the Union lines, place itself between them and Washington, and thus force Meade to attack. This time the move was to be south of the Federal lines. Lee pointed at Cemetery Ridge and said: "The enemy is there, and I am going to strike him there." He told Longstreet that he would have George Pickett's division, which was fresh on the field, and other troops from Heth's and Pender's divisions—supposedly about 15,000 men.

Longstreet did not think that such a force was large enough to make a frontal attack over nearly a mile of open ground against the well-defended center of the Union lines. He said: "General, I have been a soldier all my life. I have been with soldiers engaged in fights by couples, by squads, companies, regiments, and armies, and should know, as anyone, what soldiers can do. It is my opinion that no 15,000 men . . . can take that position."

Events were to prove that Longstreet was right, but Lee overruled him. There was no ill feeling between the two men, however, and later that morning they were seen talking amicably as they went over the ground where the attack was to be launched.

Confederate artillery had been run out on the field, and the infantrymen who were to make the assault had been assembled behind a low-lying ridge that hid them from the Federals. Shortly after one o'clock, the first Confederate gun spoke. It was followed by shots from about 140 cannon. Then the Union

The equestrian statue of Lee which now stands near the place where he watched Pickett's Charge

180

guns, about 100 of them in position, began to reply. There were more Union guns in reserve, whereas the Confederates were using everything they had. The Confederate fire converged on that point of the Union lines which was to be the center of the infantry attack. A clump of trees there served as a landmark to guide them across a field that would be obscured by the smoke of battle.

The tremendous artillery duel went on for nearly two hours. The Federal guns stopped firing first; they were running out of long-range ammunition, and the Union commanders wanted the overheated barrels to have a chance to cool so they could be used again at close range when the expected infantry assault reached its climax.

The guns had made a great deal of noise—especially when a shell hit a caisson full of ammunition and blew it up. They had made life uncomfortable for tens of thousands of men in both armies who had been pinned down under intensive fire on a sweltering-hot day. And they had killed or wounded some hundreds of men and horses. But they decided nothing. The Confederate infantrymen who had been waiting all morning while Union shells occasionally fell into their midst still had to settle the outcome of the battle by close combat.

When fire from the guns on the Confederate side of the field was beginning to slacken, Pickett received a message from E. P. Alexander, who was in charge of Longstreet's artillery. It said that if he was going to make the attack, he had better start soon, for ammunition was running low. Pickett took the note to Longstreet and asked whether he should advance. Longstreet wrote later of that critical moment: "I was convinced that he would be leading his troops to needless slaughter and did not speak. He repeated the question, and without opening my lips I bowed in answer. In a determined voice Pickett said: 'Sir, I shall lead my division forward.' "

Now the waiting infantrymen were put in motion. There were not 15,000 of them as Lee and Longstreet had estimated; 12,000 would be nearer the total of those who participated in the great march across the farmland fields of Gettysburg. Nor were they all from Virginia; troops from all but two of the

What was then called "Longstreet's attack upon the Union left center" is now popularly known as Pickett's Charge. No really authentic picture of the attack exists. This romanticized—and underpopulated—version appeared in Harper's Weekly. *It was engraved from a drawing made by A. R. Waud.*

Confederate states took part in the attack. As they went forward in formation, cannon shots from the still-distant Federal artillery began taking their toll.

Watching the lines advance across the wide stretch of open ground was the commander of the Army of Northern Virginia. Lee and his staff were at the edge of the wood that runs along Seminary Ridge. From there they had a good view of what was happening. What they saw at first must have been a fine spectacle, as thousands of men and scores of battle flags went toward the center of Cemetery Ridge, where about 6000 Union troops were grimly awaiting them. But when the Confederates approached the stone walls, fences, and trees in front of the Federal lines the picture changed rapidly. Union artillery belched fire and canister, and massed rifles swept the field with a hail of bullets. Men dropped and died or thrashed about in the agony of wounds many of which were mortal. Some Confederates reached the stone walls and leaped over them to die on the other side. The gray wave reached its crest at a high-water mark that would be forever remembered. Then it broke and receded and rolled back across the field.

Fremantle, who was going through the woods on Seminary Ridge to find Longstreet, reported what he saw: "I soon began to meet many wounded men. . . . Many of them asked in piteous tones the way to a doctor or an ambulance. The further I got, the greater became the number of the wounded. At last I came to a perfect stream of them flocking through the woods. . . . Some were walking alone on crutches composed of two rifles, others were supported by men less badly wounded than themselves, and others were carried on stretchers by the ambulance corps; but in no case did I see a sound man helping the wounded to the rear, unless he carried the red badge of the ambulance corps. They were still under a heavy fire; the shells were continually bringing down great limbs of trees and carrying further destruction amongst this melancholy procession."

A little later the British observer met Lee. He said that "he was engaged in rallying and in encouraging the broken troops, and was riding about a little in front of the wood, quite alone. . . . His face, which is always placid and cheerful, did not show signs of the slightest disappointment, care, or annoyance; and he was addressing to every soldier he met a few words of encouragement. . . . He spoke to all the wounded men that passed him, and the slightly wounded he exhorted 'to bind up [their] hurts and take up a musket' in this emergency. Very few failed to answer his appeal, and I saw many badly wounded men take off their hats and cheer him. He said to me, 'This has been a sad day for us, Colonel—a sad day; but we can't expect always to gain victories.' He was also kind enough to advise me to get into some more sheltered position, as the shells were bursting round us with considerable frequency."

Then Fremantle saw General Wilcox come up to Lee to explain, almost in tears, what had happened to his brigade. According to that careful reporter, Lee said: "Never mind, General, *all this has been MY fault*—it is I that have lost this fight, and you must help me out of it in the best way you can."

There seems to be no doubt that during the afternoon and evening Lee kept admitting that only he was to blame for what had happened. General J. D. Imboden saw him about one o'clock riding slowly back to his headquarters in the moonlight. In a brief conversation Lee said: "'I never saw troops behave more magnificently than Pickett's division of Virginians did today in that grand charge upon the enemy. And if they had been supported as they were to have been—but, for some reason not yet fully explained to me, were not—we would have held the position and the day would have been ours.' After a moment's pause he added in a loud voice, in a tone almost of agony: 'Too bad! *Too bad!* OH! TOO BAD!' "

The house near Lee's headquarters tent on Seminary Ridge

The long road back to Virginia

It was all over, and the Battle of Gettysburg—the first Lee had to fight without Jackson—had been a failure. Meade's troops were so badly mauled by three days of intensive fighting that they did not make a determined effort to follow the Confederates when they started back to Virginia in a driving rainstorm. The long column of wagons, cannon, horsemen, and foot soldiers crawled along the roads for days until they were safely across the Potomac and on home ground.

Somewhere along the way Lee learned that Vicksburg was lost, surrendered to Grant the day after the last attack at Gettysburg had failed. And he also learned that some Union soldiers had entered the house where his wounded son Rooney was staying, and had carried him off to Fort Monroe. Robert was with his brother at the time but had managed to escape. He joined his father at Culpeper where the army was resting up after the Gettysburg campaign.

The rest of 1863 was largely a disappointment for the Confederate cause. Holding actions became important. All summer long and far into the autumn, a determined attempt by the Federal Army and Navy to take Charleston went on. Wilmington, the Confederacy's main port for receiving desperately needed supplies from Europe, was also in danger. By this time there were shortages of everything everywhere throughout the South.

In September, Longstreet was sent to Tennessee to help in the defense of Chattanooga. The departure of his troops left the Army of Northern Virginia with only 46,000 men. Fortunately, there was little action, although minor affairs at Bristol Station, Rappahannock Bridge, and Kelly's Ford in October and November kept the armies in Virginia on the alert. A Confederate victory at Chickamauga on September 19–20 was followed by defeat at Chattanooga late in November. Grant's name was rising steadily in the West, but Meade remained the top Union commander in the East, even though his Army of the Potomac was inactive for months on end.

The year ended sadly for Lee. Rooney had been transferred to Fort Lafayette in New York Harbor on November 13 and was still confined there. And on the day after Christmas, Rooney's wife Charlotte died in Richmond. Nor was there any surcease from physical pain for the aging general. In October what he thought was rheumatism became so bad that he could hardly sit on a horse. And the sudden paroxysms of pain in the chest continued.

W. H. F. LEE (*"Rooney"*)

GENERAL SAMUEL P. HEINTZELMAN *and staff with their families at Arlington*

Federal troops at Arlington in 1864

ARLINGTON, FAREWELL! 1864

The winter of 1863–64 was a sorrowful one for Lee. For some time Arlington had been occupied by Union troops, and the Washington relics stored there had been sent to the Patent Office for "safekeeping." Since the house was inside the ring of fortifications which had been built around the city of Washington, it became the headquarters of the general commanding the forts on the Virginia side of the river. A Federal law had been passed which levied taxes on real estate in "the insurrectionary districts" and which had to be paid in person by the owners of the property in question. When a cousin of the Lees appeared to pay taxes on the Arlington estate, the money he offered was refused by the commissioners.

On January 11, 1864, the Government entered a "bookkeeping" bid of $26,800 for Arlington; title then passed to the United States, and the Custis-Lee House was lost forever to the family.

On June 15, 1864, 210 acres near the house was set aside as a national military cemetery. Soldiers' bodies had already been interred on the grounds. The first was a Confederate who had been buried there a month before.

Robert E. Lee never set foot in Arlington House again, although he did see the place from a distance while in the neighborhood after the war. His wife went there for a brief visit about three months before her death in November 1873. One wing of the house was then occupied by the caretaker of the cemetery; the rest stood gaunt and empty for years.

After Mrs. Lee's death, Custis became the heir to Arlington. When he tried to obtain possession, the Supreme Court ruled in his favor in 1882. But by that time, thousands of soldiers had been buried in the grounds around the house. In lieu of possession, he accepted an offer of the Federal Government to purchase the entire property for $150,000.

The estate is now the nation's most famous military cemetery. Here is the Tomb of the Unknown Soldier, and here are buried honored dead of all American wars since the 1860s.

Arlington House itself continued to fall into disrepair until 1925, when Congress approved an act to restore it. In 1933, the War Department turned it over to the National Park Service of the Interior Department. Today, beautifully restored and refurnished, it looks much as it did when Lee lived there.

On May 31, 1861, only a few weeks after the Lees left Arlington forever, Lincoln's eldest son Robert, who was home from Harvard for the summer, accompanied by the President's secretaries, John Hay and John Nicolay, rode out from Washington to visit the house. Troops were occupying the estate, and some of them were busy building earthworks on the grounds as they rode by. Nicolay left this account of their visit: "Arlington House . . . has one of the most beautiful situations imaginable. . . . The house looks quite old. I do not know when it was built, but it was evidently in its day a grand affair; and its arrangement, furniture, pictures, &c., at once carry one back to the good old 'first family' days of Virginia. . . . The furniture of the house was evidently 'stylish' in its time. The chambers are filled with family portraits—most of them indifferent as works of art. . . . Deer's antlers, the trophies of the chase in the old days, are nailed up about the hall and passages, and a historic and traditional atmosphere seemed to pervade the house."

The loss of Arlington meant a great deal to Lee. There are many references to it in his wartime family correspondence. Arlington's proximity to Washington would have made it difficult for the family to live there after the war, even if they regained possession of it.

Union soldiers on the lawn . . .

. . . and in the rear of the house

185

The seated Vannerson portrait of 1864

*The statue Valentine made
from the Vannerson portraits*

THE VANNERSON PORTRAITS

Lee did not like being photographed, but as a favor to a young Virginian sculptor, Edward V. Valentine, who was then in Germany, the busy general patiently submitted to having several pictures taken early in 1864. They were made in Richmond by J. Vannerson and were sent through the blockade to Berlin in order to give Valentine some idea of what Lee looked like when he made a 20-inch portrait statuette of him. The three Vannerson photographs are reproduced on these two pages and the next.

The statuette has a strange history. It was intended to be sold for the benefit of charity at a Southern Bazaar held in St. George's Hall, Liverpool, in October 1864. But Valentine did not have his sculptured portrait ready in time. In November he sent it to London, where it was displayed in a shop window for a while. After that it unaccountably disappeared. Fortunately, Valentine had had it photographed. The statuette portrays Lee in the general's uniform which he is wearing in the photograph on the facing page. It is not a good likeness, for it makes Lee look dumpy and squat. Actually, he was rather tall and much better proportioned than this sculptured image.

Valentine was to have other opportunities to portray Lee after the war and to take careful measurements of him (see page 239). He returned from Europe at the end of 1865 and opened a studio in Richmond, where he made a number of statues of the Confederate leaders—Jackson, Stuart, Mosby, Maury, both Johnstons, Davis, and others. A full-length bronze figure of Lee, which Valentine did in the twentieth century, stands in Statuary Hall in the Capitol in Washington (see page 250). His best work, however, is his recumbent statue of Lee in the Memorial Chapel at Washington and Lee (see page 247).

During the winter of 1863–64 the Confederacy and its armed forces were exhausting their strength. Three years of bitter warfare had drained the resources of a country that had never been rich. The Army was desperately short of food; so were its horses. Shoes for the men were always a troublesome

186

THE FULL–LENGTH VANNERSON PORTRAIT OF 1864

A comparison of this photograph with the one taken by Minnis and Cowell in 1863 (see page 167) shows an amazing difference, due probably to the change in costume, stance, and martial bear- *ing. The "booted-and-spurred" portrait is Lee at his soldierly best. Here the longer tunic, full trouser legs, and relaxed posture make him look shorter and less impressive.*

The third Vannerson portrait

*Taken by J. W. Davies in Richmond
later in 1864*

problem, and Lee's correspondence with Richmond often refers to the need for them.

On January 22 he wrote to the Secretary of War: "A regular supply of provisions to the troops in this army is a matter of great importance. Short rations are having a bad effect upon the men, both morally and physically. Desertions to the enemy are becoming more frequent, and the men cannot continue healthy and vigorous if confined to this spare diet for any length of time. Unless there is a change, I fear the army cannot be kept together."

Any one living in Richmond at this time could readily understand how desperate the Army's shortages were, for civilians were also suffering. J. B. Jones, the Rebel war clerk, said in February: "I know my ribs stick out, being covered by skin only. . . . Meal is the only food now attainable, except by the rich. We look for a healthy year, everything being so cleanly consumed that no garbage or filth can accumulate. We are all good scavengers now, and there is no need of buzzards in the streets. Even the pigeons can scarcely find a grain to eat."

Jones recorded commodity prices which reflected the inflation of Confederate currency as well as the growing scarcity of supplies. In March, 1864, which he called "the famine month," a turkey cost from $60 to $100, bacon $10 to $15 a pound, meal $50 a bushel, and flour $300 a barrel. Even more significant than his figures is his statement on March 18: "My daughter's cat is staggering today for want of animal food. Sometimes I fancy I stagger myself. We do not average two ounces of meat daily; and some do not get any for several days together." And he reported that President Davis said one day: "I don't see why rats, if fat, are not as good as squirrels."

In January 1864, the Lee family, which had been living for some time on Leigh Street, moved into the brick house on Franklin Street which Custis and his friends had been using as an officers' mess. Rooney had been exchanged for a Union prisoner and was back from the North.

Spring that year, with its dire shortages and continued threat of attack, was a hard one. But the future became even darker in March when rumors reached Richmond that Grant was in Washington, called there on March 3 from the West. At a ceremony in the White House on the ninth, Lincoln personally gave him his commission as lieutenant general. He was to command all the Union armies. On March 10 he went to Brandy Station to visit Meade; he returned the next day to Washington, made a hurried trip to the West to visit Sherman, and was back in Washington on the twenty-third. On March 26 he was at Culpeper to set up his new headquarters there.

Lee was at first deceived about Grant's intentions. In a letter written to Davis on March 25, he said: "I am not disposed to believe from what I now know that the first important effort will be directed against Richmond. . . . From present indications, I am inclined to believe that the first efforts of the enemy will be directed against Gen'l Johnston or Gen'l Longstreet [in the West]."

Lee did not remain under this misapprehension long. He analyzed the probabilities in a letter to Longstreet on March 28: "It looks now as if Grant was really going to operate the Army of the Potomac. When it was first communicated in their papers, and even upon the publication of his order assuming command, I considered it a stratagem to attract our attention here, while he was left unmolested in dealing us a blow from the West. It may be so still, but if their papers are to be believed, he returned to Washington City on the 22d instant, and was to repair to the Rappahannock on the 23d. One of our scouts even reports that he did come up in the train of the 24th, all the crossroads, stations, &c. having been strictly guarded to prevent the train being molested.

Lee's last adversary,
General Ulysses S. Grant,
photographed in 1864

If he is really going to operate here, we may expect a concentration of troops in this region. . . . It behooves us to be on the alert, or we will be deceived. You know that is part of Grant's tactics."

The young officer who had been in the Mexican War with Lee had risen rapidly to fame after an inauspicious earlier career in the United States Army. Grant had resigned in 1854, and then had been an even greater failure in civilian life than he was as a soldier. In 1861, he had been given command of the 21st Illinois. Then came Belmont, Fort Donelson, Shiloh, Vicksburg, and Chattanooga. And now he had greater power than had ever been given to any general except Washington and Winfield Scott.

Early in April, Longstreet and his men were ordered to leave Tennessee and go east to Charlottesville. Except for Chickamauga, Longstreet had done badly in the West. He had not gotten on well with Braxton Bragg and had become even more morose and hesitant than he had been at Gettysburg. He was glad to be with Lee again. Longstreet underestimated Grant. Writing to Lee on April 2, he said: "I do not think that he is any better than Pope. . . . His chief strength is in his prestige."

Lee did not make the same mistake; he knew that Grant was a capable and deadly serious fighter. But Lee did underestimate the strength of the forces Grant could bring against him. Not only did they outnumber him nearly two to one, but behind them stood the North with an apparently inexhaustible supply of manpower to replace losses in battle. And behind the Union Army were the resources of a nation which had become even more industrialized during the war, because the enormous demand for goods of all kinds encouraged manufacturers to expand their mills and factories.

THE WILDERNESS CAMPAIGN

While Grant moved against Richmond, Sherman was to drive south toward Atlanta and try to destroy Joseph Johnston's armies. And when Grant attacked Richmond from the north, Ben Butler was to come in from the east to take Petersburg. At the same time, Sigel was to operate in the Valley to tie down Confederate forces there.

The Confederates in Virginia and Georgia were, as usual, heavily outnumbered. Lee had hardly more than 60,000 men to hold off Grant's forces of well over 100,000. And Johnston had about 62,000 to oppose Sherman's army, which was nearly 100,000 strong. The Union was putting forth every effort to end a war which its people felt had gone on far too long.

Grant's troops began to move on May 3 and were soon in the Wilderness area a few miles west of the section where the Battle of Chancellorsville had been fought a year before. Lee, knowing full well that the Union forces not only outnumbered him but were also much better equipped, wanted to strike Grant while his long marching columns were stretched out in the dense woods where trees and undergrowth made it difficult for an army under assault to judge how numerous its attackers were. He permitted Grant to cross the Rapidan without opposition and waited.

Early in the morning of May 5, the Confederates started eastward along two parallel roads to intercept the southward-marching blue columns. Lee did not want to bring on a battle until Longstreet arrived with reinforcements, but sometime after 11 A.M. the Federals caught sight of Ewell's troops. They drove the Confederates back, and the battle was on. All day long, men fought in the dark woods where they could hardly see each other.

Lee's men, who knew the country and how to fight in it, used the night to strengthen their field fortifications. When morning came, the Federals in many places could not see their opponents because they were hidden behind logs against which they had piled up enough earth to stop bullets effectively.

During the day, fierce Union attacks drove many of the Confederates out of their prepared positions, and things were going badly for Lee until Longstreet finally came up. With him were three Texas regiments which hurried forward to make an attack across open ground. According to some of the many—and often contradictory—accounts of this episode, Lee apparently

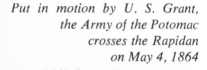

Put in motion by U. S. Grant, the Army of the Potomac crosses the Rapidan on May 4, 1864

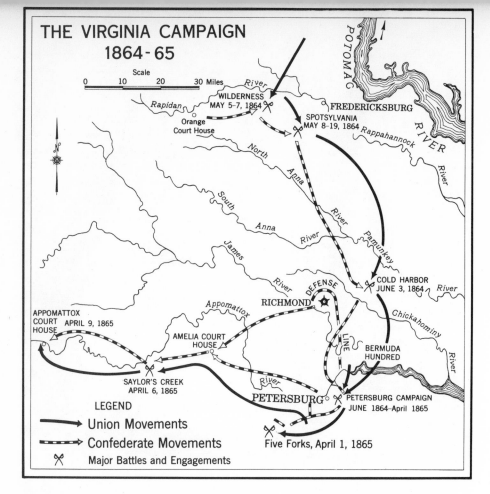

wanted to lead the charge in person. The Texans, who had no intention of letting the beloved leader of the Confederate Army expose himself needlessly to enemy fire, shouted to him to go back, crying "General Lee to the rear." One of their officers tried to dissuade him, pointing to Longstreet, who had now arrived on the field. Lee went over to greet his subordinate commander.

Longstreet promptly told Lee in no uncertain terms that he must stay behind the lines. He went on himself to fight close to the front until a bullet fired by one of his own men struck him at the base of the throat, and tore through the right shoulder. The shot, which might have killed a weaker man, took the doughty general out of the battle, but he was back in service before the end of the year.

That night the woods, which were unusually dry from lack of rain, burned luridly. The flames licked nearer to men with leg wounds who could not get away. Some were removed in water-soaked blankets; others had to remain, watching with horrified fascination as the fire came closer. The screams of the burning victims were punctuated by explosions when the heat set off cartridges in their belts.

At the end of his first encounter with Grant, Lee knew that he was up against a formidable opponent who would not hesitate to sacrifice men and matériel to win a victory. He also knew that he could not afford to meet the Army of the Potomac under its new leader on equal terms or out in the open. Only by conserving everything he had—especially manpower—could Lee hope to stave off Grant and keep him from marching into Richmond. Many people in the South had felt from the very beginning of the war that establishing the capital of the Confederacy so near the Northern states was a mistake and that Richmond would always be open to attack. There was talk now of moving the seat of government to a less vulnerable place, but Lee could not wait for that. He had to keep Grant's legions away from Richmond.

Confederates march through the burning woods in the Wilderness Campaign

SPOTSYLVANIA

No one goes around a battlefield to enumerate the numbers of killed, wounded, or missing. The casualty count for Wilderness is even more uncertain than usual. Grant's losses were somewhere between 15,000 and 18,000; Lee's were smaller, varying between 8000 and 11,000, according to the source of information.

But Grant, despite his heavy losses, did not follow the example set by previous commanders of the luckless Army of the Potomac. He had no intention of giving up or turning back. Since he realized that further frontal attacks over the same ground were useless, he set his troops in motion on the evening of May 7, heading toward Richmond. Spotsylvania Court House, only a few miles away, was his immediate goal.

Lee had ordered Anderson, whom he had put in to replace Longstreet, to proceed to the same place as soon as his men were rested. But the area assigned to them for a halt was on fire, and the new commander was eager to advance. He marched toward Spotsylvania during the night and arrived there only a short time before the vanguard of Grant's troops. He rapidly entrenched his position across the road.

During the morning of May 8, while the armies reassembled around Spotsylvania, Sheridan, in an acrimonious dispute with Meade, declared that his cavalry could whip Stuart if given the chance. Within the hour he was sent orders to do so. The next morning he rode out with 10,000 mounted men (Stuart had only 4500), moving swiftly around the Confederate Army to make a dash to Richmond.

At Spotsylvania, the Confederates used every minute to strengthen their positions. The country, although wooded, was not so densely grown up as the tangled Wilderness. The field fortifications they built under fire were in the shape of a V with the apex pointing to the north. Grant, who should have learned at Vicksburg that direct assaults on prepared defenses are costly and usually doomed to failure, nevertheless agreed to the idea of attacking the earthworks that formed the Confederates' "Mule Shoe." Late on May 10, Union troops were sent in. They fought fiercely, gained ground, and even took prisoners, but finally had to fall back at the end of the day.

May 11 was cloudy, and rain fell during the afternoon. There was a lull in the fighting because the Federals were busy evacuating their wounded in wagons that were to return with ammunition and supplies. Late that night, Union bands played softly while preparations were being made for a fresh assault. Lee, of course, had no way of knowing it, but it was on this day that Grant sent his famous message to Halleck saying that he proposed "to fight it out on this line if it takes all summer."

At dawn on May 12, Federal troops again attacked the apex which had already been named "The Bloody Angle." There they drove back the Confederates. Lee's Assistant General, young Walter H. Taylor, describes the fury of the fighting there: "Then occurred the most remarkable musketry fire of the war: from the sides of the salient in the possession of the Federals, and the new line, forming the base of the triangle occupied by the Confederates, poured forth from continuous lines of hissing fire an incessant, terrific hail of deadly missiles. No living man nor thing could stand in the doomed space embraced within those angry lines; even large trees were felled—their trunks cut in twain by the bullets of small arms."

The embattled Federals refused to be dislodged, and bitter combat with bayonets and clubbed rifles went on until late at night. During the hotly contested engagement, Lee again had to be dissuaded by his men from riding forward, and the cry "General Lee to the rear" was heard once more.

During the evening, Traveller reacted violently to a burst of artillery fire and suddenly reared. It was lucky he did, for a cannon ball went right under him. If he had had all four feet on the ground at that moment, the heavy missile would have struck his rider.

The dreadful day, which had seen some of the heaviest fighting of the war, brought yet another disaster. J. E. B. Stuart, who had been badly wounded the day before when he encountered Sheridan's troopers at Yellow Tavern, died that evening in Richmond.

Bad weather slowed down operations at Spotsylvania until May 18. During this respite, both sides strengthened their field fortifications. Meanwhile, Sigel's operations in the Valley ended in defeat at New Market on May 15, when cadets from the Virginia Military Institute supported Confederate veterans on the field. Sigel was replaced by David Hunter four days later. Inept General Benjamin F. Butler did even worse near Petersburg. Ordered to occupy City Point and stay on the south bank of the James River where he could have marched overland to Petersburg, he went instead to the north shore and succeeded only in getting his troops bottled up on the peninsula called Bermuda Hundred. Sherman, however, was now in Georgia, slowly but steadily advancing toward Atlanta.

Lee let Ewell attempt an exploratory probe of the Federal positions on May 19. He was quickly driven back. Then, on the night of May 20, Grant sent his forces moving southward, refusing for the time being to make any further direct attacks against the Confederate lines which had thus far proved to be impenetrable. Lee followed his route, keeping his watchful troops only a few miles to the west of the marching Federal columns. The two armies met and fought again on May 23, the day after Lee had received about 8000 re-

*This wooden head-slab,
put up during the war,
marked J. E. B. Stuart's grave*

inforcements from the Valley. The Confederates formed their well-tested V-shaped lines on the south shore of the North Anna River and stood off Federal attacks for two days. When Grant found that he could not break through, he continued his move southward until the end of May. Then the armies again faced each other at Cold Harbor, where they had fought during the Peninsular Campaign in 1862. And the Union Army was again within a few miles of Richmond.

During the last week of May, Lee was suffering from intestinal pains. By the twenty-eighth he was so ill that he left his tent to go to bed in a house near Atlee's Station. The ailing man, who had successfully parried the assaults of the legions thrown against him by his determined opponent, now had to face another battle, this time at the very gates of Richmond.

COLD HARBOR

Lee was so ill that he had to be taken by carriage to his next headquarters, which were at Shady Grove where he would be nearer the scene of action. His illness, however, did not prevent him from making plans for the battle. The Confederate lines stretched for about five miles from north to south, running between Old and New Cold Harbor. They took advantage of every slope, every clump of trees, and even of bushes that offered protection or concealment. The men who dug the trenches and heaped up the soil around felled logs saw to it that their rude fortifications twisted and turned along their course so riflemen stationed in them could enfilade attacking troops as well as hit them by direct fire. The Confederates who were doing the digging were weak for want of food, but they worked unceasingly, for they knew that each spadeful of earth helped to protect them against bullets. Most of the work had to be done at night because Federal cavalry were already in the area. It was amazing, though, how quickly battlewise veterans could convert open country into a hardly visible but secure series of defenses.

Late in the afternoon of June 1, Lee moved again, this time to quarters in the field near the burned-out ruins of Gaines' Mill. Sporadic fighting went on as more and more troops arrived and dug themselves in. Both sides were getting reinforcements from the stalemated section at Bermuda Hundred, and Breckenridge had brought in two Confederate brigades from the Valley.

Grant had planned a major assault for June 2, but some of his troops were late, so he had to schedule it for the next day. The scales were swinging against him, for the delay gave his opponents more time to strengthen their defenses and put their reinforcements into the lines.

At 4:30 A.M. Union troops started moving forward across land which was swampy in many places and which was everywhere dominated by Confederate artillery and small-arms fire. They did not get very far. Within a matter of minutes the field was swept by so much howling and hissing metal that no one could stand upright and live in it. Colonel C. S. Venable of Lee's staff said that "The dead and dying lay in front of the Confederate lines in triangles, of which the apexes were the bravest men who came nearest to the breastworks under the withering, deadly fire." It was all over in a matter of minutes. Those who survived hugged the ground until nightfall when they could creep back to their own lines. Grant said in his *Memoirs,* "I have always regretted that the last assault at Cold Harbor was ever made." But 7000 men had been killed or wounded in it, and one Federal officer said that "more men fell bleeding as they advanced than in any other like period of time throughout the war."

When another senseless advance was ordered later in the day, the soldiers remained where they were in mute protest against further useless slaughter. Union General M. T. McMahon said twenty years later: "In the opinion of a majority of its survivors, the battle of Cold Harbor should never have been fought."

Lee was quicker than Grant to learn that sending masses of men across open ground to take prepared positions is an invitation to wholesale slaughter. What happened at Cold Harbor presaged the kind of operations to be carried out against Petersburg when both sides settled down to the long-drawn-out attrition of trench warfare.

Union troops remained in position at Cold Harbor until June 12, when Grant began pulling 100,000 men out of the trenches to march them south of the James River. It was enormously difficult to conceal this vast movement from the watchful eyes of the Confederates, but Grant succeeded.

His hard-fought campaign, which had lasted from May 4 to June, had accomplished neither of its two objectives—to destroy Lee's army and to take Richmond. His losses were staggering: about 55,000 casualties were the price the Army of the Potomac had paid to go 55 miles from Wilderness to Cold Harbor. Confederate losses were smaller, anywhere from 20,000 to 40,000 (Southern records from this time on are inexact). But the North could afford the drain on manpower better than could the South, which was now reaching the end of its resources.

Only a fluke kept Petersburg from falling into the hands of the Federals at this time. The city was well protected by earthworks, but there were only about 2400 men to defend them. Grant ordered W. J. Smith to attack with 16,000 troops on June 15. They broke through the lines and could easily have gone on to Petersburg. But Smith delayed following up the breakthrough long enough for Confederate troops to be rushed into the lines, and the Federals lost their chance. The blunder cost them dearly, for they now had to start formal siege operations which dragged on for many months of stalemated trench warfare.

Harper's Weekly (*June 11, 1864*)
does some wishful thinking
about Grant and Lee

THE SIEGE OF PETERSBURG

Lee quickly went to work to strengthen the fortifications around Petersburg and extend them farther west. Grant ordered more attacks to be made on June 18, but as was certain when strongly built and well-defended earthworks were assaulted by men who had to charge across open ground, the assaults were easily repelled. The Federals now began to build an elaborate system of earthworks from which siege operations could be carried out.

Long-range mortars were brought in to lob explosive shells high into the air so they would fall directly over the otherwise unassailable trenches and kill or wound the soldiers in them. Sharpshooters were always ready to pick off anyone careless enough to raise a head above the parapet. Both armies built bombproofs and shelters and settled down to a long wait.

Walter Taylor found a place north of Petersburg for the general's headquarters. This was Violet Bank, where Lee had his tent pitched on the lawn. He steadfastly refused offers of staying in any of the homes offered to him. His adjutant general said that a house "was entirely too pleasant for him, for he is never so uncomfortable as when comfortable."

From here Lee wrote to his wife in Richmond, only 23 miles away. On June 30 he reminded her that it was the thirty-third anniversary of their wedding and spoke wistfully of that happy day.

For a few days early in July the North shivered when Jubal Early swept out of the Valley to threaten Baltimore and Washington. His men reached the suburbs of the Federal capital on July 11 but had to fall back when extra defenders were hurriedly put into the ring of forts guarding the city.

The 18,000 inhabitants of Petersburg went about their daily business although shells fell into the streets and tore holes in the houses. Around the city were 26 miles of earthworks which so far had proved effective against attack. Work on these never stopped; they were constantly being improved and extended farther west.

The Union Army was also busy building similar fortifications. Minor attempts to breach the Confederate lines were made at frequent intervals, but no major move was made until a young mining engineer from Pennsylvania

196

proposed an idea for blasting a way through the seemingly impregnable Confederate defenses.

This was Henry Pleasants of the 48th Pennsylvania Volunteer Regiment, which was largely made up of coal miners. Pleasants wanted to build a 500-foot tunnel at the end of which he would place an enormous charge of gunpower to blow up a Confederate fort at Elliott's Salient so troops could dash through the hole in the lines, fall upon Confederates in the trenches from the rear, and go on to take Petersburg. It was a daring scheme, and Pleasants and his miners did just what they proposed to do. But when the mine was finally set off at 4:45 A.M. on July 30, Union efforts to rush troops through the breach were so badly handled that the crater became a deathtrap for thousands of blue-clad troops who never got past the big hole in the ground.

Lee watched the Confederate counteroffensive from the windows of a house which overlooked this part of the lines. He saw the artillery duel that went on for hours and observed the hand-to-hand fighting that eventually forced more than a thousand Union soldiers still left alive in the crater to surrender.

After the Federals' ineptly managed attempt to break through the lines, activities around Petersburg quieted down. Lee clung grimly to his lines, although constant sniping from enemy sharpshooters and a steady desertion were slowly reducing his already inadequate forces. And news from other areas was consistently bad. Farragut's fleet entered Mobile Bay on August 5; less than a month later Atlanta fell, and Sherman's army marched on toward Savannah and the sea.

As the summer waned, Lee's objections to using a house with four solid walls and a roof as headquarters began to weaken. In a letter to his wife dated September 18, he wrote: "I am as sensible as you . . . can be of my failing strength and approaching infirmities and am as careful to shield myself from exciting causes as I can be. But what care can a man give to himself in a time of war? It is from no desire of exposure or hazard that I live in a tent, but from necessity. I must be where I can speedily and at all times attend to the duties of my position and be near or accessible to the officers with whom I have to act. What house could I get to hold all the staff? Our citizens are very

197

kind in offering me a room or rooms in their houses, in which I could be sheltered, but it would separate me from the staff officers, delay the transaction of business, and turn the residence of my kind landlords into a barrack where officers, couriers, distressed women, etc. would be entering day and night. I shall be very glad this winter to get a house if practicable."

In November, Lee moved his headquarters to the Turnbull house at Edge Hill, about two miles west of Petersburg. Winter was closing in, and on December 12, Walter Taylor commented bitterly that the previous evening had been unusually cold. It was a dismal time for everyone, and many people in both the South and the North wanted to see the seemingly endless war brought to an end.

The closing months of 1864 were especially dreadful for the people of Richmond and for the armies defending it. The Confederate capital was the focal point for all the bad news that poured in from the entire South. The battles of Franklin and Nashville ended in defeat for the Confederate forces in Tennessee. Sherman advanced toward Savannah and took possession of the city in December. During that month a combined Federal land-and-sea attack was made on Fort Fisher, the key to Wilmington, North Carolina, the last major port into which blockade-runners could bring essential supplies from Europe. The attempt to take the fort failed, but it was evident that another effort would soon be made by an even stronger force. Sheridan's troopers were ravaging the Valley and destroying everything needed to raise food in the fertile land which had been called the breadbox of the Confederacy.

In desperation and anger, Confederate secret-service agents stepped up their campaign in the North. They raided St. Albans, Vermont, attempted to burn hotels in New York, and made elaborate but ineffective plans to set Southern prisoners of war free.

Some idea of how badly off the people of Richmond were during those terrible months can be had from the contemporary daily record kept by J. B. Jones. Writing in December, he said: "There is deep vexation in the city—a general apprehension that our affairs are rapidly approaching a crisis. . . . Gold is $45 for one. . . . There is a rumor . . . that the government is to be removed to Lynchburg. . . . It is said Gen. Lee is to be invested with dictatorial powers, so far as our armies are concerned. . . . He is represented as being in favor of employing Negro troops. . . . I saw selling at auction

today second-hand shirts at $40 each and blankets at $75. A bedstead, such as I have bought for $10, brought $700." And on the last day of the year he wrote: "There is supposed to be a conspiracy on foot to transfer some of the powers of the Executive to Gen. Lee. It can only be done by revolution and the overthrow of the Constitution. Nevertheless, it is believed many executive officers, some high in position, favor the scheme."

Jones may have heard such talk, but if any of the would-be conspirators actually approached Lee, they were undoubtedly rebuffed. He was the last man in the Confederacy to be party to such a plot.

It is true, however, that he favored the use of Negro slaves as soldiers. He had probably made up his mind before the end of the year that this must be done, for on January 11, 1865, he committed his thoughts on the subject to paper in a letter addressed to Andrew Hunter: "We must decide whether slavery shall be extinguished by our enemies and the slaves be used against us, or use them ourselves at the risk of the effects which may be produced upon our social institutions. My own opinion is that we should employ them without delay. I believe that with proper regulations they can be made efficient soldiers."

Lee felt that slaves who fought in the Army should be given their freedom as a reward. This horrified Jones, who apparently now first learned about Lee's attitude toward slavery. On January 25, he wrote in his diary: "If it were generally known that Gen. Lee is, and always has been opposed to slavery, how soon would his great popularity vanish like the mist of the morning! Can it be possible that he has influenced the President's mind on this subject? Did he influence the mind of his father-in-law, G. W. Parke Custis, to emancipate his hundreds of slaves? Gen. Lee would have been heir to all, as his wife was an only child. There's some mistake about it."

The soldier-leader, whose idea about human bondage were at variance with many of his countrymen's attitudes, went his lonely way during the last winter of the Confederacy. The coming of spring, he knew, would bring an all-out attack against his weakened army.

Grant was well informed about the depletion of his opponent's forces. He wrote in his *Memoirs* that "it was a mere question of arithmetic to calculate how long they could hold out." And he was making detailed plans for the campaign which he believed would close the war.

Pictures of Lee drawn from life in the field are so rare as to be almost nonexistent. This one, which shows him watching a Federal bombardment of Petersburg, was made by Frank Vizetelly for The Illustrated London News, *in which it appeared on September 3, 1864.*

THE LAST CAMPAIGN

FORT STEDMAN

As could have been foreseen, the Federals made another combined attack—on Fort Fisher in the middle of January 1865. Overwhelmed by the weight of arms thrown against it, the fort which guarded the way to Wilmington had to be surrendered. After that it was almost impossible for a blockade-runner to reach any Southern port with adequate docking facilities.

During the last week in January, peace commissioners from Washington and Richmond began to meet at Hampton Roads in what turned out to be a futile effort to bring the war to an end.

At the beginning of February, Lee was made General in Chief of the Armies of the Confederate States. His first move was to propose to Davis that deserters be pardoned if they would return to their regiments. And his suggestion that Negroes be enlisted in the Confederate Army was eventually to have some effect, although it was only in Richmond that the people were ever to see two companies of black troops in gray uniforms being taught the manual of arms. The war was over before any practical use could be made of them.

Lee evidently sensed that the end was near. Acting on Longstreet's prompting—and with permission from Davis—he wrote to Grant on March 2 to propose a meeting at which they could discuss means to "put an end to the calamities of war." But Lincoln telegraphed Grant that he had no authority to settle the terms of peace and that he was to press to the utmost his military advantages. Lee's attempt to bring the war to an end by negotiation failed.

Lee now made plans for his next move. On the night of March 3, even before Grant's negative reply was received, he summoned young General John B. Gordon to Edge Hill, where he talked to him about what might be done. During the next few days, Gordon worked out the details for an assault on the northern end of the Union fortifications around Petersburg. Although the immediate target was Fort Stedman, it was hoped that the attacking force would be able to sweep on and fall upon other Union defenses from the rear. It was a desperate move, but the situation called for desperate measures. Sheridan had won the battle of Waynesboro, and was on his way from the Valley to add nearly 10,000 cavalrymen to Grant's forces.

The attack on Fort Stedman was set for 4 A.M. on March 25. It was to be a bold assault that was intended to take the Union troops by surprise and prevent them from bringing up reinforcements while thousands of hard-fighting Confederates poured through the breach.

Everything went off as planned, and as Lee watched his men advance through the early dawnlight, he had good reason to believe that his daring offensive move against a much larger army might succeed. His troops not only captured Fort Stedman but went on to take the two batteries on either side of it. But then, as the sky lightened, Union reserves were brought up in such large numbers that they overpowered the Confederate invaders, killed and wounded many of them, and took hundreds of prisoners. By eight o'clock it was all over. The Army of Northern Virginia had lost nearly 5000 men in what proved to be the last major offensive it was ever to make.

Lee explained the reasons behind the attack when he wrote to Jefferson Davis the next day: "I was induced to assume the offensive from the belief that the point assailed could be carried without much loss, and the hope that by the seizure of the redoubts in the rear of the enemy's main line, I could

GENERAL JOHN B. GORDON

200

sweep along his entrenchments to the south, so that if I could not cause their abandonment, Gen'l Grant would at least be obliged so to curtail his lines, that upon the approach of Gen'l Sherman, I might be able to hold our position with a portion of the troops, and with a select body unite with Gen'l Johnston and give him battle. . . . I fear now it will be impossible to prevent a junction between Grant and Sherman, nor do I deem it prudent that this army should maintain its position until the latter shall approach too near."

Lee had known for some time that it would be impossible to hold Petersburg and Richmond with his attenuated forces once Grant hurled his huge army against him. He had told General Gordon that Grant and Sherman had 280,000 well-armed men to use against the 65,000 ragged veterans commanded by him and General Johnston.

At nearby City Point, high policy was being made on March 27 and 28. Lincoln had come down from Washington on the *River Queen*; Sheridan was there; so was Sherman, who had been summoned from North Carolina. The Union commanders were now planning their final moves. Grant was to precipitate action by sending troops to the western end of the Petersburg lines to cut the Southside Railroad on March 29. If Confederates were stripped from the already sparsely manned fortifications in front of Petersburg to counter the assault, he would attack the vulnerable lines there. Thousands of Union troops were started in motion on March 27. Grant left City Point to go to the front on March 29. And Sheridan, with more than 9000 mounted men, rode toward the west early the same morning.

Lee's telegrams to Richmond for the next few days show that he knew very well what was happening at Dinwiddie Court House and Five Forks, where Sheridan's troopers and Warren's Fifth Corps were engaged with the Confederate cavalry and infantry which Lee had sent there to defend the area beyond his lines. And when the battle of Five Forks was over on April 1 and Union troops were overrunning the country north of the vital Southside Railroad, Lee found out that three of his generals, Thomas L. Rosser, Fitz Lee, and George E. Pickett, had been at a shadbake when Federals broke through and were not at the front to rally their troops, Lee remembered Gettysburg and the disastrous charge Pickett had led there. Just before Appomattox he removed him from command.

That night, when word of the Union victory at Five Forks reached the Petersburg area, Federal guns and mortars began a tremendous bombardment that went on for hours. Under cover of this, blue-clad troops began moving out silently into open ground with orders to attack at dawn.

At Edge Hill, Lee had been trying to get some rest, although the thunder of the Union guns made sleep almost impossible. He was not feeling well, and he was still in bed when Longstreet arrived. The veteran general, who had not yet fully recovered from the serious wound he had received less than a year before, had hurried ahead to be in advance of his troops who were being brought from Richmond by train. Before long, A. P. Hill joined them. Then a colonel rushed in to tell them that Army wagons were dashing wildly down the roads and that Union troops had broken through the lines. Hill left immediately to be with his men. He never reached them; a young Federal infantryman cut him down with a single bullet while he was riding through a grove of trees. Longstreet, too, departed to meet the train carrying his troops.

Lee got up and dressed himself. He put on his best uniform and buckled on his finest sword. Then he went out into the gray morning of Sunday, April 2. From the wide arc of Federal fortifications below Petersburg, thousands upon thousands of blue-clad troops were advancing toward the Confederate lines.

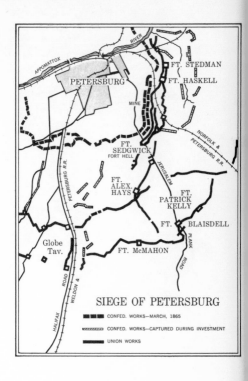

SIEGE OF PETERSBURG

CONFED. WORKS—MARCH, 1865
CONFED. WORKS—CAPTURED DURING INVESTMENT
UNION WORKS

The Union bombardment of the Confederate lines at Petersburg

to prepare the way for the massive assault of Grant's troops

Confederate trenches at Petersburg

The ruins of Richmond

THE FALL OF RICHMOND

Soon after Lee had ridden forward to observe what was happening, Hill's courier came up to tell him that the much-needed commander of the Third Corps had been killed. It was the first of many disasters on that disastrous day.

The Confederate lines in front of Edge Hill were still holding, but elsewhere they were disintegrating rapidly. Word of this reached Lee, who knew that the long battle to defend Richmond was lost. He sent telegrams to the Secretary of War telling him that he would have to abandon the lines and that he advised "that all preparation be made for leaving Richmond" that very night. A somewhat similar message was delivered at 10:40 A.M. to President Davis while he was attending services at St. Paul's Church. That moment marked the death knell of the Confederacy.

Six brass Napoleons were brought up to defend the Turnbull House at Edge Hill. Lee took personal charge of them and kept them firing when Federal batteries were sent up. Union shells fell into the house, driving out the last telegraph operators at Confederate headquarters there. As Lee and his staff rode away, the house began to burn. The flames devoured everything; only the chimneys were left standing, gaunt and tall above the ruins.

Fighting went on all afternoon as the Federals attacked one desperately held Confederate position after another. There was no staying the vast Union horde; in numbers alone it far outmatched the Confederate defenders.

At 8 P.M. what was left of the Army of Northern Virginia began to withdraw from the lines around Petersburg and Richmond. Five roads led west to Amelia Court House, the designated rendezvous 40 miles away. Over them had to pass a thousand wagons, 200 pieces of artillery, and regiment after regiment of foot soldiers and cavalry. Gunpowder and ammunition which could not be moved was blown up in the storage magazines.

And in Richmond, mobs of convicts and hoodlums were rioting through the streets, plundering stores and setting buildings on fire. The lower part of the city was a sea of flame above which smoke billowed up into the black sky. Ships and ironclads belonging to the Confederates were burned and blown up. And when the general conflagration reached the Arsenal, hundreds of thousands of shells there began to explode. Their mighty roar drowned out all the other din that rocked the former Confederate capital during that dreadful night.

Davis and his Cabinet left Richmond by train on what finally proved to be a hopeless attempt to escape the Federal armies which were overrunning the South. With them went what was left of the archives and the gold removed from the Treasury.

Before sunrise, Union troops began to occupy the city. They met no resistance and were put to work to try to bring the ravaging flames under control.

West of Richmond, the long columns of the Army of Northern Virginia stretched out for 30 miles along the roads. Every stream was an obstacle, for there were never enough bridges or fords to permit the weary troops to cross. And trouble was developing which no one knew anything about. Lee had arranged for rations to be sent from Richmond to Amelia Court House by train, but in all the haste and hysteria, something had gone wrong; the food did not get there. The hungry army was marching toward a sparsely settled area where there were few farms or towns that might have supplies. Since it was spring, the crops from the year before had been consumed during the winter. There was nothing ahead for thousands of men to eat.

What was left of General Lee's headquarters at Edge Hill

THE ROAD TO APPOMATTOX

Lee and the vanguard of his army arrived at Amelia Court House early on April 4. Artillery ammunition had been delivered but there was no food. He sent wagons out to forage for supplies and ordered a scout to ride down the railroad line to try to find a place from which a telegram could be dispatched to Danville to hurry up the missing rations. The scout was caught by Sheridan's troopers who turned his message over to their commander. The Federals now knew how serious Lee's situation was, and the number of rations requested gave them a good idea of the size of his army. It also told them that he was concentrating his forces at Amelia Court House. Sheridan was then at Jetersville, only eight miles away, and his men were blocking the Southside Railroad there. Worst of all, they were west of Amelia and could intercept any movement Lee might make in the only direction he wanted to go.

When the wagons returned at the end of the day, they were nearly empty, and a day had been lost because of the blunder in not sending rations. The desperate and starving little army now realized that it was only a matter of time. About 100 caissons were set on fire to get rid of artillery ammunition that would never be needed. And during this and the following nights, deserters began leaving. Wagon trains on the more remote roads were being attacked by Union cavalrymen who dashed in, did as much damage as they could, and then rode off to make other assaults on other parts of the slowly moving Confederate columns.

Lee pitched his headquarters tent in the garden of a private house in Amelia and remained there until shortly after noon on April 5. Then he started out with Longstreet to go to Jetersville. He did not know that the tiny railroad town was already in Union hands, but he soon heard the sound of shooting from that direction. His only chance of getting supplies was to reach Danville, nearly a hundred miles away. When he rode forward to survey the Federal lines, he realized that his army was no longer strong enough to attack the superior forces he saw waiting for him. He would have to bypass Sheridan's troopers and hope somehow to keep going. He turned away from the railroad

Captured Confederate muskets being sorted out. The poorer ones were used to pave the bottomless mud roads.

tracks and headed for Amelia Springs, which had once been a popular resort but which was now deserted.

At Amelia Springs, very early in the morning of April 6, Lee drafted a letter to young General John B. Gordon, which shows how desperate the situation was:

I have seen the dispatches (intercepted) you sent me. It was from my expectation of an attack being made from Jetersville that I was anxious that the rear of the column should reach Deatonsville as soon as possible. I hope the rear will get out of harm's way, and I rely greatly upon your exertions and good judgment for its safety. I know that men and animals are much exhausted, but it is necessary to tax their strength. I wish after the cavalry crosses the bridge at Flat Creek that it be thoroughly destroyed so as to prevent pursuit in that direction. The bridge over the same stream on the road to Jetersville I have had destroyed. By holding the position at Amelia Springs with our cavalry, which can retire by Deatonsville or up the road toward Paineville, we can secure the rear of the column from interruption. About two miles from Amelia Springs on the Deatonsville road a road leads off to the right to Chapman's into the Ligontown road, by which Farmville may be reached provided there is a bridge over the Appomattox at Ligontown. I hear there is none; therefore I see no way of relieving the column of the wagons, and they must be brought along. You must, of course, keep everything ahead of you, wagons, stragglers, &c. I will try to get the head of the column on, and to get provisions at Rice's Station or Farmville.

And at Amelia Springs, two of Sheridan's scouts, dressed in Confederate uniforms, were brought to Gordon. They answered all questions skillfully and were even provided with passes signed by General Lee. These were undoubtedly forged. An examination of the two men's boots produced a letter from Grant to Ord, instructing the commander of the Army of the James, which had evidently been brought up, to try to cut off Lee's retreat at Appomattox.

The Union spies' lives were forfeited because they had been caught wearing Confederate uniforms, but Gordon hesitated to have them shot since the war was obviously very near the end. He referred the matter to Lee, who promptly approved his suggestion to spare the men's lives. Gordon took them with him, and turned them over, safe and sound, to Sheridan on the morning of the surrender.

During the next few days the weakened Confederate columns were constantly harassed by cavalry and artillery attacks. An April 6, at Sayler's Creek, the mobile, slashing assaults developed into a bloody battle which Lee's out-

The remains of Lee's burned supply trains at Appomattox Station

207

General Lee's headquarters flag

numbered army had no chance of winning. The field became an enormous trap in which 7000 Confederates were compelled to surrender. Among them were Ewell, General Lee's son Custis, and five other top commanders. The Army of Northern Virginia was rapidly disintegrating. When Lee saw what was left of his once-invincible legions, he cried: "My God! Has the army been dissolved?" He sat on his horse holding up a Confederate battle flag as he watched the haggard survivors file past with their wounds still bleeding from the battle that had decimated their ranks.

Lee spent the night at Farmville, a railroad town, where some rations had arrived by train. But before his men could be properly fed, word arrived that Federal troops were advancing over High Bridge, where the rails crossed the Appomattox River a few miles east of the town. The trains had to be sent on to Appomattox Station while Farmville was hurriedly evacuated. Union soldiers reached the town so quickly that they took parting shots at the Confederates.

During the engagement at Farmville, Lee, according to Gordon, "was riding everywhere and watching everything, encouraging his brave men by his calm and cheerful bearing. He was often exposed to great danger from shells and bullets; but, in answer to protests, his reply was that he was obliged to see for himself what was going on. As he sat on his horse . . . watching the effect of the fire from one of our batteries which was playing upon the enemy, a staff officer rode up to him with a message. The general noticed that this officer had exposed himself unnecessarily in approaching him, and he reprimanded the young soldier for not riding on the side of the hill where he would be protected from the enemy's fire. The young officer replied that he would be ashamed to seek protection while the commanding general was so exposing himself. General Lee sharply replied: 'It is my duty to be here. Go back the way I told you, sir.'"

Grant arrived in Farmville soon after his troops had occupied the town. They held a wild celebration in anticipation of victory. While it was going on, three of Grant's top commanders called upon him and urged him to send a message to Lee pointing out that further resistance was hopeless and asking for the surrender of the Army of Northern Virginia.

When the note reached Lee, he read it, and handed it to Longstreet. Longstreet gave the answer when he said "Not yet." Nevertheless Lee wrote

One of the Lee-Grant Appomattox letters. In this one, dated April 9, Lee says: "I ask a suspension of hostilities pending the adjustment of the terms of the surrender of this army, in the interview requested in my former communication today."

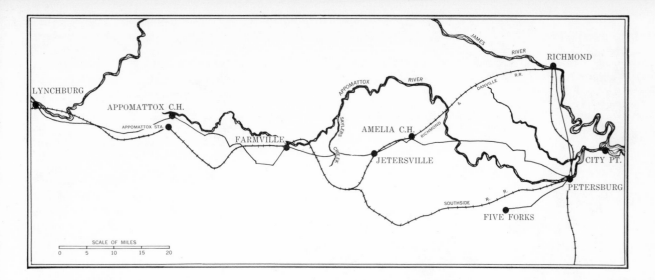

to Grant to ask what the terms of surrender would be. When he received the reply on April 8, he learned that the tough Union general, who had demanded unconditional surrender at Fort Donelson in 1862, was apparently prepared to be generous. Lee still hesitated, although his leading generals already agreed that the better part of wisdom was to surrender at once. When one of them called on Lee to notify him of their decision, Lee put him off by saying that "if I were to intimate to General Grant that I would listen to terms, he would at once regard it as such evidence of weakness that he would demand unconditional surrender, and sooner than that I am resolved to die."

The two armies kept moving toward the west. When the Confederate supply trains reached Appomattox Station, Custer's cavalrymen captured them. They burned one and ran the other three toward the Union lines. Lee's last chance of obtaining rations was gone.

APPOMATTOX. What was left of the Army of Northern Virginia after desertion, death, wounds, and capture had reduced it to a shadow of its former self was now in the vicinity of the small hamlet called Appomattox Court House.

That hitherto obscure village consisted only of the courthouse (the reason for its existence), a jail, a tavern, and a handful of private homes. One of its residents was a man named Wilmer McLean, who had been living near a creek called Bull Run when the first major battle of the war was fought there. In order to take his family out of the danger zone, he moved to the remote village of Appomattox Court House. Now the two great armies in the eastern theater of war were rapidly concentrating around his new home.

During the evening of April 8 Lee prepared his answer to Grant's letter of the same date. His words show the complexity of the problem facing him, for it must be remembered that in February he had been made the commander of *all* the Confederate armies.

I did not intend to propose the surrender of the Army of N. Va.—but to ask the terms of your proposition. To be frank, I do not think the emergency has arisen to call for the surrender of this Army, but as the restoration of peace should be the sole object of all, I desired to know whether your proposals would lead to that and I cannot therefore meet you with a view to surrender the Army of N. Va.—but as far as your proposal may affect the C.S. forces under my command and tend to the restoration of peace, I shall be pleased to meet you at 10 A.M. tomorrow on the old stage road to Richmond between the picket lines of the two armies.

General Lee's pocket revolver

209

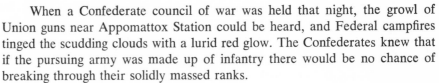

The village of
Appomattox Court House
as it looked on April 9, 1865

When a Confederate council of war was held that night, the growl of Union guns near Appomattox Station could be heard, and Federal campfires tinged the scudding clouds with a lurid red glow. The Confederates knew that if the pursuing army was made up of infantry there would be no chance of breaking through their solidly massed ranks.

The correspondence between Lee and Grant was discussed at the meeting, and there was much argument about whether they should try to cut their way through or not. It was decided that several units, mostly mobile mounted ones, would make a dash for it and try to join Johnston's forces to fight with them against Sherman.

On April 9 (Palm Sunday) there was fog over the field at Appomattox Court House at daybreak. Out of this came Fitzhugh Lee's cavalry riding madly toward the western end of the Union lines while Gordon's foot soldiers attacked the center. As soon as Fitzhugh Lee found out that not only Federal cavalry but infantry as well had come up, he rode off toward Lynchburg, taking men from other mounted units with him. The Federal forces were so large that they simply enfolded the Confederate troops on the field. Many were able to fall back, but it was obvious that further resistance was out of the question. The Army of Northern Virginia, which had always fought against great odds, was now hopelessly outnumbered. And everyone knew that still more Union troops were on the way.

When Lee arose that morning, he again put on his finest dress uniform. He tied a silk sash around his waist and buckled on a beautiful presentation sword.

Three of his generals came for a last-minute conference at which Alexander urged that the men "take to the woods and bushes" where they "would be like rabbits and partridges" and as hard to catch. But Lee understood what this would mean. He told Alexander: "We must consider its effect on the coun-

210

The McLean house
photographed a few days
after the surrender

try as a whole. Already it is demoralized by the four years of war. If I took your advice, the men would be without rations and under no control of officers. They would be compelled to rob and steal in order to live. They would become mere bands of marauders, and the enemy's cavalry would pursue them and overrun many wide sections they may never have occasion to visit. We would bring on a state of affairs it would take the country years to recover from."

In his *Memoirs* Alexander said: "He had answered my suggestion from a plane so far above it that I was ashamed of having made it." Lee's postwar career, which was to be even greater than his record as a soldier, may be said to have begun with his reply to Alexander that day. His wise decision saved the already prostrate South from years of guerrilla warfare.

Grant was suffering from a sick headache and had spent most of the night bathing his feet in hot water while he applied mustard plasters to his wrists and the back of his neck. When he received Lee's note asking for a meeting at 10 A.M. he replied that such a conference "could lead to no good." But Lee had sent flags of truce to Sheridan and Meade and was asking for a suspension of hostilities. The first steps toward surrender had already been taken.

Lee received Grant's letter while he was on the way to the meeting which he thought would surely be agreed to. Disappointed as he was, Lee nevertheless addressed another note to Grant. In it he said: "I now request an interview in accordance with the offer contained in your letter of yesterday." Firing was going on in some parts of the field, and the Federal infantry was continuing to push forward. Lee sent still another note asking for a suspension of hostilities. He waited until the advancing Union troops were only a few hundred feet away; then he rode back to join Longstreet who had drawn up his supply wagons and was ready to resist an expected attack.

Lee's messages had reached Rawlins, Grant's chief of staff. He thought

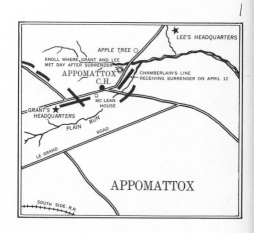

211

The surrender room

that Lee was merely trying to buy time, but his superior told him that the Confederate leader was "only trying to be let down easily." He now agreed to meet Lee and started out for Appomattox. His party made slow progress, for they had to go around part of the Confederate army, and at least once they got lost.

The courier whom Grant had sent ahead to notify Lee that he was on the way found the Confederate commander resting under an apple tree. In company with his military secretary, Colonel Charles Marshall, and a single orderly, he got up and rode toward Appomattox Court House.

Marshall met Wilmer McLean, the man who had moved his family from Bull Run to Appomattox, and asked him to help find a building for the conference. After examining one place which Marshall rejected as not being suitable, McLean offered the use of his own home for the meeting. And there Lee went to wait in the parlor for Grant's arrival.

In this humble private dwelling in an obscure Virginia village the fate of Southern independence was about to be settled. The armies had struggled for four years, and men had died by the hundreds of thousands. Armed ships had ranged the oceans of the world; statesmen had harangued and thundered; women had prayed and wept; and fire-blackened chimneys showed where thousands of homes had once stood. Now it was all over, and the South's attempt to become a separate nation had failed. Much bitterness had been engendered by the long-drawn-out conflict, and no one knew better than the man waiting in McLean's parlor how difficult the future would be for the people in the

The pen with which
the surrender was signed

*Furniture from the surrender room
in the McLean house. These pieces
are now on display in the
Smithsonian Institution,
Washington, D.C.*

The chair in which Lee sat

*The table on which
the surrender was signed*

The Secretary

General Lee riding away from the McLean house after the surrender. Drawing by A. R. Waud.

defeated South. While he waited, he had plenty of time to think, to review the events of the war and of his own life.

He knew that he had encountered Grant at some time during the Mexican War, but he could not recall what he looked like. He had met hundreds of young officers then, and most of them were only a blurred memory of faces, uniforms, and military accouterments. But Grant had made a famous name for himself during the past few years. It would be interesting to see this man who had begun his career as a professional soldier, who had taken to drink, and

214

who had resigned from the Army to go back to civilian life. Everyone knew he had been a failure at that. Only when the war had given him another chance did U. S. Grant rise to the occasion and become the kind of military leader he was evidently capable of being.

It was well after one o'clock when the Union hero arrived. He came into the McLean parlor with his boots and clothing spotted with mud from his long ride. Lee rose and walked across the room to meet him. They shook hands and sat down. Then a dozen Union officers entered the room and stood quietly near Grant to witness the historic ceremony. Outside, thousands of soldiers from both armies waited.

Lee left no written record of the occasion, but Grant described it in his *Memoirs:* "We soon fell into a conversation about old army times. He remarked that he remembered me very well in the old army; and I told him that as a matter of course I remembered him perfectly, but from the difference in our rank and years (there being about sixteen years' difference in our ages), I had thought it very likely that I had not attracted his attention sufficiently to be remembered by him after such a long interval. Our conversation grew so pleasant that I almost forgot the object of our meeting. After the conversation had run on in this style for some time, General Lee called my attention to the object of our meeting, and said that he had asked for this interview for the purpose of getting from me the terms I proposed to give his army. I said that

An autograph copy of the Farewell Address signed by General Lee

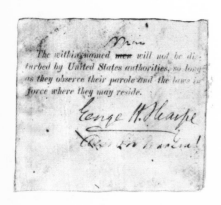

We, the undersigned Prisoners of War, belonging to the Army of Northern Virginia, having been this day surrendered by General Robert E. Lee, C. S. A., Commanding said Army, to Lieut. Genl. U. S. Grant, Commanding Armies of United States, do hereby give our solemn parole of honor that we will not hereafter serve in the armies of the Confederate States, or in any military capacity whatever, against the United States of America, or render aid to the enemies of the latter, until properly exchanged, in such manner as shall be mutually approved by the respective authorities.

Done at Appomattox Court House, Va., this 9th day of April, 1865.

The parole signed by Lee and his staff at Appomattox

I meant merely that his army should lay down their arms, not to take them up again during the continuance of the war unless duly and properly exchanged."

After some more desultory conversation, Lee suggested that the terms for surrender should be written out. Grant put the detailed conditions on paper. They were remarkably generous. (Perhaps the two generals were thinking of the terms their old commander, Winfield Scott, had offered the defeated Mexicans nearly twenty years before.)

When Lee read the document, he was pleased to note that his officers were to be allowed to keep their side arms, private horses, and baggage. "This will have a very happy effect on my army," he said. He then pointed out that his cavalrymen and artillerists owned their own horses. He wanted to know whether they would be permitted to retain them.

It was a difficult question, for no provision had been made for the enlisted men to keep their horses. But Grant again was generous. He said that he knew that most of the men were small farmers and "that it was doubtful whether they would be able to put in a crop to carry themselves and their families through the next winter without the aid of the horses they were then riding." He would not change the terms as written, but he would instruct the officers who were to receive the paroles "to let every man who claimed to own a horse or a mule take the animal to his home."

Lee thanked him, saying, "This will have the best possible effect upon the men. It will be very gratifying and will do much toward conciliating our people." He now proceeded to write a letter accepting the terms as proposed. While the various documents were being copied, Grant presented the Union officers to Lee.

Before he left, Lee remarked that his men were in great need of food. Grant told him that he would authorize him to send his commissary and quartermaster to Appomattox Station where they could obtain rations from the Confederate trains that had been captured there. The food which was supposed to reach Amelia Station five days before was at last available to the men for whom it was intended.

The fifty-eight-year-old general then shook hands with Grant, bowed to the officers present, and went out on the porch. There he drew on his gray gauntlets and clapped his hands together several times. He called for his orderly, who promptly brought up Traveller. As Lee rode away, he lifted his hat to General Grant, who had come out of the McLean house. It was all over. He had only to tell his men that there would be no more fighting, no more killing, and that they could return home. But he also had to tell them that the hope for Southern independence was never to be realized, that the Army of Northern Virginia was no more, and that it had, as of that moment, passed into history where its gray-clad troops would march forever down roads on which Roman legions, Greek phalanxes, and Assyrian warriors had preceded them into the mists of time.

He had to ride through the remnants of his army, face his men again, many of them for the last time. They crowded around Traveller as the famous horse walked slowly back toward an apple orchard where some of the engineers had formed a protective circle. On the way, sorrowful men spoke to their sorrowing general, whose face told them that the end had come. At sundown, Lee went on to his headquarters, again having to pass through long lines of troops. He asked Colonel Marshall to draw up a draft for a farewell address.

Next morning, when Lee found that the draft was still unfinished, he told his military secretary to use his ambulance as a quiet place to compose the brief farewell. Then he rode off in the rain to speak to Grant, who had come over to see him but had been stopped at the picket line. The two generals met and went to a little hillock where they could talk alone. According to Grant, they were together for about half an hour, during which they had a pleasant conversation while sitting on horseback. He reported that Lee said "that the South was a big country and that we might have to march over it three or four times before the war entirely ended, but that we would now be able to do it as they could no longer resist us. He expressed it as his earnest hope, however, that we would not be called upon to cause more loss and sacrifice of life; but he could not foretell the result. I then suggested to General Lee that there was not a man in the Confederacy whose influence with the soldiery and the whole people was as great as his, and that if he would now advise the surrender of all the armies I had no doubt his advice would be followed with alacrity. But Lee said that he could not do that without consulting the President [Davis] first. I knew there was no use to urge him to do anything against his ideas of what was right."

They parted then. They were to meet again in Washington on May 1, 1869.

Lee returned to his headquarters, where Marshall finally had the draft of the farewell address ready for him. He made a few changes in it, ordered the revised version to be copied and distributed to the corps commanders and general staff. That was all there was to it. There was no emotional reading of the document by Lee to his soldiers, no Napoleonic posturing. To him, the famous farewell address was simply General Orders No. 9.

The arduous business of issuing paroles now began. Lee remained at Appomattox until the last sad ceremony of the laying down of Confederate arms was over on April 12, but he did not witness it in person. According to the official record, only 28,231 men surrendered at Appomattox. A few thousand had ridden off to join Johnston. The rest of that mighy army were gone; many were dead, some had been captured, others had simply disappeared.

On the afternoon of April 12, after writing a report of the campaign for Jefferson Davis, Lee and a few members of his staff left Appomattox and headed for Richmond.

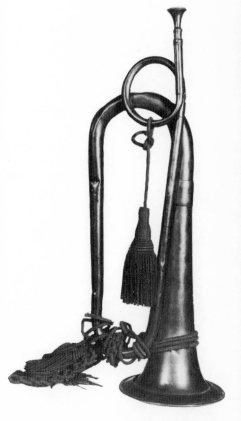

The Appomattox Bugle

THE RETURN TO RICHMOND

One of the Union generals sent an escort of twenty-five cavalrymen to guard Lee on his way to Richmond, but he politely declined the offer and rode on, accompanied only by a few members of his staff. On the way he stopped over-night at his brother Carter's place in Powhatan County. Even there he refused to stay in the house and had his old campaign tent pitched on the lawn.

The next morning, Rooney Lee and several others joined the party which so increased its numbers that there were twenty horses and several wagons when it approached Richmond from the south. Rain was falling when they came in sight of the fire-gutted buildings along the shore of the James. The bridge had been destroyed, but a temporary wooden roadway supported by Union pontoons crossed the river. They had to wait their turn to use this, and while they stood there they had a good chance to examine the desolate-looking ruins of the city which had been the capital of the Confederacy.

Most of the buildings on the streets along the river were now smoke-blackened wrecks. Rubble was everywhere, choking the passageways and impeding traffic. The fire had reached far up on the hill before it was stopped, and almost everything between the Capitol and the waterfront had been destroyed. But as Lee rode through the ruins of Richmond, people gathered around him. From them, on this sad April 15, he doubtless learned that President Lincoln had been shot on the previous night and had died early that morning. And it was being rumored that the assassin was a Southerner, a misguided man, insane perhaps, but of Southern sympathies.

When Lee reached his home on East Franklin Street, he was able to close the door on the importunate crowd and rest from the exhausting events of the last few days which had ended his military career forever. There is no record of his immediate reaction to the news of the assassination, but in a letter written a few months later, he said: "You do the people of the South but simple justice in believing that they heartily concur with you in opinion in regard to the assassination of the late President Lincoln. It is a crime previously unknown to this country, and one that must be deprecated by every American."

But John Wilkes Booth's senseless deed was to cost the South heavily. Restrictions in the occupied city of Richmond were tightened immediately. People were not allowed to congregate on the streets, and in Raleigh, where

218

*One of the portraits
Brady made of Lee in Richmond
in April 1865*

Johnston was about to surrender his army to Sherman on the same terms Grant had given Lee at Appomattox, news of what had happened changed everything. Sherman was quickly repudiated by the new government, and Grant had to go to him in person to try to pacify the peppery general.

Mathew Brady, the photographer who was making a camera record of the war, hurried from Appomattox to Richmond. Soon after he arrived, he went to the Lee house with a request to photograph its famous occupant. He was politely turned away, but Brady was noted for his persistence. According to a newspaper account printed many years later, he said of the occasion: "It was supposed that after his defeat it would be preposterous to ask him to sit, but I thought that to be the time for the historical picture. He allowed me to come to his house and photograph him on his back porch, several sittings. Of course I had known him since the Mexican War when he was upon General Scott's staff, and my request was not as from an intruder."

Brady made six negatives on April 17, 1865, only eight days after Appomattox. The best of them are among the very finest of all Lee portraits. They are the only ones which show the Confederate general in the uniform he wore

219

when he met Grant, and they show the lines of suffering and of sadness in his face.

The pictures were taken in the rear of the East Franklin Street house with daylight as the only source of illumination. Brady knew his business, and he understood the limitations of his crude camera and of the big glass plates which had to be coated on the spot. Working within these limitations, he was able to turn out masterpiece after masterpiece.

One of the many problems facing the veterans who had surrendered at Appomattox was the demand made by Union military authorities that they take an oath of allegiance to the Northern Government against which they had fought. They felt that the paroles they had signed were sufficient. When one of them came to Lee for advice, his former commander quietly advised him to take the required oath. The young man burst out in a tirade, threatening to emigrate to another country as many of his comrades were doing. "Do not leave Virginia," Lee urged. "Our country needs her young men now."

There was talk of resistance while Davis' Cabinet was still making its way south. Lee wrote to him on April 20. After explaining that at Appomattox, where his forces had been reduced to 7892 effective infantry, thousands of stragglers came in later so that more than 26,000 men finally signed paroles there, and that others had since come to Richmond to surrender, Lee said:

I have given these details that your Excellency might know the state of feeling which existed in the army, and judge of that in the country. From what I have seen and learned, I believe an army cannot be organized or supported in Virginia, and as far as I know the condition of affairs, the country east of the Mississippi is morally and physically unable to maintain the contest unaided with any hope of ultimate success. A partisan war may be continued, and hostilities protracted, causing individual suffering and the devastation of the country, but I see no prospect by that means of achieving a separate independence. It is for Your Excellency to decide, should you agree with me in opinion, what is proper to be done. To save useless effusion of blood, I would recommend measures be taken for suspension of hostilities and the restoration of peace.

In order to get away from the tense atmosphere of Richmond, Lee wanted to find a "little quiet house somewhere in the woods" for his family. Late in May or early in June the former general rode out to visit his cousin, Colonel Thomas H. Carter, at his place on the Pamunkey River. During the time he spent there, he urged his cousin to replace the former slaves still living on the plantation with white labor. When Colonel Carter told him that he had to get along with whatever help was available, Lee said: "I have always observed that wherever you find the Negro, everything is going down around him, and wherever you find the white man, you see everything around him improving."

It was at this time that the highly placed men who had served the Confederacy were being singled out as special targets by the new administration in Washington. Lee had already applied for a pardon; now he heard that he was about to be tried for treason. (Jefferson Davis had been apprehended and was being held as a state prisoner.) Lee wrote to Grant on June 13, enclosing a letter of application addressed to President Johnson in which he asked for the benefits and restoration of rights offered under the amnesty and pardon act of May 29. Grant interceded with the President for him. No positive action was ever taken, but the move to arrest and try Lee was quietly dropped.

The use of a modest house at Derwent, a James River estate above Richmond, was now offered to the Lees by its owner. And there, at the end of June, the former commander of the Confederate Army and his family went, prepared to stay for a long while.

Mathew Brady photographed in front of the Capitol in Richmond in April 1865. He is the man at the left of the group of five and is wearing a tall hat.

Another of the portraits Brady made in Richmond

*A view of Lexington, Va.
Washington College is in the center,
Virginia Military Institute at the right.*

THE LEXINGTON YEARS

About a month after he arrived at Derwent, Lee wrote to a number of his former generals asking them to send him any documents they might have which pertained to the part they played in the war. He was planning to write a book about the Virginia campaigns and he needed documentation, for many of his own records had been destroyed during the evacuation of Petersburg and Richmond and the retreat to Appomattox. The book was destined never to be written, although some of the generals sent him material for it.

In Lexington at this time a meeting was taking place which was to have an important influence on Lee's career. There, on August 4, the trustees of Washington College were trying to find a way to keep that long-established institution going. Like its next-door neighbor, the Virginia Military Institute, it had been seriously damaged during Hunter's raid in June 1864. The Institute buildings had been set on fire, and the libraries and scientific apparatus of both places were scattered or destroyed.

Washington College had been founded in 1749 as the Augusta Academy in Greenville. It was renamed Liberty Hall in 1776, a few days after the Battle of Lexington. Twenty years later, George Washington donated 100 shares of James River Company stock to the school, which changed its name to the Washington Academy in his honor. The original building in Greenville burned in 1802. The Academy was then moved to Lexington, where it was chartered as Washington College in 1813.

The college had survived the war, but in August 1865 only four teachers and a handful of students were left. Several small loans were obtained to repair the buildings, meet the payroll, and replace books and equipment, but the little institution was in desperate straits. The Shenandoah Valley had been devastated by war, the South was destitute, and many of its young men had spent so many years in the Army that they were not prepared for college. And like nearly everyone else in the Southern states, they lacked money to pay for an education.

222

At the meeting of the trustees on August 4, several names were proposed for the presidency of the college. Before a vote could be taken, Colonel Bolivar Christian addressed the board "in a somewhat hesitating manner." He told them that a woman he knew had heard one of Lee's daughters say that the people of the South were eager to give her father anything he wanted but that no one had offered him a position by which he could earn a living. Colonel Christian was asked if he was nominating General Lee for the presidency of the college. He said that he was not, but in the animated discussion that followed, he was urged to do so. The general was then unanimously elected.

No one, of course, had any idea whether or not he would accept. A letter offering him the position was drafted, and the rector of the college, Judge John W. Brockenbrough, was authorized to call on Lee to present the letter and try to persuade him to accept the position. The Judge thanked the board for choosing him, but said that he could not go because he did not have a decent suit of clothes to wear or the money to pay his traveling expenses. One trustee offered to lend him a new suit which his son in the North had sent him; another said that a local resident had just received cash for a tobacco crop and that some of the money might be borrowed for the journey. Thus equipped with borrowed clothes and funds, Judge Brockenbrough set out on his mission.

No record exists of the Judge's interview with Lee, but he was evidently persuasive enough to make the general willing to consider accepting the post. Lee had already been offered the vice-chancellorship of the University of the South in Sewanee, Tennessee, which he had refused because it was denominational. And he had politely turned away offers to become associated with the University of Virginia because it was a state institution.

Washington College was neither, but Lee was still hesitant. A letter from General W. N. Pendleton, who had been his chief of artillery and was now in Lexington as the rector of Grace Church, probably influenced him. He also went to see another Episcopal clergyman, the Reverend P. B. Wilmer, about the problem. Wilmer later said that he confessed "to a momentary feeling of chagrin" at the idea of letting so distinguished a man go to such an obscure and isolated a place when he would be welcomed by much larger and better-known colleges. But, said Wilmer, Lee's "mind towered above these earthly distinctions. . . . In his judgment, the *cause* gave dignity to the institution." And seeing that Lee felt that "this door and not another was opened to him by Providence," the bishop congratulated him on his choice.

Lee then admitted that despite nearly three years of service as head of the Military Academy at West Point, he was far from certain that he was competent to fill the new post offered to him. This sense of inadequacy—which haunted Lee all his life—was expressed in his reply to the committee of trustees at Washington College: "Fully impressed with the responsibilities of the office, I have feared that I should be unable to discharge its duties to the satisfaction of the trustees or to the benefit of the country. The proper education of youth requires not only great ability, but I fear more strength than I now possess, for I do not feel able to undergo the labour of conducting classes in regular courses of instruction. I could not, therefore, undertake more than the general administration and supervision of the institution. There is another subject which has caused me serious reflection. . . . Being excluded from the terms of amnesty in the proclamation of the President of the United States of the 29th of May last, and an object of censure to a portion of the country, I have thought it probable that my occupation of the position of president might draw upon the college a feeling of hostility; and I should, therefore, cause injury to an institution which it would be my highest desire to advance. I think it the duty of every citizen in the present condition of the country to do

The ruins of Liberty Hall

223

The oldest college buildings as they appear today

all in his power to aid in the restoration of peace and harmony and in no way to oppose the policy of the State or general government directed to that object. It is particularly incumbent on those charged with the instruction of the young to set them an example of submission to authority, and I could not consent to be the cause of animadversion upon the college. Should you, however, take a different view, and think that my services in the position tendered to me by the board will be advantageous to the college and country, I will yield to your judgment and accept it; otherwise, I must most respectfully decline the office."

The trustees, of course, had no reservations about Lee's ability and were overjoyed that he was willing to accept. They endorsed the sentiments expressed in his letter and made preparations to welcome him. His salary was to be $1500 a year plus 20 per cent of the tuition fees received and the use of a house on the campus.

Not knowing what the quarters provided for his family would be like, Lee started out for Lexington alone on September 18, riding Traveller for the three-day journey in hot weather. When he arrived in town unheralded, he headed for a hotel but was intercepted by one of the faculty who took him to the home of Colonel S. M. Reid to stay for the night.

The president's house was not yet ready for occupancy, so Lee spent a week or so at nearby Rockbridge Baths. He was inaugurated on October 2—not with a great ceremony as the trustees had hoped, but with a simple one. When he took the oath of office that day he began the last phase of his career.

The president's house was not ready for Mrs. Lee until late in November. Then the head of the James River and Kanawha Canal Company gave her the use of his private boat so she could make the journey from Richmond to Lexington in comfort. When she arrived in Lexington on December 2, her husband was at the landing to meet her. Robert, who had been ill, accompanied her. Custis, who was now teaching at the Virginia Military Institute, was also on hand. Breakfast, prepared by the wife of one of the professors, awaited them in their new home, of which Robert said: "The house was in good order—thanks to the ladies of Lexington—but rather bare of furniture, except my mother's rooms. . . . Mrs. Margaret J. Preston, the talented and well-known poetess, had drawn the designs for the furniture, and a one-armed Confederate soldier had made it all. A handsomely carved grand piano, presented by Stieff, the famous maker of Baltimore, stood alone in the parlour. The floors were covered with the carpets rescued from Arlington—much too large and folded under to suit the reduced size of the rooms. Some of the bedrooms were partially furnished, and the dining-room had enough in it to make us very comfortable. We were all very grateful and happy—glad to get home—the only one we had had for four long years."

The family silver had been sent to Lexington for safekeeping early in the war. It had been buried in the ground in two large chests to avoid seizure during Hunter's raid. When Robert dug it up, he found it so tarnished and blackened that it could not be used until it was properly cleaned. Meanwhile, the family dined with the utensils from the general's mess kit and sat on his camp stools when at the table.

Robert said that his father "at once set to work to improve all around him, laid out a vegetable garden, planted roses and shrubs, set out fruit and yard trees, made new walks and repaired the stables, so that in a short time we were quite comfortable and very happy. He at last had a home of his own, with his wife and daughters around him, and though it was not the little farm in the quiet country for which he had so longed, it was very near to it, and it gave rest to himself and those he loved most dearly."

The "old" president's house

Lee also gave his attention to the grounds and college buildings, which rapidly began to show signs of improvement. And he became acquainted with the students personally until he could greet each one by name.

The fact that the college which had offered Lee the opportunity of being its president was named Washington doubtless influenced his decision to go there. George Washington had played a prominent part in shaping Lee's career from the beginning and was to continue to do so. And just as Washington had devoted himself to public service at the cost of personal ease, so did Lee take his new duties seriously. Since he was without adequate clerical help, he had to do much routine work himself. Just answering mail was a major task, for the new president received many letters which dealt with matters far beyond the administration of the college. His former soldiers wrote to him constantly, and he regarded it as a necessary duty to reply to them—often in his own handwriting. These veterans' continuing devotion to him is the best measure of his stature as a charismatic leader—the kind who draws others to him by the magnetic force of his personality. He received several thousand letters during the five years of his presidency, and many of them show that the people of the South—ex-soldiers and civilians alike—turned to him for counsel and advice in that difficult postwar period. Letters came from the North as well as the South. Oddly enough, there were no hostile letters, although some Northern newspapers were still charging Lee with being a renegade and traitor. The old story of his abusing the slaves at Arlington was revived, and a new one was invented in which he was accused of having appropriated maps of the defenses of Washington allegedly entrusted to him by General Scott in April 1861.

Lee did not reply to such attacks even when they were obviously untrue. His attitude is best expressed in a letter he wrote to Mrs. Jefferson Davis on February 23, 1866, when her imprisoned husband was assailed by Speaker of the House Schuyler Colfax: *"I have thought, from the time of the cessation of hostilities, that silence and patience on the part of the South was the true course; and I think so still. Controversy of all kinds* will, in my opinion, only serve to continue excitement and passion, and will prevent the public mind from the acknowledgment and acceptance of the truth. These considerations have kept me from replying to accusations made against myself, and induced me to recommend the same to others."

General Lee's spectacles

About this time he also said that it would be wise "not to keep open the sores of war." And when asked to support an effort to return the remains of the Confederates who had died at Gettysburg to their own states, he replied: "I know of no fitter resting-place for a soldier than the field on which he has nobly laid down his life."

In January 1866, the trustees sent Lee to Richmond to appeal to the Virginia state legislature for funds. Then he was summoned to Washington in February to appear before a joint committee of Congress which was investigating the advisability of allowing the states which had seceded to be represented again in that legislative body.

Lee had not been in Washington since April 1861. Since Arlington can be seen from many parts of the Federal capital, his eyes must often have sought his former home on the heights across the river. The city itself had grown so enormously during the war that much of it was new to him. Even the Capitol had changed, for its great white dome, on which construction was just beginning in 1861, was now completed. And across the way from it (where the Supreme Court building now stands) was the Old Capitol Prison, where so many Confederates had been held, often without charges being brought against them.

Lee's replies to the committee did not attract much attention because they were neither novel nor sensational. He said that he had been living a retired life and had had little communication with politicians. As to the Negroes, he said that the people of his community were willing to have them educated and that it would be better for both the blacks and the whites if they were. He did not feel particularly qualified to speak about their educability, but he did not think they were as capable of acquiring knowledge as the whites. When asked "Do you not think that Virginia would be better off if the colored population would go to other Southern states?" he replied: "I think it would be better for Virginia if she could get rid of them. . . . I have always thought so."

As to secession, he said that he believed the Southern people felt "that the state was responsible for the act; not the individual," and that in his case the act of Virginia in withdrawing herself from the United States carried him along as a citizen of the state, and that her laws and acts were binding on him.

He also said that he had not known about any mistreatment of Northern prisoners. As to the Confederate soldiers' attitude toward the Federal Government, he agreed that the veterans felt more kindly toward it than any other part of the Southern people. "They [the veterans] looked upon the war as a necessary evil and went through it," he added.

Lee's answers were polite, candid, carefully phrased, and what might be expected from a man of his background and experience. The committee evidently saw that it was getting nowhere and dismissed the witness after one brief session on February 17.

During his four-day stay in Washington, Lee voluntarily saw few people other than those officially engaged in the inquiry. A group of his young friends organized themselves to protect him against importunate visitors. But nothing could keep the ladies away. Mrs. Clement C. Clay said that she saw him surrounded by them "begging for mementoes, buttons—anything . . . while he, modest and benevolent, yielded helplessly to their demands."

At this time, he was called upon by one of the former slaves at Arlington, a woman named Amanda. He wrote to her to say that he was sorry he had missed her when she came to his hotel because he wanted to learn from her "how all the people from Arlington were getting on in the world." Then he said: "My interest in them is as great now as it ever was, and I sincerely wish

MRS. ROBERT E. LEE

226

Eleanor Agnes Lee, 1842–1873

ARY Custis Lee, 1835–1918

Mildred Childe Lee, 1846–1905

Robert E. Lee, Jr., 1843–1914

George Washington Custis Lee, 1832–1913

FIVE OF THE SEVEN LEE CHILDREN

Here are photographs of five of General Lee's children. Rooney Lee's portrait appears on page 183; Annie Carter Lee apparently was never photographed, probably because one of her eyes had been injured in an early accident. And she died young—in October 1862 at twenty-three. None of the daughters ever married. Neither did Custis. But Rooney and Robert, Jr., did, and it is through them that the line has been carried on. There are direct descendants of Robert E. Lee living today.

Although Lee's daughters often went for long visits to friends in various places throughout the South, as was then the custom, they remained close to him for the last five years of his life. The eldest daughter, Mary, was said to have been strong-willed, unafraid of anything, and fond of taking long walks alone. Lee described Agnes as "very thoughtful and attentive. She has not great velocity, but is systematic and quiet." He also said that she

was a good housekeeper. In his letters he often referred to her as "Daughter."

When Lee wrote to Mildred he addressed her as "My precious Life," which he sometimes abbreviated to "Life." Agnes' health was so poor that she was often away from home seeking a cure. She died only three years after her father.

Since Custis was teaching at V.M.I., he remained close to the family. After his father's death, he succeeded him as president of Washington College. Rooney remained on his farm, the White House, until 1874, when he moved to Ravensworth which he had inherited. Robert, Jr., stayed with Rooney at the White House for some years after the war. Then he operated his own farm in King William County but was in business in Washington for many years. His book about his father, entitled Recollections and Letters of General Robert E. Lee, *was published in 1904.*

Lee autographed hundreds of photographs like this for admirers who wrote to request a picture

Boude & Miley,   Lexington, Va.

for their happiness and prosperity. At the period specified in Mr. Custis's will —five years from the time of his death—I caused the liberation of all the people at Arlington, as well as those at the White House and Romancoke, to be recorded in the Hustings Court at Richmond; and letters of manumission to be given to those with whom I could communicate who desired them. In consequence of the war which then existed, I could do nothing more for them."

The hostility toward him in the Northern press and at the inquiry made a great impression on Lee. In writing to a young friend he said: "I am now considered such a monster that I hesitate to darken . . . the doors of those I love best lest I should bring . . . them misfortune."

Back in Lexington, he devoted himself to the necessary work of trying to obtain more funds for the struggling little college. His connection with it was of enormous value, for his name brought money from private benefactors in the North as well as in the South. Among the Northern donors were Cyrus McCormick, George Peabody, and Warren Newcomb, who gave substantial amounts. Even Henry Ward Beecher, the ardent abolitionist, urged support of the fund drive for the college.

Tribute has often been paid to Lee's personal influence upon the student body which increased from 50 to 146 during his first year as president. But he went far beyond merely serving as a good example for the students to follow. The man who had been an innovator in warfare proved to be equally original in his thinking about education. He instituted an elective system instead of rigidly prescribed courses, put the students on their honor, and abolished compulsory chapel attendance.

Like most institutions of learning of the period, Washington College had always stressed a classical education. Lee realized that Southern students needed practical subjects which would help them earn a living—and also enable them to restore the shattered economy of their states. Such courses were almost unknown in colleges at that time, but Lee drew up a plan which not only involved offering such subjects as practical chemistry and mechanics, civil and mechanical engineering, and modern languages, but soon went beyond them to recommend teaching mechanical engineering, agriculture, commerce, and journalism. His suggestions for offering courses in commerce and journalism were particularly novel, for no American institution then taught them. He died before the school of commerce could be established. His death also ended his plans for a department of astronomy which was to have its own observatory.

And despite the fact that the new president had been educated at West Point, had been its Superintendent, and had spent his entire adult life in the Army, he wanted the college to be run as a civilian place of learning. The Virginia Military Institute was next door; young men who intended to become soldiers could go there. Nothing explains Lee's ambitions for the kind of school he wanted to build so well as what he told a new boy who asked him for a copy of the college's rule book. "We have no printed rules," Lee said. "We have but one rule here, and that is that every student must be a gentleman."

Fortunately for posterity, a former Confederate soldier, young Michael Miley, set up a studio in Lexington in 1866. John C. Boude, who had been a captain in the Confederate Army, provided the necessary capital. Since Miley was the only photographer in the area during the last five years of Lee's life, he was able to make a vivid pictorial record of the former general, of his family, friends, and contemporaries, and of the college and the town as they were in those days.

The photographs of Lee taken between 1865 and 1870 show clearly that he was aging rapidly. And the written accounts of his health during those

228

years indicate that it was steadily deteriorating. There are many references to illness in his correspondence, and he was sometimes so incapacitated that he had to take to his bed. This was especially true of the summer of 1867, when he was at the White Sulphur Springs and the Old Sweet Springs. He was under the impression that he was suffering from "a rheumatic affection"—which may have been true—but it is evident that his already impaired heart was failing.

One of the studio portraits Michael Miley took of Lee in Lexington

Warm Springs as it looked in General Lee's time. The big wooden hotel is gone, but the spring houses are still in use, almost unchanged.

The Lees went to the various mineral springs in the mountains of Virginia and West Virginia in the hope of relieving Mrs. Lee's arthritis. These natural springs, which the Indians had used for their alleged healing powers, were popular summer resorts then as now. Huge hotels had been built to accommodate the numerous guests who usually came to stay for many weeks. In those days, the springs could be reached only by stagecoach or carriage, and the ride over the curving mountain roads was a hard one. The Lees often went from one spa to another, as was the custom. In 1867, 1868, and 1869, they were at White Sulphur Springs' Greenbrier Hotel, where they stayed in a cottage reserved for them at the end of Baltimore Row.

Life was very pleasant in those big mid-nineteenth century resorts. And the Lee family, of course, was the center of attention. Children and young girls made much of the general, who tended to avoid male guests of military age and often went for long, solitary rides along the mountain trails. But he was known to practically everyone in the South—even to those who had never seen him. On one such ride he passed some small children whose faces were very dirty. He spoke to them gently about the need for keeping clean. A few minutes later, the winding road passed a lonely cabin out of which rushed the same children with well-scrubbed faces, fresh clothes, and neatly brushed hair. One little girl said: "We know you are General Lee! We have your picture."

But the summers were only interludes for the man who not only had to administer the affairs of a growing college, but who also sometimes had to use the weight of his authority to intervene in local affairs. There are stories of his saving a horse thief from being lynched, of disciplining his students when they became involved with meetings of the Negro freedmen or with former Union soldiers who had settled in Lexington.

There were rewards, of course, as well as duties. Early in 1867 it was proposed that Lee be made the first postwar Governor of Virginia. He declined the honor, saying that he believed his election would be injurious to the state. And in 1865 the New York *Herald* proposed that he become the Democratic candidate for President, which meant that he would have to run against Grant.

230

The *Herald* editorial paid high tribute to Lee, saying that he was a better soldier and a greater man than any of the candidates the Democratic Party was considering. Nothing came of the proposal, nor is it likely that Lee would have been willing to run.

During the late autumn of 1867, he went to Richmond to attend the wedding of Rooney, who was about to be married for the second time. (His two small children were dead, and his wife had died in December 1863.) At this time Lee was subpoenaed to appear before a Federal court in Richmond as a witness in the trial of Jefferson Davis for treason. When interrogated, he had little to say and replied as briefly and as carefully as possible to the questions asked.

The next day he went by train to Petersburg, where his son was to be married. The town held unhappy memories, for it was from there that the retreat to Appomattox had begun. He said of his visit: "My old feelings returned to me as I passed well-remembered spots and recalled the ravages of the hostile shells." But the townspeople gave him an enthusiastic welcome, and the wedding was a happy occasion. He described it the next morning in a letter to his wife: "Our son was married last night and shone in his happiness. The bride looked lovely and was, in every way, captivating. The church was crowded to its utmost capacity, and the streets thronged. Everything went off well. . . . Fitzhugh Lee was one of the groomsmen, Custis very composed, and Rob suffering from chills. . . . Regrets were often expressed that you, Mary, and Agnes were not present."

The people who lived in Lexington wanted to have a Valley railroad to end their long isolation. They succeeded in enlisting Lee's support and persuaded him to accompany a delegation which went to Baltimore in April to urge the mayor and the council of that city to help float the bond issue needed to finance the building of the line. Lee had been ill and disliked taking part in money-raising affairs, but better transportation would be of such great benefit to Lexington and its two institutions of learning that he agreed to go. It would look "ill-mannered and unkind to refuse," he said.

In Baltimore, Lee was the object of attention wherever he went. He found

*The Baltimore Cottage
in which the Lees stayed when they
were at the Greenbrier in
White Sulphur Springs*

231

One of the portraits Mathew B. Brady made in Washington in 1869

time, however, to purchase a small carriage for his wife. He was urged to go to New York to see Cyrus McCormick, the wealthy inventor, who could be of great benefit to Washington College. After thinking the matter over, Lee decided not to go. The man who was trying to persuade him told Lee that he was "shrinking from the conspicuity of a visit to New York." But he need not be exposed to any publicity, he said. He could travel in a sleeping-car compartment and would be met by McCormick's carriage when he arrived. Lee rejected the idea, saying, "I couldn't go sneaking into New York. When I do go, I'll go in daylight, and go like a man."

When the conversation turned toward the outcome of the war which Northern papers were saying had been fought by the South only to preserve the slave system, Lee protested that this was not true. "So far from engaging in war to perpetuate slavery," he said, "I am rejoiced that slavery is abolished. . . . I would cheerfully have lost all I have . . . to have this . . . attained."

The general who had ended his military career at Appomattox never saw New York again, but he did meet the man to whom he had surrendered the Army of Northern Virginia. President Grant had intimated that he would be pleased to receive him at the White House. Lee went there on May 1 and spent about fifteen minutes talking with his former adversary. The meeting had no political significance and was purely social.

While Lee was in Washington, Brady took more pictures of him. The great war photographer was in financial straits and was trying—unsuccessfully —to sell his huge collection of historic negatives to the Government. But his misfortunes did not affect his skill; the pictures he took were excellent. They do, of course, show what illness and age had done to Lee's features. He was now sixty-two.

From Washington, Lee went to Alexandria to spend a few days visiting friends. The occasion must have been an emotionally moving one, for Alexandria was the town where he had grown up. Many of his schoolmates and neighbors still lived there. And the house which had been his last home with his mother was relatively unchanged.

When he walked up from the wharf where the steamer from Washington landed, he was met by a growing crowd of townspeople. So many wanted to see him that an informal reception had to be arranged at the Mansion House. Visitors filed past him for three hours to give him the greatest ovation since Washington's time. On Sunday he attended service at familiar old Christ Church which had played so important a part in his life. With him was his brother Sidney Smith Lee. They had not seen each other since the end of the war.

On May 7, he left to return to Lexington. When he arrived there, he was asked how he had enjoyed his visit. "Very much," he said, "but they make too much fuss over an old Rebel."

Before the month was over, he had to go off on another short journey, this time to Fredericksburg as delegate from his Lexington church to a convention being held there. He went on to visit Sidney Smith at his home on the Potomac near Acquia Creek. It was the last time he was to see his brother, for Smith died two months later.

When Lee returned to Lexington on June 1, college examinations were in progress. And the new president's house was ready. Its master was destined to live in it for only sixteen months.

But there was time to finish one long-cherished project—the editing of a new edition of his father's account of the American Revolution, "Light-Horse" Harry Lee's *Memoirs of the War in the Southern Department,* which had first

Another of the Brady portraits

The entrance to the "new" president's house as it looks today

By special permission, to aid the Ladies' Memorial Association.

Gen's R. E. LEE and J. E. JOHNSTON.

D. J. Ryan, Savannah, Ga.

Entered according to the Act of Congress in the Clerk's Office of the U. S. District Court, Savannah, Ga.

Joseph E. Johnston and Robert E. Lee photographed in Savannah in the spring of 1870

been issued in 1812. The pressure of other duties, failing health, and lack of training and experience in editing and writing all worked together to produce a book of slight merit. Lee's major contribution was a lengthy introduction entitled "The Life of General Henry Lee." Douglas Southall Freeman said of it: "The picture one gets at the end does less than justice to the man and his record. . . . Lee's letters . . . were nearly always smooth. . . . But when he came to formal composition, most of the grace and all the spontaneity of his style disappeared. What he wrote became ponderous and dull." But the book sold well enough on the strength of the editor's name to go through several editions during the next few years.

In July Sydney Smith died suddenly, and by the time Lee could get to Alexandria, the funeral was over. In writing to his wife about the saddening experience, death evidently seemed very near to the aging general, for he said: "May God bless us all and preserve us for the time when we, too, must part, the one from the other, which is now close at hand."

He spent the rest of the summer of 1869 at White Sulphur Springs. It was a noteworthy season with many distinguished guests present. One of Lee's best-known photographs was made with them. In addition to many Confederate leaders, the group portrait shows George Peabody, Massachusetts philanthropist who had spent much of his life in England; W. W. Corcoran, Washington banker and founder of the Corcoran Gallery of Art, who had sympathized with the South and had gone abroad during the war; and Blacque Bey, who had married one of the daughters of the famous American surgeon, Valentine Mott, and had become Turkey's first Minister to the United States.

During the autumn, Lee caught a severe cold which persisted for some time. His health, which had been poor for years, now began to fail rapidly. "Traveller's trot is harder to me than it used to be and fatigues me," he wrote to Rooney in December. Then he added: "We are all as usual—the women of the family very fierce and the men very mild."

That month, the man who probably realized that he had not long to live refused an offer to become the president of the Southern Life Insurance Company. This was only one of many such lucrative proposals. He felt that his first allegiance was to the college, and even there he would not permit the

A group photograph taken in White Sulphur Springs in August 1869. Seated, from left to right:
(1) Blacque Bey, Turkish Minister to the United States; (2) General Lee; (3) George Peabody, Massachusetts philanthropist; (4) W. W. Corcoran, Washington philanthropist; (5) Judge James Lyons of Richmond, Va.

Standing: (1) General James Conner, South Carolina; (2) General Martin W. Gary, South Carolina; (3) Major General J. Bankhead Gruder, Virginia; (4) General Robert D. Lilley, Virginia; (5) General Beauregard, Louisiana; (6) General Alexander R. Lawton, Georgia; (7) General Henry A. Wise, Virginia; (8) General Joseph L. Brent, Maryland

*One of the last photographs
of Lee. Taken by Miley in Lexington.*

trustees to raise his salary, despite the fact that the student body had increased to 400. Nor was there any longer a shortage of funds.

Money had never meant much to him; it meant even less now, for both he and his doctors knew that something was seriously wrong with his heart. He often felt the dreadful pains of angina pectoris; he had difficulty breathing; and he was depressed and tired most of the time.

His cold had stayed with him all winter. In March, friends, family, and doctors succeeded in persuading him to go to a warmer climate. In company with his daughter Agnes, he set out for Savannah on March 24. By the time they reached Richmond, he was exhausted from the short but trying journey. Three doctors examined him and said that they would send their report to his physician in Lexington.

To his hotel came the noted partisan leader, John S. Mosby, whom Lee had met several times during the war. When Mosby left, he saw General George E. Pickett and told him that he had been with Lee. According to

236

Mosby, Pickett said that "if I would go with him, he would call and pay his respects to the general, but he did not want to be alone with him. So I went back with Pickett; the interview was cold and formal, and evidently embarrassing to both. . . . In a few minutes I rose and left . . . with General Pickett. He then spoke very bitterly of General Lee, calling him 'that old man.' 'He had my division massacred at Gettysburg,' Pickett said. 'Well, it made you immortal,' I replied.

"I rather suspect that Pickett gave a wrong reason for his unfriendly feelings. . . . Professor Venable, who had been on Lee's staff . . . told me that some days before the surrender at Appomattox, General Lee ordered Pickett under arrest—I suppose for the Five Forks affair." It was at Five Forks that Pickett had been absent, eating baked shad while Sheridan made a surprise attack (see page 201).

From Richmond, Lee and Agnes went to Warrenton, North Carolina, where they were driven to the cemetery in which Annie had been buried in October 1862. Then they traveled by rail to Augusta, Georgia. The people in every town along the route came to the train to pay tribute. It was a well-intentioned gesture, but the constant round of ceremonies took a great deal out of the man who now had only six months to live.

At Savannah a tremendous crowd was at the railroad terminal to welcome the South's most popular figure. Even some of the Union soldiers from the local garrison turned out to cheer him. There were more ceremonies and band concerts in Savannah itself. When Lee wrote to his wife, he said: "I have had a tedious journey upon the whole, and have more than ever regretted that I undertook it."

But he did enjoy meeting his old friends and companions in arms. Among them was Joseph E. Johnston, whom he had replaced at Seven Pines in 1862. They were photographed together, these two old men who seem far more than five years removed from active command. The three pictures taken of them in Savannah are not dated, but they must have been made on or very near the fifth anniversary of Appomattox.

Writing from Savannah to Mrs. Lee, he said: "My general health is pretty good. I feel stronger than when I came. The warm weather has also dispelled some of the rheumatic pains in my back, but I perceive no change in the stricture in my chest. If I attempt to walk beyond a very slow gait, the pain is always there."

With Agnes he went by steamboat to revisit his father's grave on Cumberland Island. The cemetery was unharmed, but the house in which "Light-Horse" Harry Lee had died was a fire-blackened ruin, a casualty of the war.

On his return to Savannah, Lee was examined by two doctors. He did not understand their technical language and forgot some of it, as he confessed in a letter to his wife. "But," he added, "the pain along the breastbone ever returns on my making any exertion."

On the way home, they stopped at Charleston, Wilmington, and Norfolk. At a dinner in Washington, according to his son Robert, he admitted to some of the guests that he "realized there was some trouble with his heart, which he was satisfied was incurable."

After leaving Norfolk, he visited friends in some of the great estates on the James River. This was the only time during the entire trip that he had a chance to rest. Then he spent a few days with Rooney at the White House and with Robert in his makeshift bachelor quarters at Romancoke. Mrs. Lee was at the White House, and she noted that her husband was not looking well. She said that he had gained weight and that his complexion was more than usually florid. It was May 22 before the obviously ill man was back in Rich-

237

Edward V. Valentine
in his Richmond studio

mond. During his brief stay there, he again saw the doctors who had examined him when he began his journey.

On May 25 he went to the studio of young Edward Valentine, for whom the Vannerson photographs had been made in 1864 (see page 186). The sculptor took careful measurements of his sitter for a portrait bust. When Valentine said that he was doing badly in those lean postwar years, Lee, half-humorously remarked that "an artist ought not to have much money."

There was some question as to whether the sculptor should come to Lexington then to finish his portrait or put off his visit until autumn. Lee quietly advised him to go immediately. Fortunately Valentine did, even though he had to borrow money to pay for the journey. If he had waited until fall, he would have been too late.

Valentine arrived in Lexington on June 4 and called on Lee at the new president's house. Although his sitter offered him the use of one of the rooms, he preferred to work in his own quarters and rented a vacant store for the purpose. Lee went there regularly. Valentine said that "he seemed to be fond

238

of speaking of his boyhood, swimming in the Potomac . . . of West Point, and of the Mexican War."

Valentine was responsible for having several photographs made of Lee at this time. Although he does not mention the name of the Lexington photographer, it must have been Miley. The pictures taken that summer were probably the last likenesses made.

When the bust was finished, Valentine brought it to the president's house so Mrs. Lee could examine it and give it her approval. The sculptor describes what he called an ordeal for her patient husband: "Mrs. Lee, being an invalid, could not go to the room where the bust was modeled. It had to be removed to her parlor, where were assembled a number of visitors. There he was by the good wife turned in different positions and the bust compared with the original, all of which he submitted to without a murmur."

When Valentine called to say farewell to his sitter, several people were present. The young sculptor heard Lee say to them: "I have an incurable disease coming on me—old age." That was the last time the two ever met. Valentine returned to Richmond and spent many years working and reworking the sketches and models he had made from the living Lee.

At the beginning of July, Lee went to Baltimore for another medical examination. It was a miserably uncomfortable journey, particularly the last part when the passengers had to remain for hours in stalled cars before they left Washington. "It was the hottest day I ever experienced," he wrote to Mary. "Or I was less able to stand it, for I never recollect having suffered so much." The doctor was encouraging—too encouraging, in fact, as events were soon to prove. Meanwhile, he advised his patient to drink lemon juice and watch its effect.

From Baltimore Lee went to Alexandria again to see old friends and consult his attorney about the possibility of gaining possession of Arlington. While in the home of his cousin, Cassius Lee, he discussed the war, saying that he thought that if Jackson had been at Gettysburg the Confederates would have won the battle. He was reported as saying that McClellan was the best "by all odds" of the Federal generals who had opposed him. And when asked why he did not attack Washington after his victory at Second Manassas, he said that his men were in no condition to fight any more, because they had had nothing to eat for three days. He invaded Maryland then, he explained, in

*The bust and head which
Valentine made of Lee*

*Valentine's exact measurements
of Lee's head. Note at top says
"5 ft. 11, the General's height."*

Another of the last portraits

The college chapel with the tomb of the Lee family

order to feed his army. Mention of this led him into a discussion of the mismanagement of the Confederate Commissary Department and of certain Southern newspapers which made it impossible to keep troop movements a secret because they published stories which told the enemy just what was happening.

This was one of the few times Lee ever spoke freely about the war. The only account of what he said—and he spoke at great length—was written by one of his cousin's young sons who admitted that it was regrettable that a fuller and more accurate record of the Confederate commander's recollections and opinions was not made.

Lee spent some time in August at Hot Springs taking the baths. He wrote to his wife that he found such public places wearying and hardly worth the cost. On August 29, he had to go to Staunton where a meeing of the stockholders of the Valley Railroad was to be held. The railroad's president, who was resigning, suggested that Lee be elected to replace him, which was accordingly done. The new post carried a salary of $5000 per annum, but the added income was not to be of much use to a man who now had only a few weeks left.

The college term opened on September 15. For the next few days, Lee went about his duties as president, spending most of his working hours in his modestly furnished office in the basement of the new chapel. The Franco-Prussian War was being fought at this time, and he followed the campaigns with interest. His sympathies are clearly expressed in a letter he wrote shortly before the college term began: "I have watched with much anxiety the progress of the war between France and Germany, and . . . I have regretted that they did not submit their differences to the arbitration of the other Powers. . . . It would have been a grand moral victory over the passions of men, and would have so elevated the contestants in the eyes of the present and future generations as to have produced a beneficial effect. It might have been expecting, however, too much from the present standard of civilization, and I fear we are destined to kill and slaughter each other for ages to come. . . . As far as I can read the accounts, the French have met with serious reverses, which seem to have demoralized the nation and are therefore alarming. Whatever may be the issue, I cannot help sympathizing with the struggles of a warlike people to drive invaders from their lands."

He had had enough of war and military life. "I much enjoy the charms of civil life," he wrote, "and find too late that I have wasted the best years of my existence."

One of the instructors at the College noted Lee's "aversion for military usages." He sometimes had to march in a procession alongside General Smith, Superintendent of V.M.I. On such occasions, the instructor noted, "General Smith always held himself in an exact military posture and brought his feet, especially the left one, down firmly in perfect time, whereas not even the beating of the bass drum could make General Lee keep step. He simply walked along in a natural manner, but although this manner appeared so natural, it seemed to me that he consciously avoided keeping step, so uniformly did he fail to plant his foot simultaneously with General Smith or at the beat of the drum."

On September 27, Lee attended a faculty meeting for the last time. The next day was cloudy and cold with rain beginning to fall late in the afternoon. When he left his office, he went up the little slope to his home, had his midday dinner, and took a short nap. A vestry meeting was to be held in Grace Church at four o'clock. Despite the rain, Lee put on the military cape which had served him during the war and walked to the church.

Lee's office in the basement of the college chapel. It is kept just as it was on the day he left it for the last time.

Above: A photograph of the office.   Below: A lithograph by A. J. Volck, 1873.

The death mask of Robert E. Lee

DEATH AND TRANSFIGURATION

A great storm was sweeping across the country, stripping the yellowing leaves from the trees on the mountains around Lexington, and filling the streams with torrential waters. Before the storm, the skies for several nights had been hung with the shimmering curtains of the aurora. And in the Lee house, a framed portrait of the master had fallen from the wall to land with a thump on the floor. Mrs. Lee refused to be superstitious about it, but some people whispered that a fallen portrait was a certain portent of death.

There was no heat in Grace Church, and the wind and rain made it unusually cold that day. General Lee was sitting in one of the pews, wrapped in his military cloak, and saying little during the meeting that lasted from four to seven o'clock. Rebuilding the church and increasing the rector's salary were the chief topics of business. Toward the end of the meeting, the treasurer announced that $55 was needed to pay the rector.

"I will give that sum," Lee said quietly. Some of those present noticed that his face seemed more than ordinarily flushed, but they did not sense anything wrong.

The meeting was then adjourned, and the general went outdoors to face the rain. It was very dark, for the sun had long since set, and it was the time of the dark of the moon, so there was not even a glimmer of light behind the scudding clouds racing across the sky.

When Lee entered the house, he took off his rain-soaked hat, cloak, and overshoes. His family was at tea. Mrs. Lee asked where he had been, saying that he had kept them waiting for a long time. He did not answer but stood at the table, apparently about to say grace. But no words came, and he almost collapsed when he tried to sit down. Alarmed now, the family sprang into action. The stricken man was stretched out on a couch, and two doctors, who had been at the meeting in the church, were sent for.

When they arrived and started to remove their patient's outer clothing, he complained that they were hurting his arm. The doctors ordered a bed to be brought down and placed in the dining room. The dying general was put to bed in a comatose condition. He was never to leave the room alive.

September passed, and the golden days of October began. But the man on the bed in the dining room was seldom conscious. He slept most of the time; when awakened, he took medicines and food as directed, but he showed little interest in what was going on around him. He could speak when he had to, but he uttered only monosyllables and did not want to talk or listen. He was like one already half-dead; undoubtedly he knew that he was going to die. But he was reconciled to that and did not seem to care.

Word of his illness informed the world about his condition. Messages and offers to help poured in, but he was beyond all aid. When one of his doctors tried to arouse interest by saying that Traveller had been too long in the stable and needed exercise, he got no reply. The fast-sinking man merely shook his head and closed his eyes. He knew that he would never ride again or even see his beloved horse.

During the afternoon of October 10, the general's hold on life began to weaken rapidly. His pulse became feeble, and his breathing was labored. Toward midnight he was seized with a fit of violent shivering, after which his

The dining room of the new president's house where Lee died

243

DECORATION OF THE CASKET OF GEN! LEE.
At Lexington Va. October 15? 1870.

Robert E. Lee.

FUNERAL MARCH. The Sword of Robert Lee QUICK MARCH.
by Song by by
E. MACK. (ARMAND) CHAS. YOUNG.

NEW YORK, J. L. PETERS. J. L. PETERS & Co ST. LOUIS.

physicians told the family that the end was near. But he lingered on through the next day and night, barely conscious, but still clinging to life.

During that last morning his mind was evidently again on the battlefield, for he said audibly, "Tell Hill he must come up." Then he lapsed into unconsciousness again. In his dark dreams he may have been bringing his last campaign to a close because those around him heard him say with a tone of finality: "Strike the tent." After that he sank down into a silence which was never broken. At 9.30 A.M. on October 12, he crossed over the river to rest under the shade of the trees where his companion in arms had preceded him.

Now the legends began, and as so often happens, Nature helped the birth of myth. There were no coffins in Lexington; three, which had been ordered from Richmond by a local undertaker, had arrived some time before, but the great flood which followed the storm had swept them away from the boat landing where they were stored. Two schoolboys, exploring the woods, came across one of them stranded on shore. The townspeople brought it to Lexington in time for the funeral. It was small for the corpse that was to be placed in it, but it was so obviously predestined for the purpose that the dead general, clothed in civilian dress, was buried in it but without his shoes. The body, in its waterborne casket, so reminiscent of the funeral voyages of ancient heroes whose remains were set adrift on Viking ships, royal barges, or flower-decked rafts, was taken from the president's house to the college chapel to lie in state until October 15, when the funeral ceremonies were to be held.

Word of Lee's death quickly spread around the world. The New York *Tribune,* which had been hostile during the war, sent a special correspondent to Lexington to cover the story. He describes the town in mourning: "I arrived here tonight and find the town overwhelmed with grief. . . . At the hotels, by the hearthstone, in the schools, on the streets, everywhere, the only topic of conversation is the death of General Lee. All classes of the community seem to be affected, even the colored people, who walk along in silence with sorrowful countenance and mourn the loss of 'Good ole Marse Robert.' Every house in town seems to be draped with the emblems of mourning, and no business has been transacted in any of the stores. . . . The students of Washington College, of which Lee was president, held a meeting this morning. . . . Many of the students were affected to tears. They seemed to have had for General Lee the affection of children for a father. . . . Prayer meet-

244

ings and religious services are now going on in the different churches, and a Sabbath-like stillness reigns throughout the town. The only sound breaking the silence of this twilight hour is the monotonous tolling of the bells, the knell of Lee."

The big storm had torn out bridges and washed roads away, but despite the difficulties of travel great numbers of people came to Lexington for the funeral. By 9 A.M. on Saturday, October 15, all the unreserved seats in the college chapel were taken. The day was brilliantly clear; the fine crisp air of early autumn made the distant mountains seem closer than usual, and the white pillars of the college buildings gleamed brightly in the sun. Around them were wound the black streamers of mourning.

The Reverend Mr. J. William Jones, pastor of the Baptist church in Lexington, who had fought in the Confederate Army and had served as one of its chaplains, wrote a description of the funeral ceremonies: "At ten o'clock precisely the procession was formed on the college grounds in front of the president's house, and moved down Washington Street, up Jefferson Street to the Franklin Hall, thence to Main Street, where it was joined in front of the hotel by the representatives of the state of Virginia and other representative bodies in their order, and by the organized body of the citizens in front of the courthouse.

"The procession then moved . . . to the Virginia Military Institute, where it was joined by the visitors, faculty, and cadets . . . in their respective places. The procession was closed by the students of Washington College as a guard of honor, and then moved up through the Institute and college grounds to the chapel.

"The procession was halted in front of the chapel, when the cadets of the Institute and the students of Washington College were marched . . . past the remains and were afterward drawn up in two bodies on the south side of the chapel. The remainder of the procession then proceeded into the chapel and were seated under the direction of the marshals. . . . As the procession moved off to a solemn dirge by the Institute band, the bells of the town began to toll, and the Institute battery fired minute guns. . . .

The college chapel during the funeral of Robert E. Lee

"Along the streets the buildings were all appropriately draped, and crowds gathered on the corners and the balconies to see the procession pass. Not a flag floated above the procession, and nothing was seen that looked like an attempt at display. The old soldiers wore their ordinary citizens' dress with a simple black ribbon in the lapel of their coats; and Traveller, led by two old soldiers, had the simple trappings of mourning on his saddle.

"The Virginia Military Institute was very beautifully draped, and from its turrets hung at half-mast and draped in mourning, the flags of all of the states of the late Southern Confederacy. When the procession reached the Institute, it passed the corps of cadets drawn up in line, and a guard of honor presented arms as the [empty] hearse passed. . . . The coffin was covered with flowers and evergreens, while the front of the drapery thrown over it was decorated with crosses of evergreen and immortelles.

"Rev. Dr. Pendleton, the long intimate personal friend of General Lee, his chief of artillery during the war, and his pastor the past five years, read the beautiful burial service of the Episcopal Church."

The words for the Order for the Burial of the Dead were spoken in the clear voice of the man who had barked out commands for placing artillery on the battlefield: *"I am the resurrection and the life, saith the Lord: he that believeth in me, though he were dead, yet shall he live: and whosoever liveth and believeth in me, shall never die. . . .*

"Lord, thou hast been our refuge: from one generation to another. Before the mountains were brought forth, or ever the earth and the world were made: thou art God from everlasting, and world without end.

"Thou turnest man to destruction: again thou sayest, Come again, ye children of men. For a thousand years in thy sight are but as yesterday: seeing that is past as a watch in the night. As soon as thou scatterest them they are even as a sleep: and fade away suddenly like the grass. In the morning it is green, and groweth up: but in the evening it is cut down, dried up, and withered. . . .

"O teach us to number our days: that we may apply our hearts unto wisdom.

"Glory be to the Father, and to the Son: and to the Holy Ghost; As it was in the beginning, is now, and ever shall be: world without end. AMEN."

The coffin was taken to the temporary vault in the chapel which had been prepared for it. After it was lowered into its resting place, the congregation sang the hymn "How Firm a Foundation." Then all the people filed past the tomb to pay their last respects, and the ceremony was over.

A Lee Memorial Association was formed to draw up plans for a permanent monument. Among the many donations made to it was one from a nine-year-old girl who wrote: "I have asked my mother to let me send some money— not money that she gave me, but money that I earned myself. I made some of my money by keeping the door shut last winter, and the rest I made by digging up grass in the garden. I send you all I have. I wish it was more."

When Mrs. Lee was approached by members of the Memorial Association for her advice, she suggested that Edward V. Valentine be commissioned to design a suitable monument. From pictures of various works of art, she chose one of the recumbent figure of Queen Louise, wife of King Frederick William III of Prussia, which C. D. Rauch had made in 1813 for the mausoleum at Charlottenburg. Valentine went to work and a year later had a model of the figure and the sarcophagus ready. He estimated that the projected design would cost $15,000 to complete. This sum was authorized, and he began to make an over-life-size figure of Lee, lying as if asleep on a draped couch. He had this ready to put into marble by the autumn of 1872, but the figure

The body of General Lee lying in state in the Washington College Chapel

246

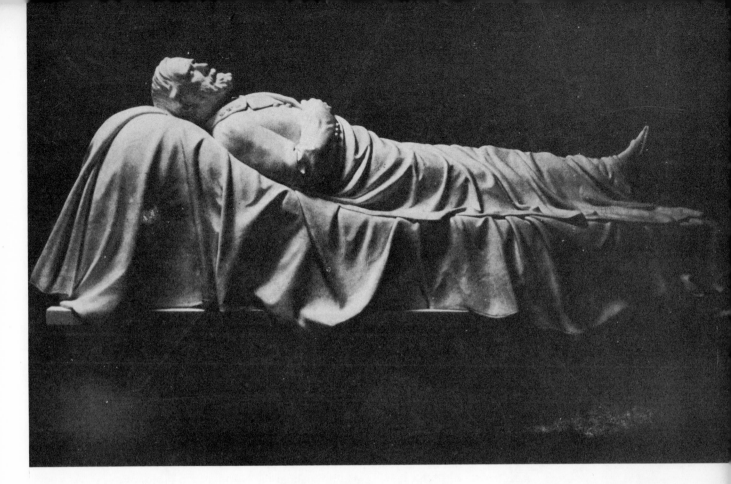

*The Valentine recumbent statue
in the Lee Memorial Chapel*

was not completed until the spring of 1875. Then the students of Richmond College asked to have the "privilege of taking charge of the monument when it is sent up to Lexington and bearing the expenses of its transportation." Accompanied by a procession of Richmond citizens, they brought the heavy statue to the boat landing and took it under escort to Lexington. It was put in storage there until a proper mausoleum could be added to the chapel. More funds had to be raised for this, but by June 1883 everything was ready for the public dedication.

Since the ceremony was held the day after commencement, many people were in town. Among them were Confederate soldiers, their wives, and—in some cases—their widows. Again a procession marched through Lexington. It visited the grave of Stonewall Jackson and then entered the college grounds where a grandstand had been built in front of the chapel. As on the day of the funeral, the weather was bright and sunny. When the recumbent statue of Lee was unveiled by Jackson's daughter, the Rockbridge Artillery fired two guns which had been used at First Manassas. The chapel and the new mausoleum were then opened, and the huge crowd filed through to pay its respects.

Since that day many thousands of people have come to Lexington to visit the chapel where the Confederate commander is buried. In the mausoleum are the remains of other members of his family, including those of his father, "Light-Horse" Harry Lee, which were brought there from Cumberland Island in 1913.

In 1871, the trustees voted to change the name of the college to Washington and Lee. The two men who had had so much in common were thus forever linked together. They had been born near each other in the tidewater country; in the mountains of their native state, the institution they had both helped is a living memorial to them.

Issued in 1955

Issued in 1937

*Lee and Jackson
on the Stone Mountain
Half Dollar, 1925*

*Lee and McClellan
on the Antietam
Half Dollar, 1937*

THE MAN AND THE LEGEND

After Robert E. Lee was dead and buried, his name began to loom larger than ever. That it would be remembered fondly in the South was to be expected, but as the years passed and the passions aroused by the war gradually subsided, his fame spread throughout the North and to places overseas. A generation after Appomattox, when Ohio-born James Ford Rhodes wrote his multi-volume *History of the United States*, he said of Lee: "A careful survey of his character and life must lead the student of men and affairs to see that the course he took was, from his point of view and judged by his inexorable and pure conscience, the path of duty to which a high sense of honor called him. Could we share the thoughts of that high-minded man as he paced the broad pillared veranda of his stately Arlington house, his eyes glancing across the river at the flag of his country waving above the dome of the Capitol and then resting on the soil of his native Virginia, we should be willing now to recognize in him one of the finest products of American life. For surely, as the years go on, we shall see that such a life can be judged by no partisan measure, and we shall come to look upon him as the English of our day regard Washington, whom little more than a century ago they delighted to call a rebel. But although Lee resembled Washington in many characteristics, he, in the judgment of the world, differed from the more illustrious man in choosing the wrong side, and lacking success he had not the opportunity to show whether the constructive statesmanship of Washington was also his."

The British, of course, had always thought highly of Lee. Lord Acton, his near-contemporary, called him "the greatest general the world has ever seen, with the possible exception of Napoleon" and admitted that he was heartbroken when he first heard about the surrender at Appomattox. Colonel G. F. R. Henderson, who came to America twice to visit the battlefields for his great biography of Stonewall Jackson, said of his subject's commander: "The campaign against Pope has seldom been surpassed; and the great counterstroke at Manassas is sufficient in itself to make Lee's reputation as a tactician. Tried by this test alone, Lee stands out as one of the greatest soldiers of all times. Not only against Pope, but against McClellan at Gaines' Mill, against Burnside at Fredericksburg, and against Hooker at Chancellorsville, he suc-

248

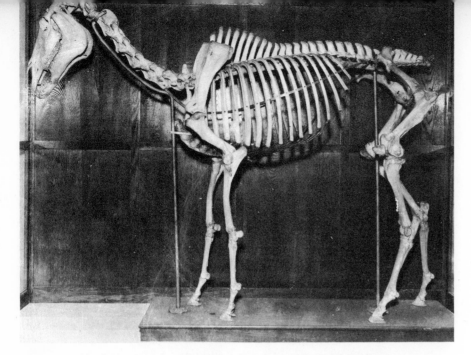

The skeleton of Lee's favorite war horse, Traveller, is kept in a glass case in the basement of the Memorial Chapel

ceeded . . . and in each case with the same result of surprising his adversary. None knew better how to apply the great principle of strategy, 'to march divided, but to fight concentrated.' It was not due to the skill of Lee that Pope weakened his left at the crisis of the battle [of Second Manassas]. But in the rapidity with which the opportunity was seized, in the combination of the three arms, and in the vigour of the blow, Manassas is in no way inferior to Austerlitz or Salamanca."

Lord Wolseley, who was Henderson's superior and who did much to mold his career, had visited the Confederate Army in 1862. He wrote of his meeting with Lee then: "He was the ablest general, and to me seemed the greatest man I had ever conversed with, and yet I have had the privilege of meeting von Moltke and Prince Bismarck. . . . General Lee was one of the few men who ever seriously impressed and awed me with their natural and inherent greatness."

These are British military men's opinions of Lee as a general. But Major-General Sir Frederick Maurice, who wrote a book about Lee as a soldier, said of his postwar civilian career: "Distinguished as was Lee's conduct while an officer in the Army of the United States, splendid as was his career as a general in the field, nothing in his life became him more than its end. His resolute refusal, in circumstances of great difficulty and temptation, to take part in any of the controversies which the war evoked, his devotion to the success of his work as president of Washington University in training young men of the South to forget the quarrels of the past and to be good Americans, all displayed even more surely than did the tests of the battlefield, high courage, sincerity of purpose, devotion to principle, and nobility of mind. No man took upon himself more earnestly Lincoln's charge, and with real abnegation of self set himself, 'with malice toward none,' 'to bind up the nation's wounds.' "

Theodore Roosevelt, an American President of Northern birth who was to have some military experience himself, commented on Lee in the 1880s: He "will undoubtedly rank as without any exception the greatest of all the great captains that the English-speaking people have brought forth—and this, although the last and chief of his antagonists may claim to stand as the full equal of Marlborough and Wellington." He also said: "As a mere military man, Washington himself cannot rank with the wonderful war-chief who for four years led the Army of Northern Virginia."

The saddle General Lee used when he rode Traveller

249

In 1907, when the hundredth anniversary of Lee's birth was about to be celebrated, a Northern writer who had been closely associated during the war with the patriotic and religious fervor of the Union cause, prepared some verses which were more remarkable for their sentiment than for their poetic quality. She was Julia Ward Howe, whose celebrated "Battle Hymn of the Republic" was still being sung at G.A.R. reunions. She wrote:

> A gallant foeman in the fight,
>   A brother when the fight was o'er,
> The hand that led the host with might
>   The blessed torch of learning bore.
>
> No shriek of shells nor roll of drums,
>   No challenge fierce, resounding far,
> When reconciling Wisdom comes
>   To heal the cruel wounds of war.
>
> Thought may the minds of men divide,
>   Love makes the heart of nations one,
> And so, thy soldier grave beside,
>   We honor thee, Virginia's son.

But outstanding among all the non-Southerners who helped to make Lee a national and then an international figure was a New Englander whose family background and personal experience made it seem unlikely that he would ever want to praise a man who had been his enemy on the battlefield. This was Charles Francis Adams, Jr., son of the United States Minister to the Court of St. James's during the Civil War, grandson of the sixth President, and great-grandson of the second President. Adams, who was president of the Massachusetts Historical Society and who had been a colonel in the Union Army, had never met Lee, although he had once seen him driving along Pennsylvania Avenue in a carriage. And less than two months before the outbreak of the war, he and his brother Henry had dined at Arlington with the Lee family while the master of the house was still en route from Texas to Washington. This was the full extent of Adams' contact with Lee. He never gave the reasons for his enthusiasm for the defeated commander of the Army of Northern Virginia, but something in his New England heart apparently found common cause with the Virginia aristocrat.

His campaign to win national recognition for Lee began in 1901 when he delivered an address before the American Antiquarian Society at its annual meeting in Worcester, Massachusetts. In the speech, entitled "Lee at Appomattox," he gave credit to the Confederate commander for terminating the war when he did rather than let it drag on in a series of guerrilla encounters. Had that been allowed to happen, Adams pointed out, the South would have been reduced to a wilderness, and the North would also have suffered from the devastating results of long-continued irregular warfare.

Then, when Adams addressed the Phi Beta Kappa Society at the University of Chicago the next year, his speech, entitled "Shall Cromwell Have a Statue?" was a plea for a monument of Lee to be erected in the nation's capital. He was asked to speak at Washington and Lee on January 19, 1907, for the Centennial Celebration of Lee's birth. He said afterward that he thought more highly of the address he gave there than of anything else he had ever done.

Toward the end of this long speech, which was delivered in the chapel where its subject was buried, Adams said: "Speaking advisedly and on full reflection, I say that of all the great characters of the Civil War—and it was

Valentine's Lee in the United States Capitol

productive of many whose names and deeds posterity will long bear in recollection—there was not one who passed away in the serene atmosphere and with the gracious bearing of Lee. From beginning to end those parting years of his will bear closest scrutiny. There was about them nothing venal, nothing querulous, nothing in any way sordid or disappointing. In his case there was no anticlimax; for those closing years were dignified, patient, useful; sweet in domesticity, they in all things commanded respect. It is pleasant to catch glimpses of the erstwhile commander in that quiet Virginia life. There is in the picture something altogether human—intensely sympathetic. 'Traveller,' he would write, 'is my only companion; I may also say my pleasure. He and I, whenever practicable, wander out in the mountains and enjoy sweet confidence.' Or again we see him, always with Traveller, the famous old charger this time 'stepping very proudly,' as his rider showed those two little sunbonneted daughters of a professor, astride of a plodding old horse, over a pleasant road quite unknown to them. Once more in imagination we may ride, his companions, through those mountain roads of his dearly loved Virginia, or seek shelter with him and his daughter from a thunder shower in the log cabin, the inmates of which are stunned when too late they realize that the courtly, gracious intruder was no other than the idolized General Lee. Indifferent to wealth, he was scrupulous as respects those money dealings a carelessness in regard to which has embittered the lives of so many of our public men, as not infrequently it has tarnished their fame. Lee's career will be scrutinized in vain for a suggestion even of the sordid, or of an obligation he failed to meet. . . . Restricting his own wants to necessities, he contributed, to an extent which excites surprise, to both public calls and private needs. But the most priceless of those contributions were contained in the precepts he inculcated and in the unconscious example he set during those closing years."

Adams was invited to give the four James Ford Rhodes lectures at Oxford in the winter of 1912–13. In the last one he made a bid to extend

Lee and a young courier, by A. P. Proctor. In Lee Park, Dallas, Texas.

Lee's fame beyond the borders of his own country: "Is Lee entitled to be numbered among the American World-Great? to constitute an additional star in that as yet not numerous galaxy? General, Educator, Virginian, by some of my countrymen Lee is still looked upon as a traitor and denounced as a renegade; by yet others he is venerated and loved—I might even say idolized. Here in Oxford, that ancient seat of old-world learning, I, an American, am simply presenting Lee's credentials on which to base his possible admission among the World's Great."

Another Massachusetts man, Gamaliel Bradford, in the short biography he wrote of Lee in 1912, said of him: "It is an advantage to have a subject like Lee that one cannot help loving. I say, cannot help. The language of some

252

of his adorers tends at first to breed a feeling contrary to love. Persist and make your way through this and you will find a human being as lovable as any that ever lived. At least I have. I have loved him, and I may say that his influence upon my own life, though I came to him late, has been as deep and as inspiring as any I have ever known."

The man who had often been denounced as a traitor in the North finally came to be recognized there for his true worth. There is no doubt that the last five years of Lee's life—the years at Washington College—did much to redeem him in previously hostile Northern eyes. Had he died during the Appomattox Campaign or shortly after it, he would have been remembered only as a general who was good at fighting but who could not—for all his military ability—win a war in which the odds were hopelessly against his side. What Lee did on the field against such odds made him famous, but what he did afterward in civilian life made him great. Lee the soldier is a dramatic figure, but Lee the educator is an even more appealing one. The essential goodness and kindness of the man—drawbacks in his military career—could be allowed free expression when he became president of a struggling little college. The man who had been forced to send so many young Southerners to their deaths was then able to utilize his power for leadership for constructive ends. It is ironic that nearly all the monuments of Lee show him in uniform; only on the college campus in Lexington is he portrayed in civilian dress.

But perhaps the best case for Lee, as the entire nation sees him today, was summed up in a speech made on his birthday, January 19, 1961, at Mercer University, Macon, Georgia, by the eminent Southern historian Bell I. Wiley, when he said:

It is inconceivable that Lee, if he were alive today, would advocate resistance to national authority or in any way abet social turmoil or racial hatred. Certainly, he would staunchly oppose the use of the Confederate flag to cloak sordid causes and shield unworthy persons. To him the Confederate flag was a symbol of suffering, gallantry, and heroism of the highest and noblest sort. He would be infuriated by the sight of self-seeking demagogues and wrong-

Stone Mountain, Georgia

253

thinking agents of bigotry, hatred and violence wrapping themselves in this revered emblem in an effort to acquire respectability and enhance their influence.

The public images of Robert E. Lee are many. There is the young, handsome officer of the Engineer Corps, the dutiful husband and affectionate father, the fighting soldier of the Mexican War, and the world-renowned commander of the Army of Northern Virginia. And then there is the peace-loving, quiet, fatherly college president. They are all Lee, all facets of the same basically simple, straightforward person.

Many of Lee's best qualities came from his mother, for he hardly knew his father. Dr. Wiley says: "He grew up to be more of a Carter than a Lee. The outstanding traits of the Carter family were geniality, devotion to family—they intermarried to a most confusing extent—loyalty to community, and devotion to church. The Carters were traditionally religious, but none was fanatic. They mixed revealed religion and *noblesse oblige* in a delightful manner, with little thought of creed or system. Lee's mother was a true Carter. She taught him to revere the Carter code, and to avoid the pitfalls into which his father had fallen; namely, recklessness, extravagance, debt, and irresponsibility in business matters. She held up constantly to Robert the axioms sacred to the Carter family: economy, moderation, self-control, courtesy, gentility, honor, and devotion to duty."

It is these old-fashioned virtues which make Lee a symbol of all that is best in the Anglo-American tradition. He should be remembered not merely as Lee the soldier or even as Lee the educator, but also as Lee the man—the man of honor, the great gentleman, good and decent human being who others—even his enemies—knew could be trusted without reservation.

> His life was gentle, and the elements
> So mix'd in him that Nature might stand up
> And say to all the world "This was a man."

INDEX